PRAISE FOR MARK MATSON
AND
Main Street Money

"This book is a must-read for Main Street investors who want to protect themselves from the Wall Street Bullies and simultaneously harness the greatest wealth creation tool on the planet."

—Arthur B. Laffer,
Economic Advisor to President Ronald Reagan
Co-author of Return to Prosperity: How America
Can Regain Its Economic Superpower Status

"Behavioral biases cause many individual investors to make costly mistakes. These mistakes often result in investors holding overly concentrated portfolios, trading too actively, and/or chasing hot stocks. Investors frequently pay high fees to mutual fund managers who they wish they'd invested with last year-i.e., the year the manager got lucky-and may regret having invested with this year. Readers can avoid these common pitfalls by diversifying their portfolios, holding equities, rebalancing for diversification, avoiding market timing, and not investing in securities they don't really understand-such as derivatives. As a result, they will have the opportunity to reap the full potential of capital markets."

—Terrance Odean,
Rudd Family Foundation Professor of Finance
Haas School of Business, University of California, Berkeley

"As long as I have known Mark, he has been an advocate for investors. If you are new to investing or a seasoned veteran, Mark's insights provide the direction and discipline that are required to succeed through good and bad markets. Change your life. Read *Main Street Money*."

—Michael Lane,
Author of Secrets of the Wealth Makers

Also by Mark Matson

Books

FlashPoint: Mastering the Art of Economic Abundance
The Dirty Filthy Lies My Broker Taught Me
101 Truths About Money & Investing
Confessions of a Commission Junkie

Television

CNBC "Kudlow Report," CNBC "Power Lunch," Fox Business News "Opening Bell," Fox Business News "Power and Money," Fox Business News "Closing Bell," and CNBC Reports.

Publications

The Wall Street Journal, Investment News, SmartMoney.com, Forbes.com, The Business Courier, USA Today, Financial Services Advisor, Advisor Today, Personal Financial Planning Monthly, and many more.

Videos

How the Really Smart Money Invests
Navigating the Fog of Investing

Audio

The Seven Deadly Investor Traps that Destroy Your Wealth
 and Three Power Strategies to Fix Your Portfolio
Taking Stock
The Curriculum for Conscious Investing
The Investor Coaching Series
Breakthrough to Abundance

Online

"Matson Money Live!" and "Mark Matson TV"

Connect with Mark Matson

www.matsonmoney.com
www.twitter.com/markmatson
www.facebook.com/markmatson
www.facebook.com/matsonmoney

Main Street Money

How to Outwit, Outsmart & Out Invest the Wall Street Bullies

Mark Matson

ISBN-13: 978-0-9853620-0-3
ISBN-10: 0985362006

For Joseph Matson—my mentor, my coach, my father.

TABLE OF CONTENTS

FOREWORD

Writing a book is a mind-numbing, soul-searching hell I wouldn't wish on my worst enemy. It's a lonely business. I promised myself many years ago I would never pen another, but some stories are worth the pain. Some stories need to be told, no matter what the price. So I pulled myself away from my business, my coaches, the media, and even my family to force these chapters into fruition. I am deeply grateful to my wife, Melissa, and my children for toughing it out with me. The heart and minds of American investors are at stake. So for you, Dear Reader, I faced the fire of writing until the tale was truly told. You are worth it.

PROLOGUE

CHANGING THE STATUS QUO

"I made a killing on Wall Street a few years ago. I shot my broker."
–Groucho Marx

YOU MAY NOT KNOW ME, BUT I KNOW YOU. Or at least, I know of most of you. Chances are you're one of the 95 percent of Americans who are destined to retire broke. It's not really your fault. Goodness knows it's confusing out there for average Americans trying to secure their financial futures. Contradictory advice and information, misleading promises, portfolio-gutting investment strategies contribute to financial meltdowns—and that's just advice from my fellow Wall Street investment professionals.

Maybe that's why the finance industry's leading lights can be counted on to take one position this year and the opposite the next. Market timing? It will never work. Oh wait, yes it can. Asset allocation? A big winner—until a real bear market comes around. Buy and hold? The best thing since sliced bread. That is, until the market tanks and the buy-and-hold model gets tossed on the scrapheap by the so-called market experts.

It seems like financial professionals desperately *want* to confuse the investing public. Where is the continuity? Where is the unvarnished truth about investing strategies? Why won't anyone step up to the podium and admit that nobody can predict the future? We scoff at astrologers and tarot card readers, but some guy in a suit hangs the "stockbroker is in" sign on his door and folks can't wait to hear what he has to say. There is no shortage of talking heads who pretend they can foresee the future, magically point you toward the best stocks, and teach you to time the market perfectly.

These phony prognosticators prey on the psychology of Main Street investors, often causing them to take risks they don't understand and lose more money than they can imagine. I call these posers Wall Street Bullies because they take advantage of investors while lining their pockets with your hard-earned money—money you need for your retirement and to fulfill your most important dreams.

It doesn't have to be that way. I can teach you how to outwit, outsmart, and out-invest the biggest Wall Street Bullies and icons. I can help you create true peace of mind in your investing experience. And the good news is that it's not that hard.

Once you are armed with the basic knowledge you need, you can adopt an investment philosophy and strategy with the potential to beat the vast majority of all the blowhards on Wall Street. You can get their hands out of your pockets once and for all by understanding this—your problems are their profits. Make no mistake, Wall Street does not want you to read this book, and they certainly don't expect you to take action.

Educating investors is an uphill battle. Only 10% of Americans actually buy a book in a given year, and many of those do not read it. The book sits useless on a shelf collecting dust. So dear reader, if you can muster the focus and discipline to read this book and take action, you will be among the truly elite Main Street investors with the guts to invest in your education. As you will see in these pages, this is the greatest single investment you will ever make for your future.

My Story

It doesn't have to be this way. Investors don't have to allow themselves to be duped.

I've always maintained that, as a longtime Wall Street observer and the CEO and founder of my own investment management firm, I have an obligation to my clients to speak the truth and to state my beliefs—beliefs that won't change like the weather off of the New England coastline. Beliefs that are clear, concise, and compelling. Beliefs that have the potential to protect your money, backed up by evidence as old as money itself.

These bedrock tenets didn't come to me through divine providence or by accident. They came from my upbringing as the son of an insurance salesman who led me on my journey to Cincinnati, Ohio, and to a calling as a financial advisor who shoots straight and practices what he preaches.

I use the term "calling" intentionally.

> *"If you're born in Kentucky you've got three choices:*
> *coal mine, moonshine, or move it on down the line."*
> –Coal Miner's Daughter

Helping people manage their money came naturally to a kid whose parents didn't have any. My mom and dad grew up in the hollows of West Virginia. Back in the 1950s, there wasn't any money in their families nor a lot of career opportunities in rural Appalachia. For a while, my Dad didn't have a job, but he wound up getting a foot in the door to Wall Street by selling insurance. I sure didn't know it at the time, but that job was the launching point for my own career in finance and investments.

I've taken a lot of cues in life from my Dad. I looked up to him the way most boys look up to football players or firemen. I knew right away I wanted to follow my father into the finance business, and that's what I set out to accomplish.

My Dad fed my passion for wealth and money. When I was 11-years-old, he gave me books like *Think and Grow Rich* and *Psycho-Cybernetics*. When most kids were reading comic books and trading baseball cards, I had my nose in a book on wealth management.

My dad wanted to be an entrepreneur, and so did I. As my father earned his financial planning license and opened up his own investment advisory practice in Cincinnati, I headed off to college at the University of Miami, Ohio. I amped up my investing lessons, taking every class I could on business and finance. During summer breaks, I returned to Cincinnati and worked at my father's investment firm. I was gung ho and hammered down on the accelerator. By the time I graduated, I had my life and health insurance license, financial planning license, and stockbroker's license.

Dreams Become Reality

I didn't have my sheepskin for five minutes before I started working for my father full time. I saw myself as a young Thomas Edison, an entrepreneur making his own way in the world. I knew even at that raw age that, like Edison, I would be my own boss, run my own show, and make a big difference for people who really needed help.

That was my dream, but the reality was sobering. My Dad was a hard worker, and he expected me to work hard, too. Burning the midnight oil became a regular habit. I also began haunting sales conventions, where I'd rub elbows and soak up the knowledge of older, more seasoned stockbrokers and insurance sales gurus.

The thing was, the more books I read and the more research I did, I began to notice something peculiar. The advice given by my broker associates and financial planning brethren just didn't ring true.

This was back in the 1980s, when Peter Lynch of Fidelity and Sir John of the Templeton Fund became stock-picking supernovas. Back in the day, it was all about portfolio performance and beating the market.

I danced to the performance mantra, too. I totally bought into what I was being told by my broker dealer. What did I know? They were the experts, and a 25-years-old kid would only know what he was being spoon-fed by the Wall Street professionals. I attended talks by economists and famous money managers. Time after time, performance and beating the market were first on the agenda.

It was always a variation of the same old story: some brilliant money manager had analyzed all the economic data, could see the future by predicting what would happen next, and would let my clients in on the amazing picks and timing moves that had made him a five-star money manager.

My gut wrenched as I did client reviews and struggled to explain why all the gurus from the biggest companies like Vanguard, Fidelity, American Funds, and Templeton were losing to the market. I felt like a failure. I couldn't eat or sleep, and the stress was mounting. If I couldn't pick the best managers in advance, what good was I? What value could I bring my clients? They could speculate and gamble with their money on their own. They didn't need my help. I was hitting bottom.

That Sinking Feeling

I was sick of being force-fed Wall Street garbage. The stuff I was being served up by my broker dealer was complete BS. With every fiber of my being, I knew what we were doing was wrong, but I had no idea how to fix it.

But a strange thing happened on the way to the coronation of Wall Street's best and brightest. It gradually dawned on me that our recommended investments weren't performing like we thought they would. Time and time again, I had to explain to client with a half-million dollar portfolio why seven of his eight funds were underperforming. It got tougher to ignore the elephant in the room.

I did try talking to my broker dealer about the raw deal we were giving our customers. It got to be a joke, with all the excuses trotted out by fund managers. It was value one day, growth the next, and REITs the day after that. Finally, I just couldn't take it anymore. I felt a bit like a homicide detective who knew the killer's identity but had no evidence to prove it. After doing some serious independent research (and some serious soul-searching), I realized that the manager could not beat the market—I just didn't know why. Worse, I had no explanation for my clients.

But what *did* I know? I knew that I didn't like commissions. I thought commissions bred mistrust between the advisor and the client. I realized everything on Wall Street was a product for sale, and the financial health of the customer be damned. It was all very disingenuous. To get new business, we would do a free financial plan with a potential client. Above all, I knew that the commission-based investment sales game was a brutal way of making a living, even though I was successful. Toward the end, my health was suffering, too. I was working all the time, not seeing my family, not exercising, drinking and eating too much. There was endless stress and bad news.

I knew a change was long overdue, but I needed a career that kept me engaged with clients. I wanted to work with them to secure their financial futures. But I needed a business model that allowed me to sleep at night and wake up in the morning to look at the guy in the mirror and hold my head up high—just like my dad had taught me.

So at age 27, I pulled the trigger and left the commission-based side of Wall Street in my rear view mirror and moved over to the fee-based advisory side. I also began the process of reevaluating how I invested my clients' money. Efficient and free markets and not a random beat the market crapshoot would be my cornerstones. Within days, I felt in my gut that I was making the right move, but a total act of serendipity confirmed that sentiment.

Shortly after I crossed over from the dark side, I attended a seminar sponsored by Charles Schwab. It paired a five-star Morningstar manager, Donald Yacktman, and a stranger to me, Rex Sinquefield. The talk was a game-changer for me when Rex stood up and made a simple, yet amazingly brilliant, argument that proved to be the last big piece of the puzzle for me: efficient markets are controlled by the laws of supply and demand.

Rex said what I had felt all along—that the free market system is an amazingly efficient machine. The free market takes into account all knowable data and also factors in the unknowns, like emotion, to determine market prices.

> *"Active management does not make sense theoretically, isn't justified empirically, and it doesn't work for your client...other than that—it's just fine."*
> *–Rex Sinquefield*

The fact is, "knowns" and "unknowns" are both unpredictable, as are stock market prices. The essence of Rex's comments at the Schwab talk—and one that I would eventually build a \$4* billion financial advisory business on—is that five-star managers are like chimps throwing darts at a board. A certain percentage of those money managers will beat the market because stock market prices are random. However, most managers couldn't do

as of 5/2013

couldn't do what their clients needed most—provide steady returns on a sustainable basis, year-after-year. Sooner or later, the law of averages would catch up with the dartboard crowd, and that's when the avalanche of excuses started. I entrusted my clients' money to a bunch of monkeys. Actually, monkeys would have been better. They work for peanuts; gurus charge huge fees.

It had become crystal clear to me that the other financial advisors in the room did not see the problem. Heck, they didn't even want to admit there *was* a problem. Leaving the room after the Schwab conference, I knew I could never again go back and offer my clients actively-managed mutual funds. That was scary, but I knew had to stop speculating and gambling with my clients' money. I swore to protect my clients from the Wall Street Bullies, the very people I had trusted for years.

David Versus Goliath

When I saw the light at the Schwab conference that day, I realized that investors were being pushed around by mega-investment complexes.

They were manipulating investors, and they were bullying their clients, a practice I found reprehensible. With this book, I want to pick up the slingshot of justice, David and Goliath-style, and fight a financial management industry built on lies.

No One Likes a Bully

As a kid, I was big for my age. This would seem to be an advantage, but older kids mercilessly picked on me. We were relatively poor, and when it rained my mother made me wear a three-dollar, bright orange rain poncho. It made me an excellent target for the bullies in my neighborhood. Every time it rained, I got taunted and beat up. At night, I laid awake in my bed praying it would not rain the next day. The older boys pushed me, hit me, tripped me, and sometimes spit on me, and I let it happen because I was too wracked with fear to fight back. Many days I hid from them and walked the long way home hoping to avoid a confrontation. To help me sleep at night, my mother bought a cheap radio at K-Mart. It soothed me to sleep, but the next morning fear reared its ugly head.

My Dad noticed that I'd been getting into fights, and I reluctantly told him how I was getting bullied. Dad told me that if I didn't stand up for myself, I would get bullied forever. Growing up in the streets of Charleston, West Virginia, my father knew how to fight. He often talked about fights he had been in as a boy and as a soldier in the military.

He was small, but he stood up for himself. In my eyes, he was the brave one. It was yet another way I wanted to be like him.

"Mark," he said, "here is what you have to do. The next time they start to pick on you, choose the leader (probably the biggest) and punch him between his eyes on the bridge of his nose. If you hit him hard enough, his eyes will water, and he won't be able to see you or fight back. Remember, you didn't start the fight. You didn't want this, but if they won't leave you alone, they have it coming. After you open up with the first punch, don't stop! Keep punching with all of your might. Don't give him an opportunity to regroup, take it to him. It won't last long. It might seem forever, but it will probably be over in two minutes."

My dad said, "Bullies are the worst kind of cowards. They hang in packs, because they are really more afraid than you are. If you take on the biggest one and hurt him, none of them will ever bother you again."

When the inevitable confrontation finally happened, I was scared, but ready. I took my Dad's advice and defended myself the best I could. I got hurt, but I stood up for myself and didn't let myself continue to be the victim. The band of bullies never bothered me again.

I had become the hero of my own story. I stood up to evil, and I prevailed. That is what I want to offer you when it comes to your investing experience. I want to give you the confidence and power to stand up for yourself so that the Wall Street Bullies can't hurt you again. In this book, I'm going to tell you about the Wall Street Bullies, show you how their games work, and put a stop to their interference in your investment success forever.

Increasingly, the public is catching on to the lies and the bullying coming from Wall Street. When the economic crash came in 2008, I felt saddened but vindicated. The financial downturn gave us a chance to change the investment landscape for our clients. We created presentations like "How to Love the Bear" and "There Is No Time to Panic." Our goal: to teach investors how to be proactive and how to be prudent, how to stand up for themselves, and how to take real control of their portfolios.

Those characteristics, along with the need for investors to stop being victims and stop help perpetuating the lies, are the take-home message. I want you to have faith and confidence in free markets. I don't want you to speculate and gamble. I want you to understand where real returns come from and how to go about the work of capturing them.

Above all, I want you to know: market returns come from the market, not the manager.

"Own" Your Own Portfolio

This book is dedicated to the Main Street investor—investors who see their money as a means to fulfill their deepest and most cherished dreams and purpose in life. This book is not for the speculator who sees money as a drug to be gambled and speculated with to create surges of adrenaline, ego, and money lust. This book is not for the speculator. You may have one hundred dollars or one hundred million, but if you want to stop falling for the traps that Wall Street has set to capture your assets and to truly gain peace of mind then you have the right book in your hands.

By the time you're done reading it, you (and not the fraudsters from Wall Street) will be the real owner of your financial future. I will ruthlessly hammer home these points because your financial well-being depends on it.

By "owning" I mean the whole enchilada—taking full responsibility for what goes into your portfolio, in what increments, and how long it stays there—understanding what you are doing and the reasons why.

When you learn how to do that, you'll also be striking a liberating blow against those bloviating barons on Wall Street. Imagine spending your career in an industry that dishes out taxpayer-funded bonuses, many of them in the billions of dollars, to so-called investment experts who blew call after call during one of the most critical periods in American financial history.

Nice work if you can get it, and the fact is, you can—at least in terms of managing your own money better than the crowd that sunk the U.S. economy during that past few years.

I'll explain how you can escape from the mediocrity that permeates Wall Street and learn how to manage your money effectively, safely, and profitably. I'll show you how to:

1. Master the critical ability to allocate your financial resources.

2. Understand the phenomenon of global markets (yes, capitalism and free markets still work).

3. Fully comprehend and, better yet, put into action the investment skills that have evaded the most polished and articulate gurus on Wall Street.

4. Maintain the discipline it takes to be a successful investor long-term.

Main Street Money reveals why speculating and gambling with your financial future is a fool's errand (one that's happily perpetuated by investment industry insiders). You'll find tools for identifying your risk tolerance limits. I'll give you detailed, easy-to-follow steps for building a financial investment framework that allows you to master the art of designing a portfolio to maximize your expected returns no matter what your risk category.

The book is full of useful graphics and flowcharts revealing insights highlighting some of the best-kept secrets on Wall Street. Practical case studies provide in-depth analysis and clearly illustrate *Main Street Money* investment concepts.

After finishing *Main Street Money*, you will come away with the tools and talent to radically change the way you look at Wall Street and how you regard professional money managers.

Above all, *Main Street Money* will trigger the portfolio master inside of every investor to rise up and take control over your own financial future, and take that future away from self-proclaimed experts on Wall Street who, by design, are the biggest threat to investors' on Main Street. Metaphorically speaking, it is time to rise up and punch these bullies square in the nose, because deep down all bullies are cowards. It is my job as your coach to inspire you with the courage to put them in their place. Our rallying cry:

"We have had enough. We will no longer fall for your forecasting parlor tricks. We see you for who you really are. We are taking control of our portfolios and our destinies."

With *Main Street Money*, changing the status quo starts now.

1
LOSING FAITH IN WALL STREET

"Wall Street: a thoroughfare that begins in a graveyard and ends in a river."
—Anonymous

AT THE TENDER AGE OF FOUR I LEARNED to be careful while making financial decisions. For months before my birthday, I begged my parents for one gift, a talking Woody Woodpecker puppet. We were very poor and it was a big deal at the time. I was repeatedly told that it was too expensive, followed by the old adage, "Money doesn't grow on trees."

After I blew out the candles and opened my present, there was Woody, wondrously staring at me from his box. It was the height of technology for its day. You pulled a string, and it said one of five classic Woody Woodpecker lines, each one starting and ending with his unforgettable Woody laugh.

I promised myself I would have it for life, but two days later I allowed myself to be intimidated by my next-door-neighbor, Bobby. He was two years older than me and a head taller. He wanted to trade a cheap plastic football for my technological wonder toy. He assured me it was a good trade. I foolishly allowed myself to be duped.

When my Dad got home, he sent me across the street to retrieve my birthday present. I proudly returned with it—along with an impressive black eye.

Even at that age, I was hardly alone. The financial industry is full of examples of how investment advice usually works out for the guy who gives it. Here's one of the best:

When asked by his church rector for some investment advice, Jay Gould, the Wall Street tycoon, made the pastor swear he would keep the advice secret; the pastor agreed. Gould said, "Buy Missouri Pacific."

The clergyman did and the stock went up for several months. Eventually the stock crumbled, and the rector was wiped out. Sadly, he went to see Gould. "I took your advice and lost all my savings," he said.

Gould said, "I'm sorry. To restore your faith, I'm going to give you $40,000 for the $30,000 you lost." Gould wrote out a check, and the minister reluctantly accepted it.

The minister said, "I must confess something. I didn't keep my word. I told several members of the congregation."

Came Gould's cheerful reply, "Oh, I know that. They were the ones I was after."

Taking Ownership of Your Financial Life

In my mind, you are like the clergyman, and the Wall Street Bullies are like Jay Gould. They're only in the game to fleece you and take as much of your money as they can and wobble down Wall Street with a wheelbarrow full of your cash.

Consequently, a big part of this book is taking these guys out—and getting you back in the game as the real "owner" of your investments.

Now, by owner, I don't mean taking on the pressure of making your own portfolio picks and deciding whether it's a good idea to add Portuguese debentures to your investments. What I mean is knowing how wealth accumulation really works, and using that knowledge as leverage to hold your actual financial advisors accountable for the decisions they make in your name. Knowledge is power for taking control of your financial future.

Let's face it. Our retirement, our health, our freedoms, ability to travel, ability to take care of our children, even ability to take care of our aging parents are all impacted by our ability to be a successful investor. So there's a lot riding on this concept of being successful with your portfolio.

The good news? It's not as steep an uphill climb as you might think, and it's a climb you can and should take without the help of Wall Street's "best and brightest." These are basic concepts that anyone can understand.

Matson Alert: Monkey Business

In December 2010, Fox TV host John Stossel conducted a vivid experiment.[1] He tossed 30 darts at a page of stocks and compared his "hits" with the top stock selections from 10 big money managers for that year. The results?

Dartboard = 31%

Money Managers = 9.5%

On the same show, Princeton University economist Burton G. Malkiel said that in the previous decade "more than two thirds of actively managed funds were beaten by a simple low-cost indexed fund, and the active funds that win in one period aren't the same ones who win in the next period."

The Three Types of Wall Street Bullies

"Know your enemy."
—Sun Tzu, *The Art of War*

You are in a battle for your financial well-being, and you do have enemies. Your primary adversaries are the Wall Street behemoths who profit and prosper by keeping you mired in problems. They create the illusion that they are the masters of the universe, and, if you just trust them to do their magic, you will make huge returns by consistently outsmarting the market with little to no risk. These people are financial predators and they prey on uninformed and uneducated investors. Often they themselves are ignorant to the lies and myths they propagate. After all, the best con artists are the ones who believe their own delusions. If you blindly trust your money to these people you can lose more than you ever imagined.

Let's look at their tricks.

The Con Man

This one is simple—think of Bernie Madoff. These are people who promise amazing returns and use a Ponzi scheme to dupe investors into handing over their hard-earned cash. They often have sophisticated names for their systems, but they always violate one big rule of investing, "There ain't no such thing as a free lunch," and its corollary, "If it seems too good to be true, it is."

This is pure Main Street wisdom that could have literally saved billions of dollars for Madoff victims. The con man first gains your trust with his great reputation and then promises high returns with no downside, a sure thing. He takes the money from early investors and pays out huge returns with the money from later investors. In some cases, he simply sends out false statements showing massive gains in the victim's assets. In reality, the con man is stealing money from their clients and the reports are bogus.

To protect yourself from the con game, never allow anyone to help you manage your assets who does not use a third party custodian. Without a third party custodian, the fox is guarding the henhouse. The custodian holds your assets in trust and protects you from theft and fraud. When investors finally catch on and ask for their money back, the con is over. Some of the world's most "sophisticated" and elite investors fell for this fraud and it devastated lives. The pain and suffering caused by Madoff literally resulted in suicides. Your investing decisions can be a matter of life or death.

The Prognosticator

The problem with predicting the future is simple—no one can do it. Nevertheless, there is no shortage of loud-mouthed crystal-ball fortune-tellers who will convincingly claim they know exactly what is going to happen next. They offer sophisticated graphs and charts, economic theories, and tons of data. These soothsayers are well-spoken and dynamic and often convince investors to make changes in their portfolios based on their market predictions. They sell newsletters, they run broker-dealers, they manage hedge funds. They prey on the desire of weary investors to have a clear view of the future. After all, if you simply know what is going to happen in the economy and which way stocks are going to go next, wouldn't your job as an investor be so much easier?

Indeed, it would! You could simply move all of your money into "the thing" that is going to make huge double-digit returns every year and never lose any money. The only problem is no one can predict the future. And those people who tell you they can are delusional or flat-out lying.

After all, if they could accurately predict the future, they wouldn't tell you. They would keep that information to themselves and extract huge rates of return without risk. If your portfolio needs a forecast about the future to work, it is already broken. Like palm readers and psychics, prognosticators prey on our fervent and childish wish to know the unknowable. When anyone tells you they know what the market is going to do in the next twelve minutes or twelve months, run—don't walk—the other way!

The Guru

It's easy to find the gurus, just go to any mutual fund rating service and look for a five-star mutual fund or buy a copy of any investment magazine, and pasted on the cover will be a picture of a well-dressed money manager who has beat the market over the last decade. And you are supposed to trust your money to this guru to beat the market in the future.

These so-called geniuses are reported to have amazing insights into which companies are "under-valued" and poised for explosive growth in the future. Perhaps you have invested your hard-earned money with a guru, a manager with stellar past performance, only to discover that his hot streak ended after you trusted your portfolio with him. Have you ever wondered why the magazines only publish the "best" stock-pickers over the last decade and never the future decade? Here is the painful truth…

No one knows who the hot stock-picking manager will be next—not even the mutual fund companies that hire them. Why? Because there is zero correlation between a stock-picker's market beating performance and his ability to repeat performance in the future. It bears repeating—*zero correlation*. [2]

These are the bullies that you must be prepared to fight. Your portfolio and your family's future depend on it. If you do not understand these tricks they will eventually seduce you with their Wall Street bravado and deception.

When I was twelve-years-old, my father took the family on a trip to New York City. Not far from Wall Street we saw a man at a makeshift table with three cups. Beneath one of the cups he had a small ball, and he asked people to guess where the ball was after he deftly shuffled the cups around. It was so simple. After allowing a few passersby to play for free, he invited the crowd to bet if they could follow it in the future.

I had ten dollars in my pocket, money I had earned from cutting grass, and I started to raise my hand to play. My father grabbed my hand and put it down. "Just watch," he said. The man next to me put up twenty dollars and after a fast flourish of the man's hands he guessed the cup in the middle. To his astonishment and mine, it wasn't there! It was under the cup on the right. My father looked at me, "See, boy, it's a con. He made it look easy, but if you trust him you will soon be parted from your money." It was a lesson I would never forget and every investor should heed.

Who Needs Wall Street?

After all, what do Wall Street's "best and brightest" know that you don't? Frankly, they're no smarter about investing and wealth creation than you.

For decades, investment industry professionals have kept that secret to themselves, burying the fact that you can handle your own finances as well as any Wall Street money manager and creating a mythical image of the financial markets as overly-complicated, only navigable with the "expert" guidance of a wizened financial guru.

A guru, by the way, who'll peel up to five percent of your money off the top, and tell you you're getting a bargain in the deal.

The reality? The myth of the savvy investment manager, steering you through the dangerous and choppy waters of the global financial markets is a myth—right up there with the Easter Bunny and the ability of leprechauns to locate gold.

The fact of the matter is, the myth is a dangerous one—a canard that promises to eliminate risk and make you wealthy in the process.

The harsh reality? Nobody, even the so-called financial Nostradamuses of the world can select the best stocks, accurately time the market, or accurately forecast the financial future.

Anyone who tells you different is selling you a bill of goods.

Want proof (and you should)? My experience over the last quarter of a century proves that most investors, when educated about portfolio design basics will make far better decisions about investing than the Wall Street elite—you simply need the right tools. Let's start with two reasons why the idea that a Wall Street Bully knows better than you is a childish one:

1. First, let's go back in time a few years, to 2008 and the unraveling of the U.S. financial markets. The next time a financial advisor tells you they know better about stocks than you do, ask them this: how do you explain the massive failure of the financial industry—especially those self-proclaimed seers—to know accurately and appropriately account for the leverage risk responsible for the massive collapse of financial giants like Bear Stearns and Washington Mutual? Even worse, ask them how hundreds of billions of taxpayer-funded bailout money, in the form of the federal government's Troubled Asset Relief program (TARP), went to the same banks and investment houses that brought the economy to its knees in the first place? Where were the crystal balls then?

2. Second, and even more important, if Wall Street was so smart, how did money managers fail to deliver positive returns to their funds and investment accounts in the aftermath of the Great Recession of 2008-2009—even as major stock indexes rose substantially?

When you ask these questions, expect a good deal of foot-shuffling, hemming-and-hawing, and a big push on the part of your advisor to change the subject ("How 'bout them Cubs!").

Just don't expect any concrete, useful answers. The dirty secret is most Wall Street types don't have a "concrete, useful answer." It's the primary purpose of this book that you get those answers, and use them to reclaim ownership of your own portfolios.

> *"Wealth is better than poverty, if only for financial reasons."*
> –Woody Allen

Why Do Financial Professionals Get It So Wrong?

The Woody Allen line is a good one, and one that accurately sums up the attitudes millions of investors everywhere in this, the glacially-moving aftermath of the Great Recession.

Let's face it, Americans want to be wealthy—and they're willing to work hard to achieve that goal. The natural inclination toward financial security, and the willingness and discipline to undertake the practices needed to obtain financial security, are all hallmarks of the great American investor.

How else to explain the trillions of dollars invested into retirement fund assets, including IRAs, 401k's, private and public pension plans, and annuities—$17.5 trillion through 2010, according to the Washington, DC-based Investment Company Institute?[2] How else to explain the rise in the number of U.S. millionaires—up to 8.4 million in 2010 from 7.8 million in 2009? [3] Or the profits U.S. financial services firms are raking in from investors' fees—about $345 billion in 2003, according to the Securities Industry Association? [4]

So, why are so many investors losing money? Why, as Venita VanCaspel notes in her epic book on investing *The Power of Money Dynamics*[5], are 95 percent of Americans doomed to spend their retirement years mired in debt, handcuffed by limited financial resources, and most likely filling out application forms at Home Depot or McDonalds to help make ends meet.

Imagine spending your golden years under the Golden Arches or as a Wal-Mart greeter?

It doesn't have to be this way. And I'm going to do everything in my power to not only prevent that from happening, but to show you how you can live out your life in relative financial prosperity—just by doing a few simple things that I've been doing for myself and my clients over the past 25 years.

My name is Mark Matson, and I teach people how to create wealth. Some of you out here in the Midwest might have heard my name or seen me on TV—Fox, CNBC, Bloomberg, Public Television—or read about me in the *Wall Street Journal* or the *New York Times*. Some might have come to my investing seminars. More likely, many of you don't know me but will be glad we met (even through the pages of this book) after you've heard what I have to say, applied my investing tenets, and accumulated genuine wealth.

My goal with this book is two-fold: I want to show you how Wall Street is leading you down a path—a toxic path—that is designed intentionally to mislead you and keep you from maximizing your true wealth potential. I also want to use this book as a wake-up call.

Wall Street gurus are intimidating but really aren't that smart, and they can easily bully you into losing your life's savings.

So when I say outwit, outsmart, and out-invest the Wall Street Bullies, the plain truth is the financial industry's best and brightest aren't the best and aren't the brightest. What they want you to believe is actually very dangerous to your financial health. They purport to possess special knowledge that allows them to take advantage of stock market prices without risk.

In other words, their genius is going to make *you* rich.

Early in my career, I fell prey to this delusion. As a young financial advisor, the first investment lesson I learned was idea of active management—the idea that there was some savvy financial manager pulling the strings behind the scenes. I gradually discovered the harsh, cold reality that no one can pick the best stocks, time the market, or accurately predict the future consistently. In my opinion, to think anyone on Wall Street actually possesses this power is a childish fantasy.

Now I know Wall Street firms have invested a great deal of money and energy into promoting the idea of stock gurus. I'm frequently on CNBC, Fox Business, and BNN, and the hosts on those networks are always asking me which way the market is going and which way the economy is headed. Make no mistake; there are plenty of financial gurus with big marketing budgets behind them who are insisting that they have phenomenal predictive abilities.

Wall Street's "Big 3" Failures

We've seen three major failures of Wall Street over the last ten years. This is further proof that the self-proclaimed experts don't know what they're talking about. Or worse, they *do* know what they're talking about, but they're *intentionally* misleading you.

#1   Mortgage crisis

The mortgage crisis was all about leverage. When I first started in the business, my father told me leverage can kill. And I believe him. Sure, leverage can be a great thing when markets are rising, but it can also destroy your business, destroy your company, and cause massive bankruptcy when markets go the other way. Any student of history, the Great Depression or other massive market dips, can tell you that financial leverage was always at the middle of a given market crash.

The problem with the mortgage crisis for large banks and brokerages was a complete failure to diversify. One of the basic tenets of investing is to understand how to properly diversify your holdings. Diversification ensures that a collapse or a crash in one sector of the market or your portfolio can't destroy all your wealth. The big Wall Street firms, be they mortgage houses, insurance companies, or large brokerage houses, failed to understand these two simple principles of deep leverage and lack of diversification.

#2   Financial advisors failed to maintain discipline.

There was another massive failure over the last ten years, one that hit close to home for me. It was a failure of advisors and investors to remain disciplined throughout the crash. Financial professionals constantly talk about the random market, about long-term investing, and about discipline (especially in buying low and selling high). Too bad they didn't take their own advice during the stock market crash of 2008. It was shocking to see financial advisors who had professed their understanding of random markets and unpredictability panic and move all of their client portfolios to cash when the market plummeted. That panic caused average investors trillions in financial losses. We'll explore the psychological and the economic elements that triggered that disastrous "rush to financial judgment."

#3   Wall Street fund managers failed to beat the market.

The third, and maybe the most telling of the "big three" failures, is the inability of Wall Street firms to beat the market and deliver more than a market rate of return back to investors. Whether it's the large mutual fund complexes or the large brokerage houses, the basic rallying cry among Wall Street titans is this: "Trust us with your money, and we'll make you rich." Of course, they never really explicitly say that in their marketing materials (legally they can't), but financial firms imply that they will beat the market, deliver stellar rates of returns, tell you what the best stocks are in advance, and tell you when to get in and out of the market to maximize your rate of return based on some vague economic forecast about the future.

Obviously, the big investment managers were wrong on just about every count.

First Steps

First things first.

Like most best-laid plans, we need to lay a solid financial foundation, a few cornerstones like my father used to say to me when I was a little boy.

The larger question—and the central thesis of this book—is how to develop your investment strategies using stocks, bonds and other investment tools. In other words, how do I maximize my power as an "owner" of my own portfolio? The traditional wealth creation model does, indeed, have stocks as its centerpiece. Because many investors have been beaten up so badly by Wall Street Bullies they have lost their faith and trust in stocks as a wealth creation tool. If you trusted these people to time the market and pick the best stocks and your experience was dismal, you are probably ready to throw out the baby with the bathwater and swear never to invest in equities again. If you are ready to give up on the market because of your past experience you are not alone. That is perhaps the cruelest blow of all. The bully has caused Main Street investors to distrust the market and give up on their future. However, there is a way to invest in markets that eliminates these failed ways of speculating, and I will show you how.

Here's another thing that gets my blood boiling. Investors have been spoon-fed the notion that future stock market trends can be accurately measured and predicted. Articles in business magazines extolling "The 10 Hottest Stocks for Fall" or "7 Big Movers That You Need to Add to Your Portfolio Now" feed that mindset. So do penny stock investment web sites and some less than scrupulous financial planners operating out on the fringes. These charlatans cast shadows over the vast majority of planners who try to do the right thing by their clients by investing their money prudently and selectively.

I've never bought into any of that nonsense.

Smashing "Predictive" Stereotypes

Allow me to explain why.

Wall Street sells the sizzle. They generate excitement surrounding star personalities. These days, it seems like everyone is an investment expert.

Consider the '90s hedge fund firm Long Term Capital Management, which loaded its advisory team with world-class economists and Nobel laureates. Trouble was, the economic dream team at the firm couldn't live up to its billing as ace predictors of stock market trends. In 1998, the Long Term Capital Management Fund had to be bailed out after hemorrhaging billions of client investment dollars.[6] More recently, the MF Global debacle appears to be the result of the same type of grotesque hyper-leverage engaged in by LTCM.

As the dream team at LTCM proved, nobody can predict the future. Look at Alan Greenspan, chairman of the Federal Reserve Board. In August 1990, Greenspan noted that, "Those who argue that we are already in a recession, I think, are reasonably certain to be wrong."[7]

There was only one thing wrong with his comment—the economy *was already* in recession. Greenspan (and most other financial seers and prognosticators) just didn't realize it yet. Greenspan, one of the savviest Federal Reserve chairmen ever, and one of the brightest lights in the economic firmament, couldn't figure out when the U.S. economy was in recession. That goes to show how difficult it is for the rest of us to figure out where the market, let alone the economy, is headed.

Unfortunately, Greenspan doesn't exactly have a monopoly on faulty economic forecasts.

Throughout the 1990s to 2005, economists tut-tutted the prospect of the economy growing at a rate faster than 2.5 percent annually. They issued disapproving clucks over an unemployment rate that was lower than six percent. The combination, they said, would trigger breakaway inflation. Not so. During the '90s and through 2006, the economy easily eclipsed the 2.5 annual growth rate[8] while average unemployment was well south of six percent.[9] And the U.S. economy experienced only very low levels of inflation.

Academic studies prove that economists are terrible at predicting the economy.

Stock market prognosticators fare even worse. Is it any surprise that *The Wall Street Journal* regularly publishes a contest between some of Wall Street's most prominent money managers and a monkey with a dart? Time and time again, the battle results in a draw, or with the monkey coming out on top more times than the Wall Street experts would like to admit (or would want their clients to know about).

Again, I'm not *intentionally* picking on the Wall Street professionals (okay, maybe I am).

I'm simply trying to illustrate a point: that it's very difficult—practically impossible—to predict stock market trends. And anyone who tells you they can should be kept at arm's length from your portfolio and your wallet. I've always believed that the job of a financial advisor is simple: he or she assumes the responsibility of helping clients define and meet their financial goals through the appropriate and judicious management of their financial portfolios. It's a big job and one that can't be successfully carried out by relying on predictions and prognostications.

Matson Alert: The Folly of Predictions
A perennial joke on Wall Street is that economists have forecast nine of the past five recessions. In my view, Wall Street experts have picked nine of the last five bull markets.

In the Prediction Game, Investors Lose

I tell my clients to lay off the so-called experts. They want to tear down the very wealth you're trying to build-up.

I see it all the time. Financial experts who fancy themselves securities industry swamis don't really mind too much if their "take it to the bank" calls evaporate when the bells rings, the market opens, and reality kicks in. They simply chalk it up to bad luck or bad timing and move on, ready to make their next big call that will empty your pockets.

Such a confident, if misguided, stance is not unprecedented. Anthropologists say that some African tribal rainmakers often cover their tracks when their elaborate rain dances fail to result in so much as one drop of precipitation (unless you count the beads of sweat forming on their brows). When no rain appears, anthropologists say that the rainmaker may shrug off the result, pointing out that he didn't exactly say when it was going to rain or that he might have missed a step in the big dance number and have to do the entire thing all over again. Some rainmakers are even known to point a finger at an unsuspecting audience member and accuse him or her of jinxing the dance ritual. The point is that it's everyone's fault but the rainmaker's.

Stock market seers are like that, too. If ABC Company's stock doesn't enjoy that 10-point bump the experts predicted, it's not their fault. The company just isn't ready to move yet, or the industry just had a bad week/month/year. The only losers in this scenario are the investors who bought the expert's forecast, hook, line, and sinker.

> **Matson Alert: Fear of Failure**
> According to the criteria provided by the journal Economics and Portfolio Strategy, when applied to the 452 managed funds from 1990 to 2009, only 13 would have outperformed the given index.[10,11]

The Prediction Racket is Big Business

As ticked off as I get at the Wall Street Bullies, you can't really blame the hucksters.

An entire cottage industry of wayward investment advice has sprung up in the form of investment newsletters, Internet web sites, direct mail campaigns, social media posts on Twitter and Facebook, and TV and radio spots. Who hasn't heard an advertisement on the radio that gold is at "an all-time high" but won't be for long. So, "lock in now before it's too late."

And you can't really even blame the investors who fall for the prediction gambits. Wall Street is a scary place that's often hard to read and understand. And, make no mistake; investors are reminded of the financial markets' complexities every day by financial services firms whose livelihoods depend on frightened and anxious investors. A pat on the hand and a seemingly knowledgeable monologue on the stock market, and the investor feels a little bit better, feels that a professional is in control of the situation.

Perhaps it's inevitable that the investor loses while the financial services professional wins.

Maybe you've heard the story of the high-rolling client who received a personal tour from the president of a brokerage firm aching for his business. A nice lunch, a tour of the building, and then a drive down to the beach to demonstrate the solid days that lie ahead

You'd Be Surprised What the Experts Don't Know

On Wall Street, nobody really knows anything.

Some very smart people populate the concrete canyons of Wall Street, but the job of guessing what will happen in the financial markets is too much for even those financial services people with the loftiest intellects.

Let me give you an example. In an issue of *Fortune* magazine, the publication noted a study of 40,000 stock recommendations made from 213 stock brokerage firms in the year 2000. The stocks that were most heavily touted lost a collective 31 percent in 2001. The stocks that were pushed to the bottom of the 'must have' list gained 49 percent in 2001. In other words, up is down and down is up.[12]

for the big-ticket customer if he signs up with the firm, but the brokerage firm president goes too far. Driving by the seaside manses, he points out that many of these homes are owned by the firm's hard-working and successful stockbrokers. Sensing a red flag, the customer turns to the president and says, "That's all well and good, but where are the customers' houses?"

That's what happens when investors fall into the trap of listening to stock market predictions. They carry virtually all of the risk and have to live with the results. The financial soothsayers are right just often enough to keep investors coming back for more. As one old Wall Street trader I know says, "Even a turkey can fly in a hurricane."

Investing vs. Speculating

Investors who rely on crystal balls and pre-packaged predictions would do well to ask themselves one question: are you an investor, or are you a speculator? The answer influences everything in your financial future. The best way to find the answer to the question is to study the two terms.

There's a legitimate school of thought that the two terms are inseparable, or at least in the "kissing cousins" category.

I maintain that the difference is significant.

Take the term "investor". By my definition, an investor is one who maps out a portfolio accumulation plan and sticks by it, through thick and thin, secure in the knowledge that the long-term is what counts. And just so there is no confusion about what long-term is, it means life-long—not three, five, or even ten years. Investors plot out plans that are based on their lifestyles and long-term objectives—not on what the market does today, tomorrow, or even next month. In other words, they dictate their strategy to the market.

Speculators don't see it that way. They get ants in their pants. Speculators could give a hoot about consistency and long-term goals and instead pray on the altar of instant gratification that the stock market can offer one who "guesses" right at the appropriate time.

Some Wall Street wit once said that speculation is a usually unsuccessful attempt to turn a little money into a lot of money. Investing, on the other hand, is an effort to prevent a lot of money from becoming a little. And it's almost always a success.

Speculating can easily destroy your wealth. As my good friend, David Booth, CEO and Founder of Dimensional Fund Advisors says, "The best way of ending up with a small fortune is to start with a big one."

How can you tell the difference between speculating versus prudent long-term investing? Simple. If you find yourself trying to stock pick, market time, or chase a manager's

---

Matson Alert: Don't Just Do Something, Stand There

According to Dalbar, Inc., an investment analysis firm, most investors would do better if they just invested in a major stock index and left it at that.

From January 1, 1991 through December 31, 2010 the S&P 500 Index averaged 9.14% annually. But the average equity fund investor only earned 3.83% over the same time.[13]

When it comes to following the so-called experts, it's actually better to do nothing, which is still a form of action.

track record, you are speculating. Any investment decision that uses a forecast or a prediction about the future is rank speculation. Most investors are really speculating with their money and they have no idea they are doing it.

True investing is quite rare on Main Street and downright non-existent on Wall Street. Investing is purposefully understanding how markets work and designing a globally diversified portfolio that eliminates stock picking, market timing, and forecasts of all types. It means constructing an allocation unique to your personal risk/return preferences and then remaining disciplined over an entire lifetime. This is nearly impossible for most investors and even most investment professionals to pull off, but I will show you how to develop and master these critical skills.

My Rules for Avoiding Speculation and Focusing on Investing

Here are a few rules of thumb to distinguish you from trading speculators:

Ignore predictions. Nobody on Wall Street has ever gotten rich predicting the future. Instead, they get rich convincing others they can forecast the future. Stay away from short-term predictions.

Don't try to time the market. Although some hucksters may tell you different, nobody can move your money in and out of the markets at just the right time, again and again and again. Sure, it can happen once in a while. Even a broken clock is right twice a day. Basing your investment strategy on someone's ability to figure out short-term market trends is akin to timing every green traffic light on your commute to work. Too many factors interfere with the process. A study by Dalbar Inc. revealed that by staying invested in the S&P 500 Index (Long-Term investment) beat the average market timing strategy by more than 2.3 to 1 over the 20 year period ending 2010.[13] People who exit the stock market to avoid a decline are odds-on-favorites to miss the next rally. Remember, for a market timing approach to succeed you have to be correct twice—when you leave the stock market and when you jump back in. Why double your chance of failure? Leave the market timing to the speculators.

Never speculate with your portfolio. You can lose more than you could possibly imagine and worse yet—you might "get lucky" with a piece of your portfolio and start to believe you have the magic ability to make easy money. Don't set yourself up to gamble and speculate with larger and larger chunks of your money. Leave the speculating to the chumps.

Stay disciplined. All successful investors share a common trait. They have discipline.

They don't panic, stay away from making emotional decisions, and don't let their ego get in the way of portfolio decisions. In short, they're not as concerned about being right as they are about making money.

> **Fast Fact: The Price of Doing Business with Wall Street**
> - If you had invested $100,000 in the average U.S. stock mutual fund in 1973, at the end of 2010, you would have earned $2.1 million.[14] Not bad.
> - If you had invested $100,000 in the Standard & Poor's 500 Index over the same period, you would have earned $3.5 million.[15]
>
> In other words, you would have incurred a more than million-dollar penalty for investing with those brilliant minds on Wall Street who tell you they can beat the market.

Your First Steps

So how do we solve the problems that are mounting up like logs on a bonfire on Wall Street? Simple—ignore them and go our own way. Specifically, go your own way and learn how to build a quality portfolio to invest for the long term.

By adopting a "value" approach to your portfolio, you're already one up on the poor folks who think they can time the stock market and build a big windfall in the process.

By avoiding speculating tendencies, you also avoid the excessive risk you take by trading in and out of the market so often.

It all comes down to human behavior, a factor that I apply into all of the investment decisions at my firm. A few years ago, my father and I were talking about an investor behavior problem and he brought up a line from *The Horse Whisperer* with Robert Redford.

> ***Annie:*** *I read this article about what you do for people with horse problems.*
> ***Tom Booker:*** *Well, truth is, I help horses with people problems.*

What a great line. I've come to believe that we don't manage portfolios. We manage behavior. We work with portfolios that have people problems.

Like a fad dieter, no amount of information on a package label is going to keep you from eating that Twinkie. Similarly, no amount of information in this book is going to keep you from mismanaging your money.

No worries. I'll show you how to solve that problem, too.

It's going to take prudence and discipline. Prudence and discipline are never popular. Prudence means when the market crashes and everybody loses their minds (like in 2008 and the beginning of 2009), you have the emotional maturity and the discipline necessary to buy equities when they're down. Most people never reach this point in their investing careers. Come to think of it, most advisors never reach this point in their investing careers.

The critical element to outwit, outsmart, and out-invest the Wall Street Bullies is to know that it's not that hard. All you've got to do is diversify, get market rates of return, and stay the course over long periods of time.

There are significant forces at work helping you to build momentum. The good news is that capitalism and free markets work. There is such a thing as return on capital, and all investors, if they plan appropriately and have enough discipline and diversification, are entitled to capital markets' rates of returns. Those returns are generous over time.

You don't need to speculate to fully leverage the power that resides in the financial markets. That's the plain truth.

It's going to take some diligence and some studying, but fewer things in life have the capacity to pay a bigger reward than figuring how investing works and how it can secure your financial future.

Let's face it, most of your future depends on your taking ownership of your own portfolio. Your retirement, your children's education, supporting your church or a charitable cause—these things all require money, and lots of it.

I'm not a big believer that the federal government's going to provide me a successful retirement or a successful health experience in my old age. It's my belief that it's absolutely critical for every Americans to understand how to allocate his financial resources to get the maximum rate of return.

Doing so is not a luxury—it's a necessity. The quality of your life to no small extent is going to be determined by your ability to successfully become a seasoned investor.

And, at all costs, to keep Wall Street out of your investment decisions.

"An economist is an expert who will know tomorrow why the things he predicted yesterday didn't happen today."
—Laurence J. Peter, U.S Educator

2

THE SIX MYTHS OF MUTUAL FUND INVESTING

"Wall Street people learn nothing and forget everything."
–Ben Graham

INVESTING CAN BE AMAZINGLY SIMPLE. Too bad Wall Street doesn't see it that way. That's why, time and time again they fail. I'm an optimist, and I fully realize that failure is in the eyes of the beholder.

While Wall Street fails to provide the prudent advice you will need to have a successful investing experience, it does provide a mechanism for companies to raise the capital they need to grow and prosper. These companies provide needed jobs, products, and economic growth essential to our economy. Your job as an investor is to tap into these investment opportunities while avoiding and eliminating the Wall Street traps of speculating and gambling—no easy task. For anyone who is willing to put forward even a small amount of effort, it is achievable.

Anyone can learn how to tap into this incredible wealth creation tool. That's the good news. Come to think of it, that's the essential theme of this book. The bad news? On Wall Street, nobody actually does it.

A big part of the problem in the financial advice industry is that marketers at big money management firms have convinced the public that investment returns come not from the market, but from money managers.

So how has the marketing machine on Wall Street managed to convince you how brilliant Wall Street money managers can consistently beat the market? It's easy. They can trot out list after list of five-star mutual funds to try to prove it. The simple truth is that returns come from the market, not the managers. In effect, managers simply don't produce the results they claim.

Study after study shows this to be true. Consider a report from Standard & Poor's, which sought to examine the percentage of actively managed stock mutual funds that underperformed their respective benchmark for a five-year period ending in 2010.

Here's what Standard & Poor's found: [16]

US Large Cap	**62%** failed	all
US Mid Cap	**78%** failed	**FAILED**
US Small Cap	**63%** failed	to beat
Global	**60%** failed	market rate
International	**82%** failed	of return
Emerging Markets	**90%** failed	
US Gov't Long Bond	**68%** failed	
US Gov't Short Bond	**75%** failed	
Investment Grade Long	**70%** failed	
Investment Grade Short	**97%** failed	
National Municipal Bonds	**86%** failed	

The vast majority of so-called brilliant money managers backed by the research of the biggest mutual fund companies on the planet failed to deliver a simple market rate of return. These results are pathetic and predictable. For the last fifty years they have not changed.

Financial Folly

"I believe the search for top-performing stock funds is an intellectually discredited exercise that will come to be viewed as one of the great financial follies of the late 20th century."
–Jonathan Clements, Columnist, Wall Street Journal [17]

Given the horrible—and there's really no other word for it—performance across the board from mutual fund managers, why do so many investors use actively managed mutual funds?

The answer really isn't surprising. The mutual fund industry has succeeded in positioning active money managers as highly trained "experts" as doctors who are critical to your financial health. We've been hoodwinked by Wall Street into believing that experienced managers must certainly have the intellectual firepower to outperform a given stock market index. After all, none of us wants "average" when it comes to our financial investments, so a "professionally managed" fund sounds like a no-brainer.

But what these investors don't know can literally kill their investment returns. Wall Street wants it that way, and they don't want you to know about it.

They have no shortage of methods to pull the proverbial wool over your eyes, and you have the right to know how they're doing it. So let's start this chapter with the six myths linked to mutual funds that *always* separate you from your money, and *always* make those fund industry fat cats richer than ever.

Then we'll get on to the business of proving why free markets are the best path to financial freedom, no matter what the so-called Wizards of Wall Street are telling you.

#1: The Myth of Reported Returns

Mutual funds don't record and present their returns to the public based on true investor returns.

Instead, fund outfits use a hypothetical model geared towards time-weighted investment returns. That gives them more leeway to brag about returns over a given period, allowing them even more leeway to tout their "over-performance" over a five- or ten-year period, even though fund shareholders may well have lost money in that time frame.

How is that possible? Simple—investors, being human, didn't buy and hold the fund over that time period. No, they sold when the fund was low and bought shares when the fund was riding high, as investors are warned not to do.

That leaves them out of the picture when fund companies cite their big gains, but that doesn't stop mutual fund companies from touting their "five star" funds.

A great example is the CGM Focus Fund, which has a stated return of 18% for the ten year period ending February, 2010. The average investor return, according to Morningstar, actually lost 11% per year! [16]

Bad Company

> *"I'd compare stock pickers to astrologers, but I don't want to bad-mouth astrologers."*
> —Eugene F. Fama, Finance Professor, University of Chicago

#2: The Myth of "Past Performance"

Another huge canard wafting in from Wall Street is the myth of track record investing.

Here's the bill of goods being sold by mutual fund marketers: finding funds that did well in the past is a reliable indicator of which funds will do well in the future. In other words, an investor might say that the average mutual fund, and the average mutual fund family, does not beat the market. Okay, fine. But what if I find the best managers moving forward?

Here's what Wall Street wants you to think. Perhaps only 10 or 15 percent of the managers beat the market, but what if there was a way that you could find only those managers, and give those managers your money from now on? Is finding funds that did well in the past really a good method of indicating which funds will do well in the future? Does track record investing, when it comes to beating the market, have any correlation to future performance?

The numbers answer with a forceful, "No." Consider a study of over and under-performing active fund managers, this one from Baird Advisory Research.[18]

According to Baird, investors habitually (and erroneously, I might add) use past performance as a top measure when choosing a mutual fund. After all, as Baird points out, "Everyone is impressed by a strong track record." However, investors who rely on the past performance model are taking a big risk.

"Investors may be making a crucial mistake by fleeing from recent losers and flocking to recent winners, especially if they act on relatively short-term results," explains Baird. "At some point in their careers, virtually all top-performing money managers underperform their benchmark and their peers, particularly over time periods of three years or less."

By chasing performance, investors fall into an ongoing pattern of buying *after* share prices have risen considerably and selling *after* they have dropped. This behavior opposes the basic tenet of investing—buy low and sell high—and can cut dramatically into investor wealth. In addition, past performance is only part of the story.

In Baird's study of more than 1,500 mutual funds with a 10-year track record as of December 31, 2010, only 600 of those funds outperformed their respective benchmarks by one percentage point or more, on an annualized basis, over the 10-year period.

Approximately 85% of even what Baird calls the "top managers" in its study had at least one three-year period in which they underperformed by one percentage point or more.

According to Baird, about half of "top managers" lagged their benchmarks by three percentage points (on average, three separate times), and one-quarter of them fell five or more percentage points below the benchmark for at least one three-year period.

Nearly 81% of managers fell to below-average in at least one three-year period—and they remained below par for an average of almost four quarters. It appears that when managers fall below their peer group median, they tend to remain there for some time.

Depending on which of the three-year periods investors looked at, they could have been highly alarmed by what they saw.

Baird also examined shorter holding periods of one year, saying that many investors make decisions based on very short-term performance. The results were even more telling. All of the top managers dropped below their peer group average at least once. Compared to their peers, there were many 12-month time periods when "it was virtually certain that all top- performing managers will go through prolonged periods where they under-perform their benchmarks and lag their peers."

Potent Evidence That Active Management Doesn't Work

"Fiduciaries and other investors are confronted with potent evidence that the application of expertise, investigation, and diligence in efforts to 'beat the market' ordinarily promises little or no payoff, or even a negative payoff, after taking account of research and transaction costs."
—The American Law Institute

#3: The Myth of the "Genius" Fund Manager

This one is almost too easy to dispel. In fact, the most accurate studies will show us that you have about as much chance statistically, even if you're a Wall Street money manager, of beating the market by throwing darts. In fact, anyone—even a monkey—can beat a fund manager.

Perhaps you've heard of Lusha, the stock-picking monkey. In 2009, Lusha went head-to-head against some leading Russian money managers and wound up outperforming the managers' funds by 94%.[19]

"She bought successfully and her portfolio grew almost three times. She did better than almost the whole of the rest of the market," said Oleg Anisimov, editor of *Russian Finance* magazine.

"Everyone is shocked," Anisimov added. "What are they getting their bonuses for? Maybe it's worth sending them all to the circus." It turns out that it's not just chimps that are making monkeys out of portfolio managers.

According to a 2009 study by State Street Global Advisors, more than 70 percent of large-cap blend funds run by a portfolio manager failed to outperform their relative benchmark.[20]

From the same study: In 2004, only 28.8 percent large-cap blend managers beat their benchmark. Tracking those successful managers out for five years to 2009 shows that only 0.1 percent of them still beat their benchmark.

That means for every 1,000 managers in this category, only one would have beaten their respective index over that five-year period.

Monkeys work for peanuts and managers charge big fees. Don't fall victim to this trap.

It's Diversification, Not Management

Here's another great question. Why would you pay a premium for a fund that does not make up for the extra cost, and is likely more volatile than simply buying a so-called hum-drum index fund?

A properly diversified portfolio, even with less-than-stellar performers, will do more for your capacity to generate returns than finding one great manager. What's more, 94 percent of the portfolio allocation comes from the mix of the assets, not the managers.[21]

This means that the vast majority of your possible portfolio returns and, coincidentally, your financial future will come from your asset allocation decision. Academic studies demonstrates that stock picking, market timing, and track record investing subtract from your return.

#4: The Survivorship Myth

There is no shortage of additional myths about stock picking.

For example, the finance industry, fresh off their bravura performance during the Great Recession, says that investment managers can consistently and predictably add value by exercising so-called superior skill and individual stock selection. If we look at the actual numbers, we see that one of the tricks that the investment community uses to hide bad performers is a gambit called survivorship bias.

Back in 1923 when the very first mutual fund was invented, there was one single mutual fund. For decades, the industry built on that one fund, adding mutual funds on a regular basis. By 1960, there were 281 mutual funds. Today, there are tens of thousands of them. Up to 1959, no funds had ever died.

But that streak didn't last.

Soon, Wall Street bore witness to a mass extinction. It was one of many extinction-level events for the fund industry. Thirty-three funds died in 1960, and another 33 funds expired in 1964. By 1969, a massive number of funds were born and died at the same time. When you think about it, the ebb and flow of mutual funds is reminiscent of the universe. Stars are born, and stars will die.

While it turns out a lot of stars were dying, what was interesting in and after that period of great flux, was that the great Wall Street Marketing Machine seemed to have a revelation—or in business parlance, a bottom-line game changer. In short, if the industry could "spin" them properly, there were just enough "winners" for the industry to hang its hat on. That's exactly what Wall Street has been doing for decade after decade, so successfully, that mutual funds became a Golden Goose.

And now 40 years later, the mutual fund universe is a thriving one (and intensely profitable to the finance industry), with 27,542 mutual funds. In fact, there are now more funds and fund classes to invest and wade through than individual stocks, making your investment choices more difficult than ever before.[14]

#5: The "Hide and Seek" Myth

Mutual fund companies are playing "hide the losers" with their funds. It's nothing less than a shell game where fund houses grease the skids by killing off the losers (1,460 of them in 2010), replacing them with brand new funds (2,134 in 2010).

Killing off the underperformers is dirty pool even by Wall Street standards, but killing them off so they can artificially pump up their performance numbers is used car salesman territory. Come to think of it, that's an insult to used car salesmen.

Worse than that, the mutual fund companies themselves have no idea which mutual funds are going to overperform, nor do they have any idea which fund managers are going to underperform. So what are we left with? An over-abundance of mutual funds for a strange, unethical reason—fund companies have no idea which managers are going to overperform or underperform, so they filter out the toxic funds and have enough in reserve to prop up industry performance numbers.

In Ohio, where I live, the motto for the state lottery is "chances are you'll have fun." The reality is "chances are you will lose your money." The advertisements only show the smiling winners with huge returns. You never see pictures of the millions of good people parted from their money. They hide the losers just like the fund industry hide its losers.

Some of those toxic funds have to be seen to be believed, but the mutual fund industry doesn't want you to see them. Take the classic case of the Potomac Internet Plus Fund, which lasted only 26 months, yet managed to lose 99% for its investors.

In fact, a list of the worst 200 mutual funds reveals an average -77.7% return for investors unfortunate enough to buy them.[14]

The Worst 200 Dead Mutual Funds

-77.7%

#6: *The Myth of Marketing Timing*

Market timing is a big piece of the Mutual Fund Marketing Machine.

Fund providers spare no expense in convincing you they can get you in and out of the market at the right time. Timing is a magic pill that can get you in before the market goes up by 30 or 40 percent, and get you out before it crashes. In other words, fund companies promise all the upside and none of the downside.

Let's face facts, market timing belongs in a magical fairy world, and our industry is rife with people who will tell you that they know where the market is going next. My opinion? Market timing is wishful thinking of the worst kind, akin to believing I can lose weight without dieting and exercising by taking some fat-loss pill. Or believing I can make money without working hard, or that I can call the psychic network hotline to see my future.

I can't predict my own future, but I can say this: it won't include any market timing.

So what is market timing? Most people are taught to think of market timing as timing two asset categories: cash and stocks. In other words, I'm either going to be out of the market, or I'm going to be in the market, and theoretically, if the stock market is trending downward, I want to get out of the market before the crash. Before it goes up again, I want to get in the market before the rest of the herd. In a nutshell, with market timing, I want to get all the upside with none of the risk.

On the surface, market timing sounds great.

Wouldn't it be wonderful if someone could just tell you where the market was getting ready to soar and the precise moment to get out? Better yet, what if someone could tell you when to get into international stocks, gold, T-bills or corporate bonds? What if I could invest all of my money into the best performing asset class for the next year and do that year after year? Wouldn't that be lovely?

Of course it would. But it is a dysfunctional fantasy to believe it is possible. And the sooner you can get this illusion out of your head the better off you will be.

Ultimately, that's why market timing doesn't work—and some pretty smart people agree with that sentiment:

*"Attempting to forecast whether the market is at a peak or in a valley—
and whether to buy or unload stocks as a result—is a waste of time.
I don't know anyone who has been right more than once in a row."*
–legendary investor Peter Lynch

*"After nearly 50 years in the business, I do not know of anybody who has
done it (market timing) successfully and consistently. I do not even know
anybody who knows anybody who has done it successfully and consistently."*
–John Bogle, Founder of Vanguard Mutual Funds [22]

I know that market timing is tempting, and I always tell my clients that managing your own expectations is a big part of your investment planning process.

We've all heard about "buy-and-hold" investing and why it doesn't really matter what the market's doing when you get in, as long as you stay in. Sure, there's a great deal of truth to that line of thinking. History shows that stocks can grow (on average) 10 to 12 percent annually and bonds can grow at a rate of up to five to eight percent per year, for Treasuries.[23] Of course, those numbers were evident in better financial times than we've seen in the past year or two. Still, combined with the miracle of compound interest (your accumulated investment returns rolled over year after year) a long-term outlook coupled with a solid, disciplined investment strategy can yield big bucks over 20, 30 and especially 40+ years.

The trick to capitalizing on free markets is in staying in the markets and not missing its sharp upticks. Market-timers who try to get in and out of the stock market at the most optimal moments—risk missing those market spikes by weaving in and out of the financial markets. And that's money that's hard to make back.

That's not all. Market timers also generally experience higher transaction costs compared to a "buy and hold" strategy. Every time an investor sells or buys securities a transaction fee will be incurred. Even if the market timer achieves above average returns, the transaction costs could negate the superior performance. Market timing does not reduce risk—it increases it. Using the time period of 10/1981 to 9/2011, an investor buying the S&P 500 index in October 1981 would have had a return of 10.81% with a buy and hold strategy. If that same investor tried to time the market and missed just 15 of the best performing months (out of a total of 360) his return would have been only 5.71%. [24]

One additional negative aspect of using market-timing techniques is the tax reporting complications. By going in and out of the market several times in one tax year (sometimes several times in a month) it generates numerous taxable gain and loss transactions which all must be accounted for on the investor's income tax return.

Market timing is a loser's game.

The Cost of Being "Out of the Market" 1982-1987*

Missing the best 10 days of a bull market is one thing. Imagine missing the best 40 days of a great bull market Consider the 1980's bull market run-up. Note the comparison between the buy-and-hold investor who remained in the stock market during the entire period from December 21, 1981, through August 25, 1987, and the market-timer who missed the top 40 days of market performance.[25]

Investment Period	Average Annual Return	Percent of Return Missed
Entire 1,276 Trading Days	+26.3%	0.0%
Less the 10 Biggest Days	+18.3	30.4%
Less the 20 Biggest Days	+13.1	50.2%
Less the 30 Biggest Days	+8.5	67.7%
Less the 40 Biggest Days	+4.3	83.7%

*Period Ended August 25, 1987 Source: University of Michigan Study

Need more proof? From 1991 to 2010, if you stayed fully invested in large US growth stocks, a $10,000 investment would have grown to $56,561, as measured by the S&P 500 Index (a 9.05% average annual gain). If you just missed five days of that trying to time the market, your rate of return drops to 6.84% and your portfolio declines to $37,535. If you just missed the best 30 days, your rate of return 30 days now out goes down to 0.85%,[24] and so this idea of playing chicken with the market—darting in, darting out, trying to guess when stocks are going to be hot, when they're not, is a sucker's bet.

All told, market timing is truly one of Wall Street's worst ideas. Nobody owns a crystal ball, even the wise guys in the fund industry. So don't believe it when someone tells you that anyone is capable of market timing to effectively predict up markets and down markets. The truth is they're random, and as a result, if you miss the markets, you will miss—even in a short period of time—massive amounts of growth.

The Sad Saga of Frontier Microcap

In 1962, the New York Mets were the worst team in baseball—they lost 120 of 160 games, one of the lousiest seasons in baseball history.

Well, Frontier Microcap is the New York Mets of the mutual fund industry. The fund lost an average of 37% each year from 2001-to-2010. How bad was Frontier? If you popped $1,000 into the fund 10 years ago, you'd have a tidy $11 remaining ten years later. [26]

Wait, it gets worse, much worse. Over 50% of the losses incurred with Frontier came from fees, which clocked in at about 4.5%. Then there's an expense ratio of about 18% a year.

Bad management. High fees. Just another day in the mutual fund industry.

You're Being Sold a Bill of Goods

The hoax of the mutual fund industry's ability to find the managers who can beat the market and pass the extra returns on to you ranks right up there with the Big Foot video footage and alien abductions. It is one of the greatest scams of all time. Of course, every prospectus says "past performance is no guarantee of future results," buried deep within its pages. What it should really say is "a manager's ability to beat the market in the past has zero correlation with his or her ability to repeat that performance in the future. "None whatsoever." It is pure luck. And that should be in huge red letters on the front of the prospectus—but of course it's not. Nor will it ever be. There is just too much money at stake to keep you believing these lies.

History shows that most mutual funds routinely fail to top their market indexes. I have a theory for that underperformance. By and large, the fees that the fund giants charge their investors are disproportionate to the money management talent provided by Wall Street's "best and brightest."

If you look closely, the bulk of the cash poured into mutual funds doesn't go to research and doesn't go to investment management—it goes to marketing. Mutual fund companies spend about $6 billion a year on advertising, according to study by Henrik Cronqvist of The Ohio State University, Fisher College of Business.[28]

The overspending on advertising is intentional. It's designed to influence financial consumers and convince them that fund managers possess magical powers that the rest of us mere mortals don't.

> **Passive Beats Active**
>
> "If active and passive management styles are defined in sensible ways, it must be the case that:
>
> **1.** Before costs, the return on the average actively managed dollar will equal the return on the average passively managed dollar.
> **2.** After costs, the return on the average actively managed dollar will be less than the return on the average passively managed dollar.
>
> These assertions hold true in any time period. Moreover, they depend only on the laws of addition, subtraction, multiplication and division. Nothing else is required."
> —William F. Sharpe,
> Professor of Finance, Nobel Laureate [27]

"The house [casino] takes a cut on each spin of the wheel, paying out less in winnings than it collects in bets. So roulette is a negative-sum game, and so is your non-index mutual fund [actively managed fund]."
–Meir Statman, Professor of Finance [29]

Here's an old joke that illustrates my point.

Late one evening, a cop pulls up next to a man on his hands and knees in the gutter.

"Hey buddy," says the cop, "What are you doing down there?"

"I'm looking for $20 I lost on Mulberry Street," the gent responds.

"But this is Maple street," the cop answers.

"I know," says the man, still crawling along the pavement, "but the lighting's better on Maple Street."

When it comes to managing our own money, many of us make like the guy on Maple Street. We try to take the easy way out, common sense be damned. The mutual fund industry is aiding and abetting our dumb behavior by promoting myths as financial gospel.

Well, enough is enough. It's time you fought back and forged a different path to financial freedom, one that doesn't rely on the myths and lies peddled by the mutual fund industry.

That path is clear to me, and soon it will be to you, too. It's all about recognizing, understanding, and harnessing free markets, without the burden of so-called professional money managers on your shoulders.

I'm going to teach you how to avoid gambling and speculating with your money, and I'll teach you how to invest prudently and effectively using free market strategies.

That journey starts in the next chapter. So let's leave the myths behind—and start looking forward with free markets as our guide.

Whether it's the loudmouth day trader who brags about his big score but can't balance his checkbook or the whackjob who stuffs his savings into a mattress "because it's a well-known fact that Martians actually run the banking industry," some people just don't want to take the time to manage their money correctly.

It's an important distinction for those who are serious about taking control of your financial lives and building your own portfolio. It's no secret that paying closer attention to your personal financial situation will not only make it much easier to build your own lifelong investment strategy, it is also one of the smartest moves you'll ever make. Chances are, if you have invested in the past, you have trusted the bullies and heard their lies first-hand. Over twenty years ago when I first experienced these problems investing money for my clients and the suffering they cause investors, I asked my broker-dealer why it wasn't working. I was essentially told, "Sit down, kid. Don't rock the boat." Well, I wouldn't sit down. And I will keep on standing tall to share the truth with investors.

We've all heard the tale of the tortoise and the hare—how slow and steady wins the race against fast and careless just about every time.

That is true on Wall Street as well.

Don't get me wrong. I'm not advocating *not* taking any risk. You have to take some risks—preferably, smart, prudent ones—if your portfolio is going to have any chance to grow.

The key to managing risk is to be disciplined with your investment style so that risk doesn't rear up on its hind legs and swallow you whole. As Warren Avis, the founder of Avis Rent-A-car once said, "As far as I'm concerned, nothing is worth going broke over."

Ah, you say. Great investment opportunities involve great risk, do they not? Sure they do. But why aim for "great" opportunity in the first place? Why swing for the fences when a few combined singles or doubles can do the job as well and maybe even better?

That's what I was talking about before. Too many investors fall prey to market prognosticators who promise big returns that they can't deliver. Yet it's investors who are victimized, lured to a "guaranteed" winner by stock market charlatans who promise investors the moon, green cheese and all.

In all my years as a financial advisor, I have yet to see a portfolio that was built on home runs. The ones that try usually strike out swinging, but this doesn't faze the Wall Street bullies. They thrive on investor ignorance.

The problem, or perhaps *challenge* is a better term, is that investors who think they can get fat on "can't miss" stocks aren't managing risk very well. In other words, they're not practicing good risk control.

The first step in standing up for your family and your financial future is to clearly see the shenanigans and smoke and mirror games the industry moguls uses to capture your money and line their own pockets. Like Toto pulling back the curtain to reveal the bumbling man pretending to be the all-powerful Wizard of Oz, you can now see the truth about Wall Street and you don't have to be a victim of its shell game.

3

FREE MARKETS AND INVESTOR PSYCHOLOGY

"The greatest discovery of my generation is that human beings can alter their lives by altering their attitudes of mind."
—William James (1842-1910)

THE WALL STREET BULLIES DON'T WANT YOU TO THINK very deeply about your investment decisions. The more they can keep you in the dark, the better. They don't want you to ask meaningful questions about whether you should invest based on your true beliefs. They don't want you asking many questions beyond, "What stocks or mutual funds should I buy?" While you do not need to be a philosopher or astrophysicist to successfully invest, you do need to align your investment strategy with how you believe the world really works.

Without your knowledge or approval, you have been brainwashed with a philosophy of investing. Like a fish swimming in a bowl of water, this belief system surrounds you. It is everywhere, and it is so commonly accepted that most investors will never admit to another way of looking at the world. Like the movie *The Matrix*, this worldview is so pervasive that we are unaware of its very existence.

We don't question the mental maps that have been thrust upon us; we blindly accept them. Like Morpheus' offer to Neo in *The Matrix*, I give you a choice—blue pill or red pill. Stay in the delusion about markets and how they work, or gain the knowledge to free yourself. Be forewarned. Once you see the truth, you can never go back to speculating and gambling. If you do, you will be plagued with the very real premonition that you are gambling with your future.

We are indoctrinated with this false reality from a very young age. Five years ago, when my son was ten, he brought home a sheet from school that described a stock picking challenge sponsored by the then largest broker dealer in the nation. Each student was instructed to study stocks and pick five to make up a hypothetical portfolio. Being in the investment business, my son asked me for advice. I told him that he had to go back to school and tell his teacher that he refused to play. He was being programmed at age ten to speculate and gamble, and the exercise was being presented as an intellectual challenge. The school may as well have sponsored a craps tournament. The assumption that stock picking, market timing, and track record investing work implies an assertion that free markets fail. This universally accepted belief has destroyed more wealth than any other. So what will it be? Blue pill and live a life of delusion, or red pill and see the unvarnished truth? Decide for yourself. If you pick the blue pill, you might as well throw this book in the garbage because it will be useless to you. If you choose the red pill, read on…

Dear investor, it is my job to help you see the truth, choose your worldview, and make an informed decision about how to invest your money instead of blindly following the path of the Wall Street Bullies.

Why do investors get caught up so easily in believing what clearly cannot be true—that anyone can predict the unpredictable? The problem lies within, and this is where most investors mentally check out. They prefer to pretend that investing is simply an "outside job" of understanding facts, statistics, and data, and then slapping together a bunch of investments. Nothing could be further from the truth. Investing is an inside job. You must be willing to look at how your own mind operates to be a successful investor. As bad as the bullies are, you are your own worst enemy. Wall Street bullies know how your brain works, and they are masters at turning it against you.

The Investor's Dilemma

The natural state of an investor is anxiety, confusion, doubt, and fear. The world can be a scary place (what with wars, recessions, market crashes, and Wall Street protests). What once seemed like an indestructible global market expansion quickly imploded into massive deficits, mortgage bubbles, double-digit unemployment, political uncertainty, and outright fear.

Even in good times, investors are plagued by fear mongering messages. Fear sells magazines, news shows, books, and financial products. If it bleeds, it leads. In the midst of all this, you may have witnessed your retirement funds and 401k devalued and wondered if you can maintain your lifestyle.

For the first time in American history, many people are questioning whether their children will grow up to be better off than their parents. The American dream is in doubt.

Fear of the future is the first element in the investor's dilemma, and this fear makes us easy prey for Wall Street bullies.

Even if fear is not in the forefront of our minds, it lives in our subconscious doing push-ups. How can you know if you are caught in the investor's dilemma? You can easily identify it by its symptoms.

Common refrains from those suffering from The Investor's Dilemma:
- Am I getting high enough returns on my investments?
- Am I going to be able to maintain my standard of living in retirement?
- Can I afford a quality education for my children?
- What about the next market crash? (I think that one is habitually on people's minds.)
- Are we going to have a double-dip recession? Will it be a W or a V?
- What's the recovery going to look like?
- What's the market going to do?
- What about the next market boom?
- When should I get into the market, and how long should I stay in it?
- What's going to happen with the economy?
- What's going to happen during wars, or recessions?
- What's going to happen with the U.S. debt?
- What's going to happen to energy prices?

These are the stresses that can easily cause us to lose sleep and creep into other areas of life. They can affect our health, happiness, relationships and work performance. If you find yourself wondering or worrying about these issues—you are experiencing the effects of the dilemma first hand.

As human beings, when we are subjected to doubt or fear, we all want a way out—it is only natural. The faster and easier it is to get out of the pain we are experiencing, the better. We all want a fast and easy solution to our problems. Freud called this wish fulfillment or fantastical thinking, and it makes us want to believe things that just are not true. When you are in this state of mind, you are an easy mark.

When investors experience pain and fear about the future, they understandably want an easy out, and what better way than to find someone who can forecast what is likely to happen next. My life would be so much easier and I could stop worrying and someone could just tell me what is going to happen next in the economy, what stocks to buy, and whether the market was going to crash or rocket to new heights. Who wouldn't want that information? You could stop wondering and fretting about the state of the world and rest easy knowing your Wall Street forecaster has you covered. The desire for clear knowledge of the future is the second step in this vicious cycle and it sends you in a dangerous direction—right into the hands of the bullies.

If you are looking for someone to predict the future of the market, it only seems reasonable to find the person who was able to do it in the past and expect that they will continue their "brilliance and clairvoyance" into the future. It is here that the quest for magical investment begins. If I can just find the stock picker or mutual fund manager who beat the market over the last 20 years (in desperation we falsely reason) they can surely do it again. Or if I can locate a manager who predicted the last market crash, he can save me from the next one. The search is on for the Wall Street guru or prognosticator who has this incredible skill. What leads every investor to the next step in the cycle is information overload. What exactly are you looking for - the best mutual fund manager, hedge fund, broker, financial planner, ETF, index fund, individual stock?

Sure, we have some ways of keeping score of what's happening in the present day. When it comes to investing, for example, we look for a track record. Who was able to beat the market in the past? Who earned the highest returns in the past? Who was the fund manager of the year? What's the latest five-star mutual fund?

There are literally a million options to choose from on any given day. This is when information overload takes control. I just Googled the word "investing" and found over 204 million pages.[30] Good luck wading through all of that! Most investors believe that technology makes investing easier but the truth is, technology makes it more confusing and complex.

Investors finally make a choice, and the vast majority of the time, it involves trusting a manager who has had five years of stellar returns or dumping a major portion of his portfolio in a sector that has recently shown stellar growth. This is called track-record investing or chasing hot returns, and this is what investors do. This is what Wall Street does. The result is a temporary sense of relief. After all, everybody loves a winner and if you have ever done this, it seems that you can rest assured that this magnificent manager is going to relieve you of the stress of wondering and worrying about your portfolio forever—all is well, except it isn't.

Now you are going to compare your portfolio to every other option out there and you will soon see that your five star manager isn't shooting the lights out like you thought he would and that wonderful sector you bought to "diversify" your portfolio crashed. You look around and you see other investors or friends making high returns and you are decidedly unhappy. Allow me to prove to you that investing can be amazingly simple.

Three Basic Rules

Rule #1   **Own Equities.**

They are the greatest wealth creation tool on the planet.

Rule #2   **Diversify.**

Use many stocks to reduce risk and offset equity risk with short-term fixed income.

Rule #3   **Rebalance.**

Periodically reallocate your assets by selling the segments that are relatively high and purchasing segments that are relatively low.

It really is this simple, but virtually no one left to their own devices can actually do it and this includes so-called investment professionals.

No one actually follows the rules because emotions now take over. Eventually, investors sell the asset categories that crashed or dump their previously hot five-star manager. Often, especially after a market crash, they make the colossal error of dumping their assets into cash.

I recently conducted a study of over 14,000 real portfolios of investors who were trapped in the dilemma.[31] Five years ago (before the market crash), they were 70% in equities and only 30% in fixed income. After years of stellar market returns, they thought they were bulletproof. They had no idea how much risk they really had assumed.

After the Crash of 2008, the average investor was only 30% in equities and 70% in cash and fixed income. They had violated every rule. They chased returns and track records. They panicked after the crash and, instead of buying more equities, they sold their stocks and bought more fixed income. This is a slippery slope to a truly destructive process.

At this point in the dilemma, investors break the simple rules of investing and suffer larger losses than they could have possibly imagined. As they encounter huge setbacks and watch their portfolios get decimated, they feel renewed fear and doubt about the future. How could these brilliant managers have lost so much of my money? Why couldn't they see what was about to happen? Thus, the cycle repeats itself ad infinitum.

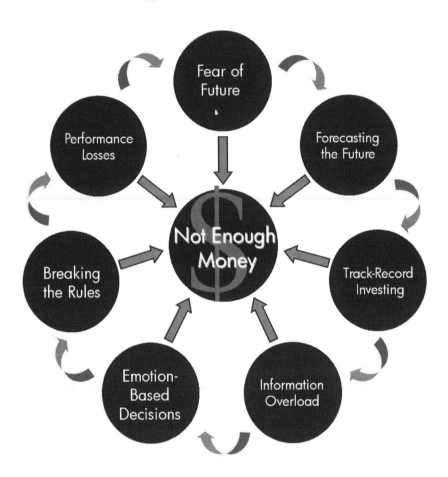

The Investors' Dilemma is an emotional and psychological paradigm that, if left unchecked, can destroy your portfolio and the long-term returns you need to reach you life's most important dreams and goals.

I recently spoke at a charity event in Indianapolis for 300 investors. The fundraiser benefitted the March of Dimes and many families including children were in attendance. I spoke of the dilemma facing families and investors to grow their wealth successfully for their children and grandchildren. After my talk, several mothers and fathers shared with me the fears and the challenges they were facing. In the pain in their eyes and the wavering tone of their voices, I could see the effects of the dilemma. They had been seduced by the Wall Street Bullies, and they were experiencing the emotional roller coaster of their devastating and dysfunctional way of speculating. Whenever I get to speak with investors face-to-face, I am reminded that their problems are all too real. You can also see the results of this tragedy in third party studies.

We know it's true, because we have the cold, hard evidence.

Research from DALBAR[13] shows us that from 1991 to 2010, the S&P 500 benchmark averaged 9.14% growth (on an average annual basis). When my analysts and I studied all those wealth destroyers—those big goliath mutual fund companies that destroyed so much wealth in the last decade—the average equity fund during this period of time adjusted for inflows and outflows was only 3.83%. That's a big difference, akin to losing over five percent versus a simple market rate of return. If you compare that to inflation, it barely keeps pace; and after you subtract taxes, you're actually running behind inflation (talk about anxiety).

That's the exact opposite of the dream, the wish, and the fantasy of every investor. They want stock market rates of return with Treasury bond risk. In reality, what they get is Treasury bond rates of return with stock market risk. They get the exact opposite of the fantasy that they actually want.

The Result

CATEGORY	1991-2010 ANNUALIZED RETURN
S&P 500 INDEX	9.14%
AVERAGE EQUITY FUND INVESTOR	3.83%
INFLATION	2.57%

*DALBAR, Inc., *Quantitative Analysis of Investor Behavior*, 2011
Results are based on the twenty-year period from 1991-2010

"The ideas of economists and political philosophers, both when they are right and when they are wrong, are more powerful than is commonly understood. Indeed the world is ruled by little else. Practical men, who believe themselves to be quite exempt from any intellectual influence, are usually the slaves of some defunct economist."
—John Maynard Keynes [32]

The most powerful thing you can do to protect yourself from this destructive cycle is to develop your own personal investing philosophy. If you never develop your own philosophy of investing, you will always revert to the commonly accepted but untrue belief that free markets fail. This is the fundamental ideology propagated by Wall Street Bullies to keep you in the investor's dilemma and keep you perpetually gambling with your future.

My job is to show you the alternative and empower you with the knowledge to decide for yourself. Once you have developed a clear market belief system, we can delve deeper into implementing a strategy based on this. Most investors mindlessly fall into myths and traps without even considering market beliefs. This is a fatal portfolio mistake—one that you should avoid at all costs.

A belief is a state of mind in which confidence is placed, and the market is a place where buying, selling and trading occurs. Your market belief system will guide your most critical investing behaviors because beliefs always trump knowledge. Let me explain. Perhaps you cognitively know or understand the fact that exercise is good for your health. You even express a commitment to consistently stay fit and exercise to your friends and family, but somewhere deep down you "believe" that exercise is just no fun or even painful. Perhaps you rationalize your lack of exercise by telling yourself that you are too busy or other things are more important. You see, deeply held beliefs will always trump information, facts and statistics when it comes to determining behavior. Because of this, we have to help you develop a strong belief system about the market—one that will protect you from the Wall Street mayhem that you see all around you. Successful investing is more about developing the right mindset and beliefs than about the right portfolio mix. Without the former, the latter is useless.

There are two basic market belief systems and based on which one you adopt, you will pursue drastically different portfolio behavior. One has the power to deliver you from the ravages of the Investors' Dilemma; the other will doom you to forever suffer its dire effects on your money and your mind.

Let's examine the "markets fail" belief system. This is the belief system propagated by large brokerage houses, mutual fund complexes, investment newsletters, and Wall Street Bullies everywhere. The "markets fail" belief presumes that prices of stocks and bonds react to information slowly, which allows some individuals to consistently and predictably identify under–priced investments and buy them to allow you to enjoy returns in excess of the market.

In short, people who subscribe to this belief system feel that they are smarter than the market. Stocks are predictably mispriced, stocks that are going to beat the market can be purchased systematically, and stocks that are going to underperform the market can be systematically sold. Based on the "markets fail" hypothesis, managers and investors should be capable of consistently beating the market without taking on additional risk. Who wouldn't want that?

In a broader sense, this is the same market belief suggested by Karl Marx, the Father of Communism. Free markets fail to set appropriate prices for goods and services; therefore, a centralized committee should know what the true price should be to maximize wealth to society as a whole. Certain stock pickers and market timers believe that markets mis-price stocks and bonds and a committee of managers can identify "true price and value." Ironically, Marx believed that markets failed to price everything and that a centralized government committee could set more effective prices. No Wall Street Bully would ever admit that they share a belief system with the mastermind of communism, but their basic market ideology is the same. In their infinite wisdom, they believe they are smarter than the invisible hand of the free market.

> *"So who still believes markets don't work?*
> *Apparently it is only the North Koreans, the Cubans, and the active managers."*
> –Rex Sinquefield [33]

There is another way. It is the "markets work" hypothesis. The belief that markets are random and unpredictable. Adam Smith suggested that free markets are the best determinate of price and communicate all available information into the pricing system. Based on this philosophy, the market price is the best available price, and it represents the general consensus of seven billion people on the planet.

If you subscribe to the "markets work" view, there is no way to consistently and predictably extract return from the market without regard to risk. In academic circles, this is often referred to as the Efficient Market Hypothesis and it implies that there is no way to consistently stock pick, market time or track record invest and beat "the market" after costs. This is the basic belief system as laid out in *The Wealth of Nations*. It is the foundation for our free market system and capitalism. If you adopt a "free markets work" belief system, it will be your job to eliminate stock picking, market timing and track record investing. Eventually, you will see it as your job to prudently allocate your resources into the global market and allow the awesome force of free markets and entrepreneurship to grow your wealth.

To help you choose your market belief, it may be useful to understand what really goes into setting stock prices. We will call the first component "rational data." These are facts, statistics, balance sheets, and economic information. This information is good and "knowable" data, but take it with a grain of salt because sometimes data can be inaccurate or intentionally misleading.

The second type of market mover is irrational. Things like fear, greed, love, shame, guilt, and individual plans. For example, one individual may cash in his or her stock to buy a house or send kids to college. This is "unknowable" information.

No single person on the planet can measure all the emotions and individual plans of all market makers. It would take a massive ego to believe yourself capable of this, but it doesn't stop Wall Street bullies from telling you they know.

So both rational and irrational information goes into setting stock prices. As information shifts and changes, the price changes with it—simultaneously. So you might ask, "What will change the rational and irrational factors?"

I think you already know—unpredictable information. Can anyone consistently predict the news? Somewhere in your mind should hear a resounding—NO! So if no one can predict the news, no one can predict how all of these things are going the change. Therefore, no one—and that means no one—not your broker, not Jim Cramer, not Peter Lynch, not even Warren Buffet—can tell you what stock prices are going to do next.

In other words, all knowable and predictable information is reflected in the current price and the only factors that can change prices are unpredictable events in the future.

I am 48 years old now, and I can remember as clear as day the exact moment that this realization hit me right between the eyes. It happened twenty-one years ago. It shook me to my very core then and resonates with me now. Free markets work. I had always believed it, but I had been investing my money and my clients' money as if markets failed. My gut was telling me it was irrational to believe that one manager, no matter how brilliant, was smarter than the collective knowledge of all market participants. I didn't have the deeper understanding of markets to explain the failure of all the active managers I had ever used. In a single flash, I knew the failure of my previous actions. Then and there, I knew I never had to speculate or gamble with my client's money again.

When you grasp the concept that free markets work, you'll have more than just supply and demand creating wealth for you and your family, you'll be channeling the power of the entire free market system.

"We who live in free market societies believe that growth, prosperity and ultimately human fulfillment, are created from the bottom up, not the government down. Only when the human spirit is allowed to invent and create, only when individuals are given a personal stake in deciding economic policies and benefiting from their success—only then can societies remain economically alive, dynamic, progressive, and free. Trust the people. This is the one irrefutable lesson of the entire postwar period contradicting the notion that rigid government controls are essential to economic development."
–Ronald Reagan [34]

Free Markets Explained

So how do you begin to describe an issue as complex, yet crucial, as free markets?

First, any market economy is forged in the fires of supply and demand. For free markets to work, governments have to step out of the way, a practicality that drives central-planning types crazy. In a free market economy, buyers and sellers are encouraged to trade, buy, or sell freely based on a mutually agreed price without state intervention in the form of taxes, subsidies, or regulation.

What drives the free market? Ideally, it's fueled by individual innovation and the implied promise that a good work ethic, creativity, ingenuity, and investment will be rewarded. It's no secret that all commercial enterprises exist to make a profit. Consequently, in a free market environment, a thriving business is one that posts a profit on a regular basis, even as competitors work equally hard to take as much market share as possible. Competition is a vital cog in the free market wheel.

Competition in the marketplace provides the best possible product to the customer at the best price. When a new product is invented, it usually starts out at a high price. Once it has been in the market for a while and other companies begin to riff on it, the price goes down as new competitive products emerge. In a competitive market, the lousy and overpriced versions of the product are pushed out of the market because consumers will reject them.

The free market ultimately picks the winners and losers in each industry based on customer demand and the ability of companies to meet the demand in a cost-efficient manner.

Before I delve into the concept of free markets and how they apply to the investment world, let's list some key advantages of free markets. That should give us a good foundation to work from through the rest of this chapter:

Benefits of a Free Market System

Free markets enjoy a healthy dose of freedom, free of state interference (as I said above, that's a prerequisite for success in capitalistic economies). That's one of my favorite takeaways from free markets: the decision of what to produce, for whom to produce, and in what quantities is all up to the private enterprise and is not determined by the state.

The state can play a significant role in a free market economy. For instance, government acts as the official arbiter on key issues like contracts, ownership, and in enforcing health and safety issues (the better to protect workers and consumers).

Companies may establish their own unique costs to attract customers and use those costs to gain leverage over the competition. Ideally, the state has little influence over how businesses set their prices.

There are few limits in a free market system. For example, a vast array of goods and services can be produced that even the highest-demanding consumer needs (think light bulbs or gasoline). That enables businesses to focus on creating goods and services that the market wants and leaves low-demand products on the sidelines, where they belong.

Consumers have a horse in the free market race. Customers, by asking for products they want (creating demands) can steer companies to address their needs and wants. If a business can't meet those demands, it will be culled from the herd, assuring quality companies will exist in a free market economy. Again, as it should be.

Fledgling businesses with a strong idea and a good business model can compete with businesses that have been in the same market for decades (think Apple and IBM). Low barriers to enter a no cost marketplace economy make this achievable without government control.

Free markets allow for maximum flexibility, too. If a demand for a product or a service is off the charts, a business can marshal its resources (like human capital) to meet that demand. In a free market society, companies don't have to gain permission from anyone, especially the state, to turn on a dime to meet consumer demand.

The Link Between Free Markets and Your Investments

How do free markets impact your investment portfolio?

That's the beauty of it. With free markets, the sky's the limit. Without free markets, your portfolio—and your chance at financial security—are grounded.

Here's a great story that perfectly sums it up.

The billionaire Andrew Carnegie was once visited by an ardent socialist who spoke at length about the evils of Capitalism and its tendency toward inequality. Carnegie called his secretary and asked for two numbers: his estimated net worth and the approximate global population.

"Give this gentleman sixteen cents," he then instructed her. "That's his share of my wealth."

Most people don't begrudge Carnegie his wealth. That's what free markets are designed to do: reward those who take the risks necessary to accumulate wealth.

But over the past few years, people have begun to doubt the validity and the effectiveness of free markets.

Hey, I understand. Considering the downward direction of the U.S. economy, who can blame them? I don't care if you're 25 or 105; there are basic issues that haunt investors.

After all, the Wall Street bullies and crony capitalists have created massive mistrust in the street. But don't confuse Wall Street with the thousands of companies that bring amazing products and services to Main Street.

Not only are free markets the best determinate of stock and bond prices (and everything else for that matter), they are also the engine that will drive the long-term wealth accumulation of the companies in your portfolio, if you let them. Now it's your time to choose—let's review your options.

Markets Work

Under this belief, markets are basically random. Through a process of buying and selling, supply and demand, the free market does a better job at pricing goods and services to maximize the wealth of an economy. So, when a stock is traded at $50 a share, it's because all market participants vote for that price by either buying it, not buying it, or selling it. A stock's price is virtually set by about seven billion people, the entire population of the planet, and thus makes it the best price for the stock—the free market price. This was the theory put forward by Adam Smith, the famous Scottish economics philosopher, who created the theoretical model of supply and demand.

From that point of view, economists conclude that all knowable and predictable information about the future is in the price today. Therefore, only random and unpredictable events will change the price moving forward. This is the efficient market hypothesis that Adam Smith first hit upon, and that was popularized by market experts like Burton Malkiel and Eugene Fama, the Father of Modern Finance, who hammered away at the theory that all markets were efficient ones. What they were not so subtly hinting at was this: *No individual money manager, no matter how brilliant, can have more information or more knowledge than the market itself, which incorporates literally millions of pieces of information into the pricing system.*

Markets Fail

This hypothesis was put forth by Karl Marx almost one hundred years after Adam Smith. Of course, Marx was no fan of free markets. In a historic blunder, he predicted that free markets fail and that what you need in a successful economy is a centralized planning committee to set the price and actually own the means of production. If you trust "central planners" to set the prices, you can maximize the price to society. We all know how that theory turned out, as Marx's political model in for the Soviet Union crumbled under its own dead weight in the late 1980s.

Unfortunately, this is the same argument that active managers make: that markets fail, we can buy and sell stocks based on our perception of the real value, and pass returns onto the investor. But we already know that every investor already has a belief system. No amount of persuasion can convince a person to change that belief system. Occasionally someone who believes markets fail can, with enough education, be converted to a "markets always work" investor.

Yet very seldom have I seen a person who believes markets work ever switch to the markets fail worldview.

Now as an investor, it's absolutely crucial that you choose your market belief system.

Most investors allocate their assets by investments without first choosing what their investment belief is. Once you have your investment belief, then *that's* going to tell you how you're going to allocate your assets.

So, which will you choose? What do you believe? Markets work? Or markets fail?

It is time to make a choice.

What makes most sense to you?

MARKETS WORK   **MARKETS FAIL**

If you believe that free markets work, focus on a structured fund approach.

If you believe that markets fail, keep gambling with your money.

If you believe that markets work, focus on asset class investing.

If you believe that markets fail, focus on speculative investing.

Let's go a bit deeper. If you believe markets work, you'll want to focus on market returns, you want to focus on market allocation, and you want to have a lifelong investing process. If, on the other hand, you believe in the markets fail hypothesis, you want to stock pick, market time, track-record invest, and find some guru who's going to help you follow that path. Be prepared to take a lot of abuse from the bullies.

But that leaves many investors right back where we started at the Investors' Dilemma.

When I teach these market beliefs, the vast majority of my audience is in my market belief camp; they believe that free markets work. If you believe free markets work, and you have mutual funds and other types of investments, brokerage accounts where you're using stock picking, market timing, track record investing, or you're having an investment professional doing it for you, then you're still speculating with your money.

If that's you, then the best approach is to diversify, allocate your assets, and invest for a lifetime. There isn't a need to be concerned with short-term, get-rich-quick schemes, so you can disregard media hype, and all those other timing and picking tricks that don't work. The end result should be confidence and peace of mind. Once you've aligned your investment philosophy with your belief system, that's really where you want to be as an investor.

On the other hand, you may believe that markets fail, and you're *really* gambling with your money. Hey, I realize there are some people that just like to gamble. I'm not here to pass moral judgment on anyone. That said, I would encourage you not to gamble and speculate with your financial future. If you want to go to gamble a little fun money in Las Vegas, go ahead and set aside some money for that fun vacation from your entertainment budget. Please, just don't use your retirement funds.

Some investors actually find themselves in a gray area, floating between speculative investing and asset class investing, and they never really achieve sure footing in their investments. Investors in that free-floating environment try to be prudent with their money, but they always keep slipping back down to the speculating side of the slope. It's like trying to be on a diet, but always eventually binging on chocolate ice cream.

Such uncertainty doesn't mean that you are weak—it means that you are human. Being human, we all have our weaknesses. Sometimes people believe that markets work, or they've tried asset class investing, but in their heart of hearts, they just can't stand the discipline and the long-term commitment and eventually they fail. I've seen many advisors do that, unfortunately.

In my mind, the only two places to be as an investor are in the "free markets work" and "asset class investing".

On the "markets work" side, make sure to follow these action steps. If you are in this camp, I will show you how to:

- Eliminate speculative investment techniques.

- Work with a financial professional who believes that markets work.

- Ignore the media hype.

- Set lifelong financial goals.

- Focus on capturing market returns.

- Use asset class or structured funds.

- Prudently diversify.

- Identify your risk tolerance.

On the "markets fail" side, consider the following if you believe that markets fail, then you are morally obligated to:

Pursue speculating techniques.

Work with the bullies who actively gamble with your money.

Stay connected to the Internet, magazines, talk shows, news shows, Internet shows, and download apps to your cell phone so you can track up-and-down markets.

Read every article about stocks and options that you can find, wonder and worry about the market and what might happen next. Whatever you do, don't miss the next hot stock tip if you believe markets fail.

Free Markets Work

Okay, that was tongue in cheek, but really, now that you have the evidence, what kind of investor do you really want to be?

I know where I want to be.

The stock market is the greatest wealth creation tool known to mankind. The good news is that if you trust that markets work, you can shed the Investors' Dilemma because you're no longer trying to forecast. You can stop trying to pick the best stocks, and you can allocate your assets to take advantage of global capital markets.

Above all, you can rest easy with this powerful idea in your back pocket. Free markets work, and there's the opportunity for a bright financial future when you stick to your beliefs.

How Wealth Is Created

*It took 12,000 years to inch from the $90 per-person hunter-gatherer economy
to the roughly $150 per-person economy of the Ancient Greeks in 1000 BC.
It wasn't until 1750 AD, when the world gross domestic product (GDP) per person
reached around $180 that the figure had finally managed to double from our
hunter-gatherer days 15,000 years ago. Then in the 18th Century, something
extraordinary happened—World GDP per person increased 37-fold in an incredibly
short 250 years to its current level of $6,600, with the richest societies,
such as the New Yorkers, climbing well above that.
Global wealth rocketed onto a nearly vertical curve that we are still climbing today.*
–The Origin of Wealth [35]

It is wealth to be content.
–Lao-Tzu

Hᴏᴡ ɪs ᴡᴇᴀʟᴛʜ ᴄʀᴇᴀᴛᴇᴅ? As we discussed previously, Wall Street would have you believe wealth is created primarily by stock brokers and mutual fund managers. They—and only they—possess the wisdom and intellect to divine the financial markets for the rest of us mere mortals.

But if you are still reading, I am sure you have decided that you believe markets work and you are eager to tap into their awesome power. But not so fast—before I get into the mechanics of building your portfolio, it is essential to truly understand how real wealth is created.

In reality, the vast majority of Ph.D. economists do not understand the underlying dynamics that have created the world around them. They create sophisticated graphics, study demographics, chart supply and demand equilibriums, and they have complex jargon to convince you that they have the keys to unlocking the secrets of economic prosperity. But they are blind to the true drivers of the wealth creation mechanisms that you must utilize if you choose to harness the forces of global capital markets.

Matson Money Rule

Never invest in anything you do not clearly understand.

It is crucial that you truly understand the wealth creation forces that are going on all around you and have been for over a thousand years. Having a deep and meaningful understanding of these forces will make you a much better investor. You will truly understand how, and more importantly, why you allocated your assets. This will also give you a greater ability to focus on the long-term, which is critical for your success and shrug off short-term bad news and temporary market downturns. In addition, it will provide a much broader view to understanding current events in their proper perspective.

If you do not understand how wealth is truly created then you will all too easily become frightened when economic news is negative and panic by going to cash. I have seldom witnessed any investor remain disciplined over a lifetime who did not, at least at a gut level, have this understanding.

Wealth creation is inside all of *us*, and has been since the dawn of time.

To kick off Chapter Four and our conversation on wealth creation, let's start at the very beginning and use what we learn here as a foundation for your own lifelong wealth creation campaign.

Origins of Wealth

The philosopher Ayn Rand once said, "Wealth is the product of man's capacity to think."[36] I like that quote, but believe it's important to add that need and want have as much to do with wealth creation as intellect.

A big part of that concept is the need to survive, and to think about how you're going to do that. Think about that for a moment. From the onset of civilization as we know it, what has always served as the "ultimate" form of barter and trade? In fact, food has always been the bottom line when it comes to currency, because even today, given a catastrophic circumstance or conditions, you would surrender everything you had in exchange for food.

That's not so far-fetched. In the dark days of the Great Recession, there was no shortage of Internet "survival" sites that promised to teach people how to live in a great period of need and want. Most of their advice centered on hunting and gathering for food and water and then defending your resources with your life. Talk radio was filled with commercials for "seed banks" and prepackaged foods for the "coming apocalypse."

This also explains why television shows like *Survivor* and *Man Versus Wild* are so popular with viewers (especially with guys). At the most basic level, we know in our guts that when we are left with nothing, stuff like food, water, fire, and shelter become highly-coveted objects of desire, far more important to our survival than billions of dollars to an investor on Wall Street.

Let's fast forward a bit through western history to the Renaissance period. If you needed to borrow some money in this age, where did you go? You would pay a visit to the

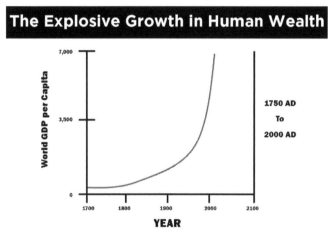

The Explosive Growth in Human Wealth

World GDP per Capita

1750 AD
To
2000 AD

YEAR

Source: Estimates for 1 million BC to 2000 AD from J. Bradford DeLong, University of California, Berkeley. Estimates for 2.5 million BC to 1 million BC are an extrapolation. GDP per capita is measured in 1990 international dollars.

goldsmith. Instead of giving you a gold coin, the more sophisticated goldsmiths would draw you a fancy piece of paper that represented the value of one gold coin. That piece of paper was "as good as gold," and could be freely spent as if it were the real thing. Collectively these pieces of paper were known as warehouse receipts.

Fast forward a little bit more: the King of England is waging a war and needs some way to pay for it. Baron Rothschild says, "Here's what you do. Open up a goldsmith's shop and call it the Bank of England. Parade a cart load of gold into it with a lot of pomp and circumstance, so everybody believes that there is gold in there." So began the Bank of England—which started with the King himself as the primary customer. They, too, would write up warehouse receipts that were good as gold. On each slip of paper was written: "Payable to the bearer on demand one ounce gold coin." (This currency, of course, was the precursor to the U.S. dollar).

In no time at all, the warehouse receipts greatly outnumbered the number of gold coins that stockpiled to back up the receipts. This process is what's known as monetary inflation. Here's a good example. Let's say I put my house up for sale and you come to me wanting to buy it, offering warehouse receipts as payment. But I refuse your currency, and insist that you pay me in gold. My lack of confidence destroyed the value of that money. If more and more people within a society all refuse to acknowledge a currency's implied value, you get monetary inflation because people want extra money to back up your purchase.

But back to England: when the King catches wind of what is going on, he declares that the warehouse receipts are now valid as legal tender. If people are reluctant to use it this paper as money, he tells them they have no choice. So by the King's decree, the people of England are forced to use the paper as money or go to jail. The money is now *fiat*—Latin for government decree.

Money is not wealth. Money is simply a sum of value or a means to an end to make transactions more efficient and effective. It is a representation of wealth not wealth itself. Many investors spend massive amounts of time attempting to forecast and predict monetary policy and currency rates. This is a dead end. Don't confuse money with wealth.

You cannot create wealth simply by moving money around. Many economists make the mistake of assuming if you simply move money around to the "right" places it will create wealth. For example, if you tax and redistribute money to others it will create net additional wealth. Or if the Fed manipulates markets by buying or selling bonds, it will create wealth by "stimulating" the economy. Or the notion that through deficit spending you can use money to "jump start" the economy. All of these failed attempts at creating wealth and prosperity work off of the childish wish fulfillment that by simply moving money around, you can create more of it, but true wealth creation is a much more dynamic and amazing process.

To create wealth, someone has to DO SOMETHING. Once you truly understand what that "something" is, you will be capable of becoming a seasoned investor, and may I add, capable of creating exponentially greater results in your career or business as an entrepreneur. In fact, until you understand what this something is, you will be doomed to mediocre results at best.

Let's first examine why simply moving money can never create more of it. Many people go through their entire life without understanding it.

Let me offer an easy example of why simply moving money around can never create wealth for you or society as a whole. For real wealth to be created in your portfolio, in your career, or for your business, value must be created for other people.

Take a simple monetary exchange as an example. A farmer works all year long to grow corn. At the end of the growing season he harvests it and now has more than he can eat. In a small town nearby is a farmer who raises pigs, he is very good at it and he has more than he can eat. The hog farmer would love some corn and the corn farmer would love to treat his family to a barbecue. The farmers could pack up their corn and hogs and make a trade but that would be cumbersome. Luckily, they can sell the fruits of their labor and exchange cash money instead and—voila—wealth is created! In this exchange, both parties are enriched and new wealth is created. It is a classic win/win scenario—everybody is better off (except the pigs). Wealth creation always entails free will. In other words, true wealth creation can never be the product of coercion.

In our simple example, pretend each farmer exchanged one hundred dollars to purchase food to meet their wants, needs and desires. There is an exchange of money that was "moved around" and wealth creation resulted.

Now let's pretend this, after leaving the bank with one hundred dollars to buy corn, the hog farmer is robbed. Someone points a gun at him and demands all of the money in his wallet. The farmer, not wanting to risk fatal injury, complies and hands over the cash. Moral explanation aside, the robber has been "enriched" but he received the funds as a direct result of coercion. The farmer was not made "better off" and did not receive value in the transaction. Wealth creation requires the free will of both parties to a transaction. Wealth creation cannot occur when one party is being forced, against their will, to participate in the exchange of goods, services, or monetary currency.

Where there is no freedom, there is no wealth creation. You might be thinking "this is all well and good but why do I have to know this stuff? Can't you just give me a pie chart and a list of funds to buy and let me get on with my life?"

And, indeed, I could but it would be useless to you without a deeper understanding of the underlying wealth generating capability of your portfolio. In other words, if you do not know where returns really come from, you will panic at the least market downturn or chase the latest super-hot asset category. Becoming a successful investor may be one of the most challenging tasks you will ever set out to master. I should know, I have dedicated the last twenty-five years of my life to just that.

My Biggest Mistake

When I first became aware that free markets work and that stock picking, market timing and track record investing were equivalent to rank speculating, I imagined a great enlightenment where advisors and investors would see the academically proven research and work to eliminate gambling from the investing process. I believed it would get easier to be a prudent investor—I was dead wrong. What I couldn't see twenty years ago was the massive proliferation of technological wizardry that would actually push investors and advisors to be more imprudent than ever. Two decades ago we did not have 24/7 investing news channels, smart phones, Internet investing sites, E-trade, hedge funds, ETFs, and wall to wall flat screen TVs with tantalizing economic data. Technology has made it possible to bombard you 24/7 with messages crafted to get you to speculate with your money. It is sad to say that today it is far more difficult to eliminate speculating and gambling than ever before. And unlike the naiveté I possessed twenty years ago—this time I only expect it to get harder.

If you hope to navigate this minefield of speculating traps, it is going to require some work on your part.

Money Isn't Everything

I know, I'm a money manager and it's heresy to say that money isn't the only path to happiness—but it's not.

My biggest client early in my career convinced me of this. Up until that point, I had always believed that it was my job to help investors become financially secure by aiding them in growing larger portfolios. My rookie thinking was that the larger the portfolio, the greater the financial resources available, the greater the peace of mind the investor would experience. In some cases I found the exact opposite to be the case.

My largest investor at the time had over five million dollars. She was far from a Main Street investor and by my simple reasoning she should have been my most happy or at least content and peaceful client. But nothing could be further from the truth. Having watched her parents suffer through the Great Depression, her money became a great burden to her. Ironically, the more she had the more she felt burdened by the responsibility to manage it. She lived in perpetual fear of becoming a bag lady living on the streets. In my experience, money can cause resentment, fear, doubt, and even shame. And for some the more they have, the greater the burden of managing it.

Eliminating the tendency to speculate with your assets and stand up to the Wall Street bullies is only the first step of becoming a seasoned investor. The goal is to experience money as abundant in your life and use it as a medium to empower yourself and others to live more fulfilling lives. The great news in this is that you can accomplish this and make the world a better place.

Personal independence and freedom are more important to people's well-being than wealth, a new study concludes.

Researchers at the Victoria University of Wellington in New Zealand analyzed the findings of three studies that included a total of more than 420,000 people from 63 countries and spanned nearly 40 years. [37]

Their key finding: "Money leads to autonomy, but it does not add to well-being or happiness."

The studies looked at data from three different psychological tests familiar to therapists:

The General Health Questionnaire, which measures distress in terms of anxiety and insomnia, social problems, severe depression and physical symptoms of mental distress, such as unexplained headaches and stomach aches.

The Spielberger Anxiety Inventory, which evaluates how anxious respondents feel at a particular moment.

The Maslach Burnout Inventory, which screens for emotional exhaustion, depersonalization and lack of personal accomplishment.

The analysis revealed "a very consistent and robust finding that societal values of [freedom and autonomy] were the best predictors of well-being," wrote psychologists Ronald Fischer and Diana Boer in an American Psychological Association release.

"Furthermore, if wealth was a significant predictor alone, this effect disappeared when individualism was entered," they added.

In other words, living a deep and meaningful life and serving others creates more happiness than any amount of money.

From Zero To 60—Economically, At Least

Okay, history lesson over.

But it was a good appetizer for the main course—and my main point in this chapter—that knowing how wealth is created isn't a luxury, it's a necessity for regular investors.

After all, how are you going to beat Wall Street if you don't understand how the basic engine that creates wealth and prosperity, not only here in the United States but on a global basis works? Despite the ongoing debate about government's role in the economy, you may be surprised to know that it's not through the often misguided efforts of Uncle Sam. And not from the large corporations that are often "in bed" with them.

In fact, it's not even close. Yes, it turns out that it's not through big government intervention, high taxes, high spending and control of the economy through centralized planning. It turns out that's really not how wealth is created. So how is it created? If it's not stock picking, and it is not government intervention into the economy, what is it?

And how are you going to harness its power? Even though we are in tough economic times at the outset of the second decade of the 21st Century, overall, if you look at the long term, we are still in the midst of the greatest wealth-creation explosion in the history of mankind.

As crazy as that sounds, it's actually true. I love watching CNBC, Fox Business News, and CNN, and I love listening to Sean Hannity and Rush Limbaugh. But when I listen to some of the talk show hosts who are conservatives, the one thing about them that really irks me is their lack of ability to put what has happened in context over a longer time period.

My main problem is that they act so negatively toward the financial markets. I've heard conservative pundits say things like "you shouldn't own stocks," and seen Glenn Beck pushing gold like Midas, and I've heard critics claim the economy is never going to get better. We need to understand that all that negativity at some point becomes destructive.

Let's look at the good parts of what's been happening.

If we look at the first stone tools, some 2.5 million years ago, they were the first piece of technology on the planet. Yet interestingly, for most of this time period, going back to the invention of the first piece of technology, there was no increase in the "wealth value" of those tools. Using the gross product per person on the planet, or the world GDP per capita, for basically tens of thousands of years nothing happens at all economically. But then all of a sudden at the very end (basically in the last 10 minutes of human history), there's a massive increase of wealth starting about 2000 A.D.

First Value Creation: Hand Axe 1.2 Million Years Ago

So What Happened?

Let's take a look at the historical timeline of wealth creation that started this chapter.

It took 12,000 years to inch from $90 per person in a hunter-gatherer economy to roughly a $150 per person economy for the ancient Greeks in 1000 B.C. In other words, everybody on the planet at that time had a "wealth value" of about $150 per person.

But wealth creation grew at a glacial pace for 2,700 years. In fact, things don't get better until 1750, when the world's gross domestic product hits around $180. It wasn't until 1750 that society finally managed to double the real wealth value of the hunter-gatherer some 15,000 years ago (see what I mean by "slow"?).

But world economic growth, as measured by wealth creation, really took off right after that. In the next 250 years, the "wealth per person" ratio skyrocketed to its current level of $6,600. So, it basically increased 37-fold in only 250 years. You read that right. Global wealth rocketed onto a nearly vertical curve that is still (even though temporarily on the downside) climbing today.

> *Two amazing things happened about 300 years ago:*
>
> *1. America is born.* One was the invention of the greatest country that has ever existed on this planet, the United States of America. I say that because the United States of America had forefathers who understood how to create a government that supported the rights of the individual, something that had never existed on the planet before, and does not exist to the extent that it exists here in the United States.
>
> *2. Science and technology take flight.* At pretty much the same time as the U.S. comes onto the world stage, and starts dominating global economics, the invention of modern-day science takes hold and begins merging into global economies. Those two things, scientific inquiry and the birth of the United States of America, both happened about 300 years ago.

Thus were the seeds of wealth creation sown, beginning the longest wealth creation explosion the world had ever seen. And it's not going to stop any time soon. We looked at a simple example of two farmers, how does wealth creation apply on a global scale?

That's a vital point in this chapter, and in this book. Real wealth creation happens when random information is organized. I'll give you a second to absorb that one—when random information is organized. For example, 1.2 million years ago, the only form of technology that we had at the time was the hand-axe, basically a rock that early humans used to hammer away at things.

Compare the ancient axe to the latter day computer mouse. One kills game and the other directs the user to information. Interesting, they're essentially the same size, and they both fit in your hand. But the modern-day mouse is a much more sophisticated object than the hand axe and is much more useful at creating wealth. That's how advanced modern technology has grown. We're a much more innovative society than we were 30,000 years ago.

It took man 1.1 million years to evolve from the hand axe and invent the handle. If the axe were invented today, within 10 seconds, somebody would invent the handle. Because of the Internet and the way information travels around the globe so quickly, technology mutates faster and faster and faster.

Another perfect example of a technology that fits in your hand is the iPhone, also a mutation of technology. But the iPhone is also another great example of wealth creation. It is the direct result of ordering of matter that is unsurpassed in the development of humankind. When you create wealth, you're taking matter from a less-ordered state—a random state—to a state of greater order and complexity, but not just any order. It's order that creates perceived utility, meaning in other words, somebody wants a product like the iPhone. Wealth creation only takes place when someone creates something of value that other people prefer to trade their *own* wealth to obtain.

In a free market if we're going to maximize wealth, it basically is a perception of what people want, whether it's hula-hoops or the pet rock, and it's a willingness to trade for it. If the government has to force you to buy something, that's not real wealth creation. There is no perceived value in the transaction.

That's an important cornerstone to wealth creation. For example, you might see a Ferrari and say, "I don't want to part with my $300,000 to buy a Ferrari." You might say, "I don't own a Ferrari, but I will rent a Ferrari for the day." I was once willing to trade financial assets for the pleasure (perceived enjoyment) of driving a Ferrari up and down the Pacific Coast Highway, which ended up by the way being a very nice day, I might add.

Riding along the highway in an awesome classic car was a lot of fun. And that was my choice. There's no government official pointing a gun at my head, or forcing me to buy health insurance, or telling me I have to make that transaction. For wealth to be created, the trading must stem from free will, not coercion.

In the great health care debate of 2009 and 2010, the government ultimately forced mandatory health care on to the nation—we didn't have a choice. That's coercion—the polar opposite of true wealth creation.

> Wealth creation only takes place when someone creates something of value.

In a free society, the consumer determines value. The consumer also determines who has wealth. The government doesn't determine who gets wealth (although it does determine what portion of that wealth is payable back to the government), the consumer determines who receives wealth by voting with their dollars to purchase certain combinations of goods and services.

Who decides what's valuable in a free society? You do. You decide what's valuable with your purchases and your buying power. In modern commerce, there are a wide variety of products and services we can buy. Go to any Wal-Mart, and you'll see what I mean. There are literally thousands of items that you can buy at a Wal-Mart, and anybody can walk in and share the experience. In fact, according to the retailer's own data, there are over 100,000 different items in stock in your local Wal-Mart.

That's just for starters:
Most cable networks carry 200 or so channels
Satellite television carries over 500 channels
There over eight million book titles on Amazon.com
Kroger's grocery store has over 275 breakfast cereals alone.
Nordstrom's has 150 different types of lipsticks.
In New York City, there are 50,000 restaurants to choose from.

There are over one trillion estimated pages on the Internet. No one really knows, and more are being created every minute of every day.

So how can such a massive increase in human productivity, wealth and choice explode so furiously in the last 250 years?

It's a process of differentiation, selection, and amplifying. In essence, economic growth is an evolutionary process that is the DNA of capitalism, and has created immense wealth creation on our planet, and as an investor you can hook directly into its incredible power.

> **"Who decides what is valuable? You do!"**

The Library of Babble

In the English language, there are 100 English language characters, including small letters, capital letters, numbers, and punctuations. Let's say we create a library, and we're going to call it the Library of Babble. In it, there are going to be 500-page books. We're going to take these hundred letters, and we're randomly just going to organize the data. The average book is going to be 2,000 characters per page, and the average book is going to be one million characters per book. We're calling it the Library of Babble, because most of the books are absolutely going to make no sense at all. They're just going to be gibberish.

That means there are going to be $100^{1,000,000}$ possible books. That's how many possible books are in our library, a number vastly larger than the universe itself. Of course, most of the books are going to be complete gibberish. But also, through random ordering, we're going to have *War and Peace*, the *Bible*, *Don Quixote*, *Moby Dick*, *Romeo and Juliet* and *Hamlet*, and we're even going to have the complete story of your life.

In our library we'll also have a business wing—we'll call it the Mark Matson Wing, because after all, it's my library. Within this section we'll shelve the business plan for Apple, the business plan for IBM, and the business plan for Matson Money. In fact, there will be business plans for all the businesses that have ever existed and that have ever failed. I'm sure there's a business plan in there for each of the technology companies that went bust in the 1990s and early 2000s (we can call that section the "broken wing" of our library).

But there's a caveat, and it's a big one. All of our business plans have to exist in an environment, and the environment is the economy in which they exist. So if I come up with a business plan, even though it might be great today, if I wrote that business plan 200 years ago, the plan may not work. The supporting technology wouldn't exist. In fact someone would read it 200 years ago and say, "That's science fiction. There's no way that's even possible."

On the other hand, I can take a perfectly valid business plan for making horse-drawn carriages mass-marketed in New York City. That business plan might have worked 200 years ago, but may not work today because it would be hopelessly outdated. So a business plan that works in one business environment may not work in a future or past business environment. The design space is going to shift and change.

Whether or not a business plan is valid is based on something very simple. In the design space in which it functions, is it profitable? Does it make money? Does it create more value for the economy and for society than the assets it actually uses up?

That's the Holy Grail of wealth creation. A society that grows wealth is constantly exploring and innoating new business models. As soon as someone stumbles upon a new business model, whether it's Facebook or Microsoft or Apple, there's someone right behind them trying to duplicate that model and make it even better, and mutate it, and change it into other models. So products, services and technologies are always mutated. What happens is that someone will invent a new technology, like a clicker or an Internet live stream. The entrepreneur that invented LiveStream, for example, had no idea that my firm, Matson Money, would specifically be using it, or that thousands of people would be watching it, mutating it and using the technologies at home.

That's how commerce, and by extension, wealth creation goes. Society takes these technologies and they mutate into new, unimaginable technologies, which initiates wealth creation in society. Another way of saying that is that when electricity was invented, or first discovered and captured, no one could have imagined a nuclear power plant on one side of the grid and the Internet on the other side of the grid because of mutating technology.

Within this framework, there are winners and losers. Some business models are going to be profitable; but most are not. The selection process of profitability will pick those healthy ones that survive and thrive in that design space, and weak or defective ones will evolve out of the system. Successful models are replicated and expanded upon, are magnified, and mutated into even newer models, and the wealth creation continues.

But here's what many people don't understand. Nobody owns a crystal ball that can peer into the future, no one knows what business model will work in advance. Profitable designs are retained, they're replicated internally and externally, and then they're mutated to even newer, more profitable business models.

Wealth and Our DNA
Why do entrepreneurs pursue wealth creation and magnify successful business models, mutate new technologies, and reorder matter? Because they want to help other people. It's part of the human condition to be altruistic and to want to help. It's hardwired in our DNA.

Free market theory says no one knows what's going to work in advance, not me, not Obama, not Chavez, not Putin, and not the heads of the world's largest mutual fund companies who pretend they can "see" the future.

No one knows what's going to work in advance. It's all an experiment. We must have maximum freedom to explore and discover success and failure. When people fail, the model has to allow for new business models to evolve out of the system. No entity is too big to fail. Just as the dinosaurs were wiped out by an asteroid, we experienced an economic asteroid of our own recently with TARP in 2008 amid the big bank bailouts. You heard the argument that, "Well, these companies are too big to fail. The fabric of society will collapse. We have to save these companies." Even staunch conservatives like Congressmen Paul Ryan and John Boehner got onboard with that sentiment. Politicians on both sides of the aisle were tricked by the crony capitalists that they had to prop up. Leaving voters to simmer over the fact that, once again, Washington chose Wall Street over Main Street.

Wealth Creation and "Central Planning"-Style Governments

When I was in eighth grade, my grandfather came to visit us in Cincinnati. He had worked his entire life in the hills and hollers of Charleston, West Virginia. Most of it he spent driving a truck or working for Union Carbide, a large chemical manufacturer.

My father, on the other hand, was a small businessman. He was a young financial planner and he helped people plan for their retirement and protect their families from death and disability. We were far from rich. We lived in what today would be an average size house of $115,000. We were Main Street America. My Grandfather did not see it that way. He walked into our house and the first thing out of his mouth was "how many people did you have to steal from to get this place? You must think you are a real big shot."

My grandfather's view was that the only way you get money was to take advantage of other people. My father said he worked hard for his money and helped a lot of people. I can vouch for that—ten to twelve hour days were the norm. He worked tirelessly to help his financial planning clients. My grandfather slaved away for years watching others create the wealth that he desired and loathed. Unfortunately, he never understood that the "pie" isn't fixed. My grandfather rejected free markets but my father embraced them.

When you understand the true wealth creation mechanism around which everything on Earth revolves, you become aware that it's a non-zero sum game. It's not that you have to take from one part of society to give to another part of society. In capitalism and free markets, everybody can win. The rising tide raises all ships. The pie gets bigger. Live or die based on fulfilling the needs, wants and desires of the consumer.

English economist, Alfred Marshall said, "Entrepreneurs are today's medieval knights. They're heroes of capitalism—entrepreneurs." Why? Because entrepreneurs explore design space and order information to create true wealth for the society. When entrepreneurs no longer create value in a free market system, they're allowed to die, metaphorically speaking. And the resources of their companies—employees or buildings or equipment or computers—are allowed to be used in new models, unpredictable ways, and reallocated by the society in the free market.

> Free markets reward experimentation; governments do not.
>
> Free markets provide quick feedback; governments do not.
>
> Free markets represent the broad needs of the population; governments do not.
>
> Free markets shift resources to useful models and away from unfit models; governments do not.

As a matter of fact, governments take resources from profitable models and allocate them to unprofitable models where wealth is destroyed. Note Amtrak, the US Postal Service, Fannie Mae, Freddie Mac. Free market societies create wealth faster and more efficiently, because they explore design space and multiple successful models, and provide an immediate fitness factor tested by the profitability motive.

> Free markets are a magnet for wealth creation.

If you look throughout history, immigration flows from big man societies to market-driven ones. There's nobody trying to get into Mexico, there's nobody trying to get into Cuba, except for a vacation and some cigars, I suppose. They don't want to go there to live. Nobody's dying to get into North Korea. Vaclav Havel—the former dissident jailed in communist Czechoslovakia, later President of the Czech Republic—once said, "The essence of life is infinitely mysteriously and multi-formed, and therefore it cannot be contained or planned for in its fullness and variability, that any central intelligence." What he's hooking into is that free markets work and people sitting at the head of centralized economies trying to play God destroys wealth creation.

> But capitalism does work, and so do free markets.

In fact, free markets have always found a way. Sure, free markets kind of ebb and flow, and if you look throughout history, this progression to freer markets throughout the planet is a long-term progression. While there may be fits and starts, the long-term trend is positive for those of us that keep fighting for free markets.

Government and Wealth Control

- Feudal Monarchies – 80% of economic capital under control of king (Big Man)

- Modern Europe – 47% of GNP under control of government

- Prior to Bailout – 33% of GNP under control of United States Government

- Estimated "Stimulus" Post-Bailout – 40% of GNP under control of US Government

Source: see endnote 38

Wealth Creation and Investing

It's critical for investors to actually understand how wealth is created, because if they're going to allocate their capital in available markets all over the world, they have to understand the underlying engine that drives this wealth creation process. It's not a manager on Wall Street—that won't work, as I've already pointed out. It's entrepreneurs evolving new technologies and serving the needs of consumers on a global basis, spreading prosperity and helping others, creating value for others. *That* is the engine that drives wealth creation. If you don't get that, you can never hope to have faith and security and confidence in your underlying investment strategy.

That said, I think people on Main Street do get the picture. At one time, it was thought that people couldn't grasp Einstein's theory of relativity. While it's true that most people can't comment at length on the ins and outs of relativity or quantum physics, most people can tell you the basics and have a rudimentary understanding of Einstein's essential concepts and principles.

It's the same deal with free markets and wealth creation. It's critical that investors know this information, absorb it, and make it their own.

That mindset will keep investors from being pulled off track once they understand where the engine of wealth and prosperity really comes from.

And why free markets—and only free markets—are the engine that makes wealth creation work for them.

No Monopoly on "Too Big To Fail"

Lehman Brothers was not the first time that big companies went belly up. In 1669, the Dutch East India Trading Company, had 150 merchant ships, 40 war ships, 50,000 employees—they were virtually the Wal-Mart of their day—and 10,000 soldiers. They employed one-fifth of the world's population. Two hundred years of existence paying an 18 percent dividend per year.[39] Still, the Dutch East India Trading Company was not too big to fail—and it did because free markets allowed it to—to make way for better things to come.

SAVE THE INVESTOR, SAVE THE WORLD

"Just as a cautious businessman avoids investing all his capital in one concern, so wisdom would probably admonish us also not to anticipate all our happiness from one quarter alone."
–Sigmund Freud

SEVERAL YEARS AGO, I WAS BRAINSTORMING A MOTIVATIONAL TITLE for a conference my company was sponsoring to help educate and motivate investor coaches to better guide their clients. Earlier that year, I received a DVD series of the television show *Heroes*. I had started watching the series with my family. It is the classic super hero plot line of Good versus Evil. Certain characters are born with mutant genes, and their mutations give them special abilities like seeing the future, flying ,or the power to regenerate limbs. The cheerleader in the show has the unique "ability" of being indestructible. She can jump off of buildings, walk through fire and be stabbed repeatedly with a knife and no problems. One of the genetic heroes gets a premonition telling him to "save the cheerleader, save the world." The rest of the first season unfolds as the bad guys try to destroy the cheerleader (a tough task) and the good guys seeking to protect her.

While watching the show, it came to me, "Save the Investor, Save the World." At first, it was just an amusing idea, but I later realized it made for an excellent title for the event. As the event grew closer and closer, the question kept nagging at me—was it possible that by saving individual investors here on Main Street, we could save the world or at least make it a better place to live? Is there a greater purpose that most investors and advisors miss? And if there was, could understanding this greater purpose help investors actually build better portfolios and be better equipped intellectually and emotionally to demonstrate the proper behavior in chaotic markets? Is there a greater meaning or purpose behind how we managed money and how investors on Main Street should invest? It was obvious to me that without a greater purpose for money, most investors default to the position that, "I just want to make as much money as I can." I had discovered that money without purpose was never enough and could actually become a burden—there had to be something more. Are purpose and meaning important when you invest your money?

Investing is not simply a pie a chart or graph. Your investing results will be made up of the accumulated behavior over a lifetime. It is never what you know that matters. It is what you actually do that will determine outcomes. Actions speak louder than words. Investing is simply a subset of actions that make up your life like: eating, exercise, working or relationships. Like all of these areas, meaning and purpose will play a big role in the results you can achieve. For you to have the opportunity to be a successful investor and to achieve true peace of mind, you must find the answer to the question, "Why am I investing and to what greater purpose?"

Cycling has been one of my greatest life passions. At the age of 31, I was regularly riding my bike over 200 miles per week. It kept me lean and fit, recharged my batteries and reduced my stress. It was a major part of my life and so too was asthma as I struggled with it from childhood. It was especially challenging to breathe in the spring when the pollen poured into the air. While training for a 700 mile cycling event, my asthma spiraled out of control and the doctor prescribed me an oral steroid produced to get it back into control. After a myriad of treatments (including massive doses of steroids), my breathing eventually returned to normal and I resumed my aggressive training schedule assuming all was well. As the event drew near, I noticed a nagging pain in my left hip. I assumed it was a muscle strain. I took Advil, iced it and returned to the training. The pain intensified. Every time I rode, it became more debilitating. After a month of trying to push through it, I gave in and scheduled a meeting with an orthopedic specialist. He took my medical history and promptly ordered an MRI. Several weeks later, he called my personal cell phone.

"Mark?"

"Yes."

"This is Dr. Swank."

"I need you to come in and see me as soon as possible." (He sounded concerned).

"Why? Am I ok? Is it anything severe?" as my mind instantly went to the worst case scenario.

"I don't have a tumor do I?"

"No, nothing like that. Nothing life threatening, but I do need you to get in here."

The next day, I found myself waiting for him to give me the news. He tried to force a smile as he entered the room.

"Ok doc, what the heck is going on?" I blurted out.

"Well, you have a disease called osteonecrosis."

"What is this doc? I was finance and accounting major," I tried to joke, "I never took a lick of Latin."

"Osteo means bone and necrosis means death."

It hit me right between the eyes. I could feel the fear run through my body.

"You mean I have bone death? How do you fix it? Give me a pill or something. I need to get up and get training."

"It's not going to work like that. There really is no cure. We don't even know exactly why it occurs. We do know that in some patients Prednisone can trigger it. It is a particularly nasty side effect."

"So it is just going to stay like this and I just have to learn to deal with the pain?"

"Not exactly. The head of your femur is crumbling. As the weight of your upper body presses down on the joints the head will continue to flatten out. It will become progressively painful. I can give you painkillers, but eventually you won't be able to walk."

"How long will that take?"

"My best guess is about a year."

"Then what?"

"Then you will have to have a total artificial hip replacement. I am sorry to have to give you this news; I know you are only thirty-two."

"Is there anything I can do to stop it?"

"There are some experimental surgeries, but nothing permanent to reverse the process."

"Oh," I was looking down at the floor. My eyes were beginning to tear up.

"And, Mark, you have it in both hips."

At first, I couldn't believe the diagnosis, "I want a second opinion. This can't be happening to me." After confirmation, I quickly fell into a state of depression and self-pity. "Why is this happening to me, it isn't fair?" I desperately sought a cure. But after months of research it became clear that this was indeed to be my fate. Self-pity became depression and I was crippled by self-doubt and fear about my future. I was riddled with both physical and emotional suffering. The feeling of daggers in both hips slicing into me resulted anytime I put weight on them and the pain became a physical burden that I could not escape.

In my last attempt to find a cure, I went to see a blood specialist. There were several theories that the bone destruction was a result of microscopic blood clots brought on by the drug Prednisone. He would not cure my disease, but I found the answer I needed in his waiting room. You see, he was also an oncologist who specialized in treating various forms of cancer. I was surrounded by men, women, and, even more sobering, children battling for their very lives. In an adjoining room, they received their chemo treatments. In an instant the primary question in my mind went from the self-pity-driven, "Why me? Why is this happening to me?" to "Why not me? Why do I think I get a free pass at life with no pain or struggles? I have youth, friends, loving parents, and amazing children, and I have the financial resources to deal with this. Why not me?" Then it hit me, "Mark, you have to use this to help other people. You have got to turn this into good."

I left the doctor's office, and for the first time in months I was smiling. The physical pain was still there and I limped back to my car. But I had defined and forged meaning and purpose from my personal suffering. I resolved to have the needed surgery as soon as possible and get on with my life. I also made it my personal mission to educate as many people as possible about this disease and the dangers of Prednisone to help them avoid my same outcome. I had no idea how important that mission would be.

Several years later, my daughter, Mallory, suffered a severe bout with asthma. Her doctor prescribed Prednisone. Because of my personal experience with the drug I was able to get both of our blood tested. Buried in genetic code was a single marker that I had passed on to her. Our blood clotted just a little too fast and did not break up fast enough. If they had administered the drug, chances are she would have acquired the same disease I had. For an adult the results are dire—but for a child, still growing, the results are catastrophic often resulting in the destruction of the growth plates in the hips and lifelong crippling deformity. Because I had my hips replaced, I was able to save my daughter from an even worse fate. What seemed like a cruel and destructive twist of fate was (after giving it proper meaning and purpose) an actual miracle.

Perhaps you too have had setbacks in your life that at the time seemed insurmountable and devoid of meaning only to "reframe" the experience to turn it into a way to empower yourself and others to survive and even thrive. Maybe you have even experienced painful and unexpected losses in your portfolio that have triggered the same voice, "Why me? Why has this happened to me?" If you have, you are not alone and finding meaning in that experience and defining a greater purpose for your money will be a huge part of finding the peace of mind you are seeking.

Even in the most tragic and horrific events there is transformative power. In his groundbreaking book *Man's Search for Meaning*[34], Viktor Frankl describes his experience in surviving a German concentration camp. He writes:

> *A thought transfixed me: for the first time in my life I saw the truth as it is set into song by so many poets, proclaimed as the final wisdom by so many thinkers. The truth—that love is the ultimate and the highest goal to which man can aspire. Then I grasped the meaning of the greatest secret that human poetry and human thought and belief have to impart: The salvation of man is through love and in love. I understood how a man who has nothing left in this world still may know bliss, be it only for a brief moment, in the contemplation of his beloved. In a position of utter desolation, when man cannot express himself in positive action, when his only achievement may consist in enduring his sufferings in the right way—an honorable way—in such a position man can, through loving contemplation of the image he carries of his beloved, achieve fulfillment. For the first time in my life I was able to understand the meaning of the words, "The angels are lost in perpetual contemplation of an infinite glory."*

If you don't believe in something, you will fall for anything. That is the central theme of this chapter. The meaning and purpose you attribute to your portfolio will give you the strength, courage and foresight to be disciplined and follow the simple rules of investing while others are bowing their heads and lining up to buy the Wall Street bullies' snake oil. The pursuit of purpose and meaning is not a luxury, it is a necessity. So is it possible to prudently invest for your family and make the world a better place? The answer is a resounding—Yes!

> *"Free enterprise will work if you will."*
> —Ray Kroc, founder of McDonalds

Saving the Globe, One Investor at a Time

One key cog in my investment philosophy involves saving the investor from himself or herself and from external economic and wealth issues that loom large all over the world.

As I've said, free enterprise is what enables a society to prosper. But don't take it from me—take it from one of the greatest leaders in history, Winston Churchill. Here's what Churchill had to say about the value of free enterprise:

I do not believe in the power of the State to plan and enforce. No matter how numerous are the committees they set up or the ever-growing hordes of officials they employ or the severity of the punishments they inflict or threaten, they can't approach the high level of internal economic production achieved under free enterprise. Personal initiative, competitive selection, and profit motive corrected by failure and the infinite processes of good housekeeping and personal ingenuity, these constitute the life of a free society. It is this vital creative impulse that I deeply fear the doctrines and policies of the socialist government has destroyed.

Nothing that they can plan and order and rush around enforcing will take its place. They have broken the main spring and until we get a new one, the watch will not go. Set the people free. Get out of the way and let them make the best of themselves. I am sure that this policy of equalizing misery and organizing society—instead of allowing diligence, self-interest and ingenuity to produce abundance—has only to be prolonged to kill this British Island stone dead. [41]

Like Churchill, I believe that the factors I've introduced so far in this book are actually helping to save the investor here in the United States—factors like capitalism, and free market investing and mutating technology. These are the very DNA of wealth creation.

Together those two wealth drivers are making the world a better place. Those are the cornerstones on which we can build a wealth creation platform that can solve big, geopolitical problems like human rights abuses, massive poverty, and healthcare issues around the globe. If you look at just the last 100 years, the quality of living has increased sevenfold throughout the planet, and the general health of the world's population has gone up dramatically. Consequently, the world is becoming a better place, contrary to what many people would have you believe.

But we're not there yet—not by a long shot. Remember when I discussed the investors' dilemma in Chapter Four? Well, there's a global dilemma infecting the planet, as well.

It starts off with fear of the future, and it includes fear of recessions, depression, wars, rioting, and other toxic social issues. Even though we've always had underlying fear and angst, and we've always had wars, poverty and social unrest, history has shown that societies deal with these monumental problems in different ways.

Myriad political figures have tossed out childlike answers, many in the form of communism and socialism. We've already focused on how Marx, Lenin, Stalin and other communists have basically told people, "Don't worry about the future. We'll take care of you." Or, "Trust us. Just give the government control of your life, give government control of setting the prices, and with that control we, the central planners, will take care of you."

The problem is that communism creates despotism. Socialism over the long term creates an environment where despotism breeds in its own toxic stew. The Nobel Prize-winning econommist and social observer F.A. Hayek in his books, *The Road to Serfdom* and *The Fatal Conceit,* does a great job showing how people who grasp onto socialism and communism wind up living in a society where the police state grows and mutates. The reason for that is simple: you have to control people's lives to control their wealth and then transfer that wealth to the state. You have to tell them where to work, what to eat, how to act, how to behave in society, and as you allocate resources—*not* based on freedom and independent liberty, but on the goals of the State—you wind up creating a police state.

To survive, the police state has to grow, which it can easily do as the central planners confiscate wealth from those that earn and transfer it to those that don't. When that cycle perpetuates itself, you start confiscating human rights and alienating human values. You also end up creating massive amounts of fear and pain and poverty because ultimately when you don't allow a society to evolve through free markets, you create massive poverty and suffering, and we see plenty of that throughout the world.

But it's a cycle that can't continue unless wealth is being confiscated. Eventually, the government runs out of other people's money. The people who were the engine of the economy and job creation—in other words, the private sector—get tapped out.

History shows this to be true. Ultimately, when the despots have run through the wealth of their own society and drained it, they look to other people and other countries to grab their vital resources (think oil or land). That's what World War I and World War II were all about, despots running through their stores of resources, decimating their own society, and then eventually needing to take the resources from other societies. But that only leads to the grim reality of genocide, the mass killing off and murder of large percentages of the populations of the countries these despots take over, and on to the inevitable abuses of human and fundamental rights (think Nazi Germany and Communist Russia).

Make no mistake, socialism and communism go hand-in-hand with the abuse of individual personal rights and freedoms, and we still see that on a global basis, which leads to immense human suffering. That's the global dilemma.

Global Dilemma

Where there is pain and suffering, people want easy answers. Socialism and communism promise equality and prosperity for all, the only problem is– it does not work. No idea has created more human poverty, fear, pain and suffering than communism and socialism. Absolute power corrupts absolutely, a central fact that cannot be denied. But there is a better way and you can be a part of the solution to the global dilemma we face today.

When entrepreneurs abuse their power, they are evolved out of the system by consumers and competitors. Not so with despots. They will use force to stay in power forever.

Can greater amounts of wealth and prosperity make the world a better and safe place to live in? It's questions like this that I focus on every day and I am prepared to dedicate the rest of my life to creating systems, processes, and tools to help Main Street investors realize the independence they deserve and make the world a better place.

So, to address both the investor and global dilemma, we start by looking in our own back yard and focus on your problems as an investor. I have to teach you how to ask the right questions. Most people spend more time planning Thanksgiving dinner than giving thoughtful attention to their investments. It is sad, but true. In fact, they ask all the wrong questions.

I know, because when someone learns that I help my clients invest money, the barrage of questions is not far behind. Of course, they like everyone else are searching for quick, easy answers they really don't have to think much about. It goes something like this:

> *"Hey, what do you think is going to happen to the economy?"*
>
> *"I have no idea, and neither does anyone else. No one can predict the future."*
>
> *"Oh, okay," they stammer. "What stocks should I pick?"*
>
> *"We don't pick individual stocks," I tell them.*
>
> *"What do you think the market is going to do?" Now they are clearly frustrated.*
>
> *"Anyone who tells you they know what the market is going to do in the short-term is either delusional or just flat out lying—I certainly don't know."*
>
> *Clearly struggling, "Can you at least tell me what mutual fund manager I should put my money with?"*
>
> *Now I really blow their minds, "A manager's past performance has zero correlation with future performance."*
>
> *"Well, if you can't tell me these things, how the hell do you manage money?" they blurt out angrily.*
>
> *"The truth is," I tell them, "that you don't need to know any of those things to pursue successful investing. You are asking all the wrong questions."*

I have extreme confidence and peace of mind about my personal investment decisions and those I make on behalf of my investors. So I started to address their problems with—you guessed it—a question. What is it that I (and those few investors who have mastered prudent investing) know that gives me peace of mind no matter what the market does on a day-to-day, month-by-month basis? If I could identify this and help other investors learn what I had discovered for myself, I could help them out of the Investors' Dilemma. That is how I created the Twenty Must-Answer Questions for creating peace of mind. They are designed to raise your consciousness about what you are doing and why you are doing it with your portfolio.

If you know the right things, you don't have to know everything. With the right education and coaching, I can help you discover all of the answers for yourself. Very few investors, no matter how sophisticated they believe they are, can answer more than a handful of them the first time they are presented with them. Thankfully, with just a little honest effort, everybody can discern the answers. In future chapters, I will coach you on how to answer these questions and that will transform how you invest.

When you focus on the right things it will enable you to eliminate all the forms of speculating with your portfolio.

Stemming the Tide

How can we possibly help to stem not only in the Investors' Dilemma, but also the Global Dilemma? It all starts with investors understanding how they are allocating their money and then having positive investment experiences that encourage the spread of free market benefits on a global basis.

You also have every investor understanding the answers to the Twenty Must-Answer Questions for how they should allocate their resources. The answers to those 20 questions will help those investors raise their consciousness about what they're doing and why. That helps them eliminate all speculating and gambling from the investment process, and helps them live powerfully so they can affect the world in positive ways.

The Questions Are the Solution

My dad is my greatest teacher, coach, and hero. Somehow he escaped the overwhelming poverty of his childhood. I can remember as a ten-year-old watching him shave in the morning and hanging on every word of wisdom he imparted to me.

In between swipes of the razor, "Boy," he would say lovingly (he still calls me that), "A man's greatest security is in his own shoes. You've got to be 100% responsible for your own success in life. Focus not on yourself, but on how you can create value for others."

"Dad, tell me about the house by the railroad tracks." I could never get enough of that story.

"When I was your age, we lived by the tracks. My dad was driving a truck for a living and my mom was raising us. We had no indoor restrooms, no plumbing, and no central air. It was basically just a shack. We lived on beans and potatoes. Once a week, if we were lucky, we got to eat a chicken. We had to nail the tops of instant Carnation milk cans to the holes in the bare floorboards to keep the rats from getting in."

"Dad," I coaxed, hanging on every word, "How did you get out of there? How did you learn to make money?"

"Well," he said thoughtfully, "it's really about asking the right questions."

"But that doesn't make any sense. How can that be?"

"Okay, think of it like this. If I had consistently asked myself questions like, 'Why am I doomed to live a life of poverty? Why am I going to have to work in the coal mines? Why am I going to be destitute and waste my life away in these hollers and hills or live on welfare?' my life would have turned out very different. Instead I constantly asked, 'How can I use my God-given abilities to create the wealth and prosperity that I deserve? How can I work harder and smarter than the next guy? How can I meet the men and women who have achieved greatness in their business and lives and what can I learn from them?' But mainly when I was your age, I asked, 'How can I grow up and get the hell out of this place?' You see these questions led my focus, goals, and actions on a completely different path. The questions are the answer."

It is a lesson I have never forgotten. Even today, every day when I drop my kids off at school I say, "Don't forget to ask a good question." To which they reply, "Oh, Dad," and roll their eyes. I smile to myself as they gather their backpacks and books and saunter into school. I think to myself, "You may think it is corny now, but someday you are going to need that skill." So I drill it into their minds relentlessly. The quality of your life will be determined by the quality of the questions you ask.

Ask the wrong questions, and doom yourself to negative outcomes. Ask the right questions, and a whole new world opens up to you. This is true in business, true in relationships, and certainly true in how you invest your money.

I also observed that the questions that make the biggest difference to individuals and the world do not have easy answers. On the contrary, some questions, if they are powerful enough, can define and drive a whole lifetime. Walt Disney asked, "How can I create the happiest place on earth?" Henry Ford asked, "How can I bring cheap and affordable transportation to Main Street?" Steve Jobs asked, "How can I bring the personal computer into every household and transform people's lives?" These are huge life-altering questions. They transform the people who are asking them, and they make the world a better place to live.

The questions that drive me are: "How do I help investors achieve true peace of mind? How do I help investors stop speculating and gambling with their life's savings and find meaning and purpose greater than money itself? And how do I actually create and allocate your resources to achieve the maximum expected return for your personal risk preference?" In twenty-five years of advising thousands of investors, I have found that average investors have absolutely no idea about how much risk or volatility they are assuming for the mix of assets they have created.

Wall Street v. Academia

Instead of taking our lead from the Wall Street bullies, we will turn to academia. It is in the hallowed halls of economic universities that we will begin to find some answers. You will see in subsequent chapters there are not just stuffy theories; they are sound investing principles that have real Main Street investing applications. One of the keystone principles I will teach you is how to implement a concept called Modern Portfolio Theory. This is a Nobel Prize-winning concept developed by Dr. Harry Markowitz. All you need to know now is that it will help you understand what true diversification is and how to apply it to your personal portfolio. Once you have eliminated speculating and gambling and applied academic principles of investing to your money by understanding the Twenty Must-Answer Questions, you will be able to create a deep sense of peace. Not because you can forecast or predict the market, but because you will understand how markets work and why.

This will allow you to move from a state of scarcity, never enough, constantly craving more, and a nagging feeling of doubt and fear to a state of abundance, a sense that you have more than enough, a surplus of resources. Sure, who doesn't want the finer things in life—a nice home, cars, travel, leisure time and the latest technological gadgets? And surely becoming a wise steward of your portfolio can help you achieve that. It will also empower you to help others.

Think of a time in your life when you experienced significant stress and anxiety from a feeling of scarcity. Perhaps you experienced not enough money to pay the bills, excess debt, economic downturns in your business, or perhaps fear of losing a job or watching your portfolio drop in value. This puts many people at a loss to empower others. When fear and anxiety take over, it affects all aspects of our lives. We may lose sleep, stop exercising, overeat, be less effective at work and less attentive to our loved ones. It can even affect our health. On the other hand when you are confident about your financial decisions and achieve a state of abundance around your wealth, you are much better at becoming a powerful leader and helping others. Over the many years I have been working with investors, I have also observed that when they have peace of mind about finances, they are also more empowered to help charities and causes they care about.

By applying the academic principles of Modern Portfolio Theory as the primary tenet, you can escape the Investors' Dilemma and move from a state of fear and anxiety to a state of clear understanding of what you are doing and why at all times.

But what about the Global Dilemma we are facing today? As an investor should you even care? Even in our age of relative abundance, nearly two billion people on the planet live on less than two dollars a day.[35] There are global recessions, disease and malnutrition, abuses of basic human rights, terrorism, and war plaguing our planet. These are massive challenges and the stakes are high. So is it possible that by investing your money and solving your own problems you could help save the world? Not only do I believe that the answer is yes—it might just be the most important and powerful thing you could ever do.

How could prudently investing your money for your family to reach your life's dreams, seemingly a self-interested act, make the world a better place for everyone?

The answers to these questions lie in how you allocate your assets to tap into global free markets and the seemingly miraculous power that free markets have to create wealth.

The government doesn't want you to think this way, nor does the mainstream media, but it's free markets that drive global wealth, not global governments. Think about it. When investors allocate their resources, they're actually helping people save the world because their resources are allocated on a global basis. Here's a list of free market economies that investors can currently harness:

SAVE THE WORLD

Argentina, Australia, Austria, Belgium, Brazil, Canada, Chile, China, Columbia, Czech Republic, Denmark, Egypt, Finland, France, Germany, Greece, Hong Kong, Hungary, India, Indonesia, Ireland, Israel, Italy, Japan, Malaysia, Mexico, Netherlands, New Zealand, Norway, Peru, Philippines, Poland, Portugal, Russia, Singapore, South Africa, South Korea, Spain, Sweden, Switzerland, Taiwan, Thailand, Turkey, United Kingdom, and the United States of America

The Rise of Free Markets

We haven't always had it so good.

If you go back 50 to100 years, you'll find a dramatic reduction in the availability of global free markets. If we actually look at the long-term progress of the United States and other free markets, we might expect that 50 to 100 years from now we'd have even more free markets that can accommodate private investors and spur faster and more substantial global wealth. In fact, only in Africa and part of the Mideast do we see an absence of free market economies. Not coincidentally, those regions harbor some of the worst totalitarian regimes of the modern age.

From a wealth standpoint, this is how you make the world a better place.

Global wealth is achieved not by forcing people to buy or sell, but by helping free markets grow and create prosperity for everyone. I'm talking about the expansion of human rights and global wealth, as investors provide the capital to feed the rise in global free markets. In London, in Tokyo, in Vienna, in New York, in Rome, in Brazil, in New Delhi, in Hong Kong, in Madrid and Amsterdam, all over the world we're seeing a remarkable rise in global entrepreneurism. And *that* spirit spreads the ability to create wealth. People like Bill Gates, Henry Ford, Steve Jobs, Thomas Edison, and Mark Zuckerberg—all spreading global entrepreneurship and innovation.

Free markets and entrepreneurship evolve technologies that make our lives better. They give us more leisure time, better food, education, jobs, travel and better toys to work

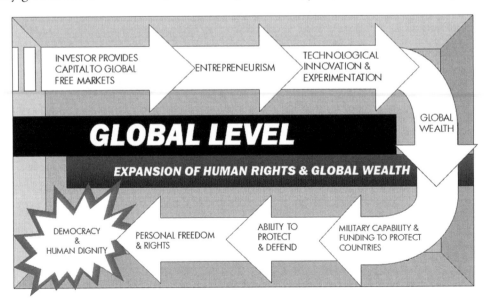

and play with like cell phones, laptops, and iPods. In fact, looking back on human history, you live in the greatest period to be alive on the planet, not the worst as some would have you believe. And over the last one hundred years things have only gotten better, not worse. Our standard of living has increased seven times over the last one hundred years [43] and lifespan has rocketed from 50 years to 78 years.[44, 45] Yes, it is an awesome time to be alive! But it can be better. By allocating your assets globally, you are firing the engine of free markets and global expansion that makes the world a better place. That also helps reduce war and conflict because when free countries trade, they do not fight with each other. No army has ever crossed a border of a free market ally to attack it.

But if you pursue free markets, you are going to create wealth and prosperity, and there are going to be those on the planet who think that wars were just an effect of misunderstandings, lack of communication. You know, "People just need to understand each other better." But as a 48-year-old man, I've come to believe that there is both good and evil on the planet, and I don't ever expect there to be (in my lifetime or in the near future) a shortage of dictators who seek to oppress and confiscate the wealth of others.

That's why it's vital to protect and defend other free-market economies.

It's critical because our personal freedoms can so easily be taken for granted. Sometimes we actually throw them away for no good reason at all. Personal freedoms, such as freedom of speech, freedom of religion, freedom of the press, freedom of democracy, freedom to vote—and to supply the human dignity that enables me to choose a job I desire, to pursue my own liberty—all of these freedoms fuel economic growth on this planet.

So not only are we helping the investor create wealth with free markets and tools like Modern Portfolio Theory, but I think it's important for investors to know that they are actually making the planet a better place. They're saving the world by aiding free enterprise and innoation to spread human dignity and prosperity on a global scale. This is a noble endeavor for any investor, and I find that comforting.

> *"It is discretionary capital that finances most of what is original and idiosyncratic in our culture and economy."*
> –George Gilder [46]

Its Science

"A lot of people are afraid to tell the truth, to say no. That's where toughness comes into play. Toughness is not being a bully. It's having a backbone"
–Robert Kiyosaki

The Strings of Poverty

Most eight-year-old boys look forward to gym day at school. They see it as a wonderful opportunity to get out of class and play, but Joe was dreading it that day in 1953. He knew they were playing dodgeball, and that meant physical and emotional pain. He was small for his age but tough as nails. Where he grew up, street fights were just a part of everyday life. You learned to defend yourself or else, and Joe could whip a boy twice his size in a fair fight, but what was getting ready to happen was not fair—not even close.

Joe's mother and father were, as the saying goes, dirt poor. For a while, they even lived in a ricketty shack with dirt floors, and when you are that poor, you surely do not have the money for gym shoes. In fact, Joe only got one pair of shoes per year in the fall before school started and they were always black street shoes. So as the other children were putting on their sneakers, Joe took his shoes off and looked woefully at his feet covered in nothing but socks.

The gym teacher would not allow street shoes because they left black marks on the floor, so as the other kids ran out to the middle of the gym floor, Joe lagged behind, knowing what was to come. Gym balls in the 1950s were hard red orbs, and it was important to put as much space between yourself and your pursuer lest you get blasted. But this was impossible for Joe, and the other boys knew it.

"Hey, little Joey, you going to cry to your Mommy when I light you up?" the boys taunted.

Joe could feel the fear growing in his gut, but he also began to feel something else, something strangely empowering. He couldn't quite place it, but it was there.

The whistle blew, and the gym-shoed boys ran to get the balls. Joe slipped and slid in his hole-torn socks. Three boys instinctively converged on Joe drawing within several feet of him. He was surrounded. There would be no escape. The bullies fired the balls at Joe simultaneously, and the pain ran through his body and, against his will, his eyes began to mist over.

"Don't let them see you cry," he told himself. "Don't ever let them see your tears. You fight this. You stand tall. Don't let them beat you."

He stood up and walked to the sidelines as he watched the game, but he never shed a single tear.

Later that night, safely in the walls of his house, Joe took off his shirt. He was covered in welts and bruises. He had that feeling again that he couldn't quite place, but this time it was mixed with anger. The anger covered over the fear, and that was good.

His mind raced. "I will get out of this. I will free myself from this poverty. I will not be a victim. I will not let them hurt me. I won't let them win. I won't."

Many years later, that boy would grow to become my father. He patiently drilled the mindset, values, and principles into me that gave him the means to escape his poverty, and that I have found are critical to long-term investing success. Whenever my father shares part of his life he is always careful to include the "moral of the story" just in case I missed it, and the moral in this story is key for understanding the next chapter. First, that you must be 100% accountable for your own life. Second, if you want anything in life you have to work hard to get it, in other words, "There ain't no free lunch."

When it comes to investing, that means that you must not take a back seat in your portfolio design. You must be accountable for understanding how your portfolio is designed and exactly how much risk and volatility is involved. And as for the "free lunch" part—you must assume risk in the investment process. No matter where you invest your money there is risk. The goal is to understand how to control, manage and respond to risk and volatility in your portfolio.

There is no free lunch in investing, no magic formula to get great returns without risk, even though the bullies of Wall Street want you to believe it.

There is no substitute for the hard work of understanding markets and being 100% accountable for your decisions.

Wall Street is not the only place you find bullies who claim to have your best interest at heart. Washington, D.C. is full of bullies who tell you daily that they know what is best for you and they will fix everything from unemployment to your retirement. So as an investor, how much should you count on Washington, or the federal government to help you stay on track and reach all of your life's dreams, and maximize your wealth?

While I'll spend most of this chapter examining the key issue of managing investment returns, I want to set the table for that discussion by talking about how external factors, most recently the buffoonish and dangerous strategies deployed by the U.S. government that have stalled the economy and how you can prudently invest despite them.

It's no secret that we've been in the worst financial crisis since the 1930s. That much is set in stone. The question is: what are you going to do about it?

Government Gone Wild

If only the policies coming from Washington were concrete. Wildness is usually the natural habitat of bald eagles, college keg mixers, and erratic relief pitchers—it's not supposed to be the natural order of economic policy handed down by the Federal Reserve and the federal government. To call the policies coming from our nation's capital "extreme" is not mere hyperbole. There's little doubt that the federal response to the economic crisis has vastly increased market uncertainty, prompting some investors to seek safe havens in more conservative assets, while others have stood paralyzed as the stock market has taken a sizeable chunk of financial security out of their lives.

But financial markets are ever-dynamic and the landscape is shifting—to the good, as I will explain. First, though, some background data must be laid on the table.

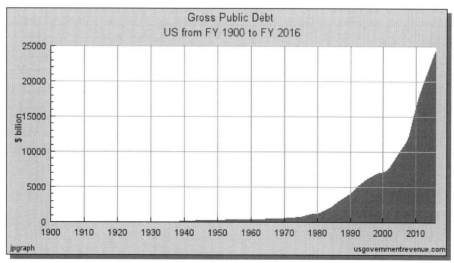

Source: US Government Debt. See Endnote 47.

Bailouts, and Stimulus, and Easing—Oh, My!

In retrospect, there is plenty of blame to go around for the real estate and mortgage crash that escalated into a global debt crisis. Overzealous banks making insane loans with little or no money down, real estate speculators on small salaries leveraging their third "investment property," investment firms packaging the risky loans into security products, and last, but not least, the federal government who gave birth to the monster Freddie and Fannie to guarantee the whole mess. So who is to blame? Everybody. Everyone drove this bubble that would eventually lead to recessions, real estate devaluations, and nine percent unemployment.

In response to the crisis, the government stepped in to bail out banks and brokerage firms as well as GM and Chrysler to the tune of $750 billion. This was crony capitalism at its worst. The ire and mistrust engendered by bailing out the bad actors who misjudged their own business models can still be witnessed in the Occupy Wall Street movements and Tea Party meetings. Truly, nobody likes it when you bail out the bully, and rightfully so. Those bullies should have been allowed to devolve out of the system so that better and more sound businesses could evolve. In their infinite wisdom, they took on a massive "stimulus" program to jump-start the economy with $800 billion. Needless to say, it did not bring the economy back to life. It instead froze the needle of unemployment at slightly over eight percent. And, to add insult to injury, the Fed began a loose money policy. Has any of this been helpful to Main Street? No!

Although claiming to have the best interest of Main Street at heart, these policies have done nothing to create jobs or free the entrepreneurial genius and capital in this country. The answer to our problems is not on Wall Street or in Washington, D.C., but it resides on Main Street. After all, Washington borrows forty cents out of every dollar it spends. Every Main Street investor knows, as they sit across the kitchen table from each other paying their bills, that spending this amount of money is unsustainable.

This is a recipe for bankruptcy for any company, investor, or country. It's not even science; it's common sense. As I was growing up my father always told me, leverage kills. You do not leverage your business with massive debt. He was right, and I am sure you know that, too—but not the massive Wall Street banks and investment firms. They were clueless. How ironic that they want to "handle" your money when they can't even keep their own house in order. When that doesn't work, well, it's time to print money!

Poor budgetary habits are an unfortunate habit in Washington. That's what a $14 trillion debt load can do to a country. The last time the deficits were this high as compared to gross domestic product was during World War II. Our current level, however large, is still only half of its highest peak. No matter that the current federal response is generating deficits that will make last year's numbers seem downright quaint. That's already out of the private sector's control. The question is this? How are the markets absorbing the huge amount of debt the government will issue in new Treasury auctions?

Just exactly how do they plan to keep funding all of their deficits?

By and large, the U.S. government can raise money two ways. By fattening the federal tax coffers (not a popular option in a steep recession) or by issuing more Treasury notes, often to foreign investors in emerging economic behemoths like China and India.

In fairness, the Federal Reserve is trying to help the U.S. economy grow, but it's wandering far off the policy-making reservation to do so. Case in point: after exhausting conventional methods by pushing the federal funds rate to zero, it is now stepping up to unconventional methods known as "quantitative easing." In 2009 and 2010, the Fed bought over $1 trillion in mortgage-related securities and $300 billion in long-term treasury bonds to improve liquidity as their new method.

The theory was simple but flawed: make money cheap and borrowing easy by expanding the money supply, banks will lend, businesses will borrow to put capital to work, and the economy will grow. However, the social engineers in Washington forgot one main thing. The growth in the economy must be fueled by the "little guy" the small business people who run a modest company that hires two or three employees. People who run a family dry cleaner or a restaurant or a plumbing company are the entrepreneurs who will eventually save this country. These are Main Street entrepreneurs. While they see backroom bailouts and stimulus waste and the Fed printing money, they do not see anything out of Wall Street or Washington that is inspiring them to take risks and grow. In fact, quite the opposite, investors and businesses are sitting on all-time high cash positions. They are afraid that the endless spending and deficits will end in more regulation, risk, and higher tax bills. It is the Main Street worker and investor who will lead us out of this recession into greater prosperity and freedom. Main Street you are the answer. In the meantime, how much should you depend on Washington's help?

Uncle Sam is playing the shell game, too. In fact, the government's high-stakes version of the shell game is one that would make any street hustler blush. It's a classic bait-and-switch that keeps the average American's eye off the ball. Think about it. Many investors had been worried about a great global depression (and may still remain so). Even more investors fear massive inflation, which cuts into corporate earnings and household spending.

Who can argue with that? Fear is both a natural and rational response to this Caligula-style bacchanal of fiscal and monetary stimulus now being injected into the economy. The government doesn't want you to worry about any of these things. That's why the printing presses have been rolled out and numerous diversions put into play to keep you from figuring out that Uncle Sam also has the shell-game ball in the palm of his hand.

You simply cannot depend on the central planner at the federal level to create the set of economic circumstances that will save you from this or any other recession. *If politicians knew how to create jobs, they would be entrepreneurs.* In fact, all of this planning is much more likely to hamper job creation and growth. Similarly, you must not depend on them for your retirement. If you receive Social Security or other financial support, great, but you better not count on it for your dreams and retirement security.

The centralized planners in both Washington and Wall Street want you to become dependent on them, but centralized planning does not work at a portfolio level or government level. You need to take charge of your own financial destiny. To do that, you are going to need an understanding of where returns really come from in your portfolio.

Hopefully, I have smashed the illusion that returns come from a brilliant guru or prognosticator omniscient enough to grace your portfolio with his elitist stock-picking and market timing prowess.

Before we can have a meaningful discussion about rates of return and where they really come from, it is necessary to understand what they are and how they are actually calculated. Most investors have no idea what the total rate of return is in their portfolio. They may know what one fund did in a certain year, but they have no clue about the total long-term compound rate for all of their assets. Nor do the various broker-dealers or even so-called money managers clearly calculate performance. This is not an accident. The more the bullies can keep you in the dark, the better. First, there are different types of rates of return.

What's the difference between compound rates of return and simple rates of return? In short order, compound rates are derived from linking each year's return through multiplication. Simple rates of return are derived from adding each year's return. For example, consider a fund with annual returns of +20%, +25%, and -15% over three years. The value of an initial investment of $100 in the fund would be calculated as follows: $100 x 1.20 x 1.25 x 0.85, or $128, equivalent to an average annual compound rate of +8.3%. However, when the returns are simply added, the final value of the investment would be $130, a simple average rate of +10% annually.

Let's look at an investment that provides a return of +100% in the first year and

-50% in the next, or vice versa. The average return would be +25% (100 - 50 ÷ 2), but the average compound return would be zero. Since the reality is that you would have seen your initial $100 double to $200, only to fall back to $100, it is clear that zero is the appropriate figure. So you should rely on what is called the geometric rate of return, which is annualized on a compound basis and will precisely reflect the total return that you would have actually received, rather than the simple arithmetic rate.

When you analyze performance, you must always focus on compounded rates of return and never average rates, and for our purpose all of the numbers we discuss will be compound returns. As if that were not complicated enough, you also want your returns to be time-weighted and dollar-weighted. This will ensure that inflows and outflows of funds in our portfolio do not skew the numbers artificially high or low. It is also essential that any money manager or advisor you work with provide audited Global Investment Performance numbers. Audits help ensure that your returns are accurate and not deceptive. Also insist on a third-party custodian who actually holds the assets. Simply following these rules would have saved the Madoff victims billions.

Once you understand the basics of compound returns, you can allow their "magic" to work for you. Albert Einstein is attributed with saying, "Compound interest is the most powerful force in the universe." While it is impossible to directly attach him to the statement, it is truly an awesome force. A force you will need to harness to reach your dreams and drive your portfolio long-term. Just a small increase in portfolio efficiency (by adding 1 to 3 percent higher expected return for your given level of risk) can make dramatic increases in portfolio value.

Seemingly small differences in annual rates of return can result in enormous differences in total return over long periods of time. For example, a +12% rate of return from a good performer produces a +211% cumulative return over ten years. For a mediocre performer, a +11% rate produces a +184% total return. And for a poor performer, a +10% rate produces a +159% total return. Even as you use annual rates of return as your standard of choice, then, do not ignore the magic of compounding.

Inflation, the Dream Killer

Even if you are retired today, the greatest detriment to your future is not short-term portfolio swings, but the long-term devastating effects of inflation on your spending power. Just as compound interest can work for you in your portfolio, it will work mercilessly against you in everything else. Everything you need to enjoy life simply gets more expensive—cars, housing, food, clothes, energy, and medical treatments. If you need it, surely it will be more expensive in the future.

Impact of Inflation on Investment Returns

I've discussed this issue at many investment seminars, and it's at the heart of total return issue. It's all about buying power, as measured by inflation and the U.S. dollar. By any measure, the value of the dollar these days—and its subsequent impact (perhaps burden is a better term) on U.S. consumers—is in retreat.

History, recent and otherwise, tells just how much in retreat. Take the average duration of a Baby Boomer's lifetime. Using CPI as a measure of inflation, the decrease in purchasing power can be seen over the following time periods: [27]

In 1958, $1.00 had approximately the same buying power as $7.38 in 2008.
In 1968, $1.00 had approximately the same buying power as $6.19 in 2008.
In 1978, $1.00 had approximately the same buying power as $3.38 in 2008.
In 1988, $1.00 had approximately the same buying power as $1.82 in 2008
In 1998, $1.00 had approximately the same buying power as $1.31 in 2008.

The average annual inflation rate over the entire period between 1958 and 2011 was about 4%, fairly consistent with inflation's historical growth.[9]

Here's another way of looking at it:

In 1930, $0.56 would buy you a gallon of milk vs. $2.79 in 2010.
In 1930, $0.08 would buy you a loaf of bread vs. $1.37 in 2010.
In 1930, $0.10 would buy you a gallon of gas vs. $2.73 in 2010.
In 1930, $640 would buy you an average car vs. $28,400 in 2010.

As a result, no matter where you live, the real impact of inflation on consumers has become a burden. Now, thanks to rising inflation, millions of Americans are paying more for goods in an economic climate where their homes are worth less and their debt levels are climbing.

Don't make the mistake many investors do when they project they will need less income as retirees than they do today. Will the effects of inflation change the fact that most people spend more money when they have leisure time (think family vacation versus work time)? More time to play and explore the world means more spending, not less. To become a successful investor, you must balance the long term devastating effects of inflation with the short-term volatility of your portfolio. Many investors have become far too focused on short-term swings and have underestimated the effects of inflation.

That begs the question I hear a lot at these seminars: "How does inflation impact my investments, and what can I do about it?"

People living off a fixed-income, such as retirees, see a decline in their purchasing power and, subsequently, their standard of living. While your income is etched in stone, the price you pay for goods and services rises, meaning more money going out the door. Fixed income investors fare no better. Take a bond investor who pays $1,000 for a treasury bill with a 10% yield. You may earn $100 from your investment, but higher inflation eats into the value of that as well. In portfolio management terms, inflation just eats bond investments alive.

That's why the end game is vital to your financial future. Beating inflation is the number one goal of portfolio performance.

Is There a Science to Investing?

Just look around and you will see the amazing advances science has brought into your life. Science is simply the idea that it is possible to discern how the world and the universe actually work. In the scientific process, a scientist or academic hypothesizes how they believe the world works and then devises an experiment to observe how the world reacts. These experiments are backed up with mathematical models but are never said to be "valid" until they are observable and (this is very important) repeatable. Through this process, it is possible to understand and put to good use the laws that govern how matter "acts." For example, the law of relativity gave us $E=mc^2$. Although most of us would be hard-pressed to express all of the implications of this formula, we understand that it has real world implications.

Modern science has given us the microchip, Internet, smart phones, flat screens, and laptops. Science has transformed every aspect of our lives. While we have unlocked many of the formulas that the universe seems to follow, much remains a mystery. But is there a science to investing, or at least a way to look at investing the way a scientist or statistician would? Are there any formulas that can aid you in the search to build an efficient portfolio? The answer is yes—by applying advanced statistics there are a set of "laws" that seem to drive investment returns over the long haul. They describe where returns "come from" and why we believe it is likely they will continue to drive these returns in the future.

The Three Factors: Taking Control over Investment Returns

The next step in amping up your investment returns is to figure out where they come from. Let's face it, figuring out where returns come from is a mystery to most investors, and indeed, most advisors too.

While Wall Street bullies have been busy trying to convince you and others that they alone know how to predict and time markets, academics were busy studying the mountain of data that conclusively proved they couldn't and tirelessly studying and researching the seemingly simple question, "Where do returns come from?" Some of the leading academic theorists to tackle this question are Eugene Fama and Kenneth French and what they found in their studies would literally start a revolution in the investment world. Not only is it a theory that has real world applications for Main Street investors, the theory eliminates the traps of stock picking, market timing, and track record investing.

Scientists and academics love simplifying equations. When an academic principle can be summarized into a short equation, scientists call it "eloquent," and the kernel of what they found is eloquent indeed. They surmised from researching thousands of stocks throughout the recorded history of the market that returns did not come from the manager—the return came from the market itself. In other words, all investors were entitled to a market return, and the investor's primary job was not to mess it up. This is the basic equation:

The Return on Capital = The Cost of Capital

In other words, capitalism needs capital. It needs funding. So when an entrepreneur is building a company, building a new process, building a new system, building something that he or she thinks the world needs that can add value to other people, they need capital, either their own, or many times other people's capital to help build their business.

When you allocate a portion of your assets to a company in the form of stocks or bonds you are on the left side of the equation. The company must provide a return to you equivalent to their cost to raise money to grow. And how is their cost determined? It is based on risk. As an astute investor, you simply wouldn't purchase stock in a more risky company unless it had the expected benefit of a higher long-term return on your capital. And as it turns out, capital markets are amazingly efficient, and pricing is what we will refer to as "risk premium." These risk premiums are where returns come from. Most investors believe it is their job to avoid risk, but if you hedge all the risk in your portfolio, the expected rate of return is zero.

No, your job is to understand which risks are likely to maximize your wealth given your personal risk tolerance. As a provider of capital, you are entitled to a return. It really is that simple. Your job is not to mess it up.

There are three basic factors that constitute equity returns. We will cover each separately. Together they constitute what is known in academia as the Three Factor Model. Keep in mind that one of your goals must be to outpace inflation, the primary component is the market itself.

Let's look at the time period from 1927 to 2010, and the growth of a dollar. If $1 were invested in the S&P 500, all in all, it grows to over $2,600.[49]

During that same historical time period, equities have provided about on average a 7.88% premium over fixed income.[42] Why? Because equities have volatility. Conventional wisdom holds that investors don't like volatility. Not so. Most investors just can't tolerate downward volatility. Upward volatility is just fine. Indeed if the market were not so volatile, it would not offer the premium associated with higher rates of return. In other words, when you kill volatility, you kill the premium.

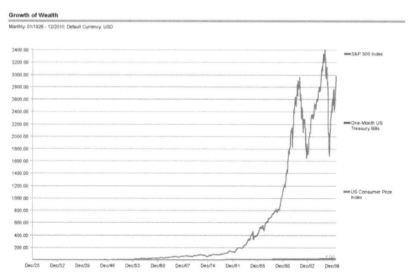

Source: 2010 Dimensional Fund Advisors Returns Software. See Endnote 49.

Historic Market Premium = 7.88%

Past performance does not guarantee future results.

The addition of nearly eight percent is the long-term reward investors would have received by simply allocating a portion of their portfolio to a simple index of Fortune 500 stocks. This is 8% versus the "risk free" rates of short-term government securities. Also note that the return to investors far exceeded inflation during this period, and the amazing power of compound interest escalated $1 to $2,600.[49] Keep in mind, no stock picking or market timing was required!

An additional cost of capital is what we call the "small" premium. You can think of it in very simple terms. Small companies incur more risk than large companies; therefore, investors who are willing to give small companies capital to grow their business have a higher expected rate of return. If we look at the timeline from 1927 to 2010 once again, you can see the premium for small stocks dwarfs the standard premium (i.e., the market premium itself). Historically, the small premium has been around 3.24% in excess of the market premium.[49]

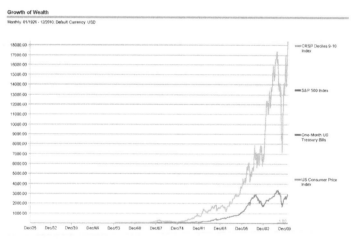

2010 Dimensional Fund Advisors Returns Software. See Endnote 49.

Historic Small Premium = 3.24%

Past performance does not guarantee future results.

The difference in historic wealth creation in micro-cap stocks versus Fortune 500 stocks is staggering. While one dollar invested in large company stocks grew to $2,600, micro-cap stocks skyrocket to over $19,000 per dollar invested.[49] Putting this into perspective, with a $10,000 initial investment in 1927, Large U.S. stocks grew to over $26,000,000 and in Micro-cap stocks over $190,000,000. While I know these numbers are staggering, and you do not have an 84-year time horizon to invest, this should demonstrate the incredibly awesome effect of equity returns compounded over time. These numbers reflect the inspiring ability of capital markets to provide return to investors who are smart enough to allocate a portion of their assets into companies that are morphing technology and creating great benefits to consumers—truly a win/win scenario. The pie gets bigger, and a rising tide raises all boats.

In an age of high-speed Internet, movies on demand and drive through fast food, we like everything now. We love instant gratification and quick fixes. I have a good friend who often says sarcastically, "Instant gratification is not fast enough for me." He needs to get over it. It is absolutely mission critical that you adopt a long-term perspective toward your portfolio. Focusing on the short-term is a recipe for disaster. Most investors want to see the thing that performed best over the last five or six years. They are seduced by easy money and quick fixes. They don't want to be bothered to look at history or scholarship. With my help, you won't make this mistake.

The final premium is something that we call the value premium, or the distressed premium. These are companies that have a large book value relative to their outstanding market price. Historically the value premium has been in the ballpark of about 5% per year.[49] If we combine the small and value premiums you can observe the effects of historic performance on only one dollar invested in small value stocks, which grows to $124,000 as measured by the Fama/French small value index, dwarfing the returns for both large and small stocks alone. Past performance is not a guarantee of future results, but even a casual observer can see the stunning affects in the mountain chart of this graph.

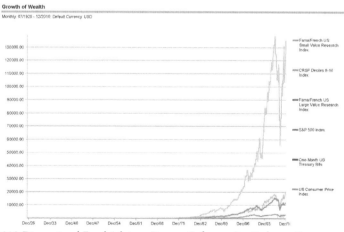

2010 Dimensional Fund Advisors Returns Software. See Endnote 49

Historic Value Premium = 4.82%

The historic risk premium for value or distressed companies versus growth is 4.82% per year.[49]

If you take these three factors—the market premium, the small premium and the value premium—and you analyze the average portfolio, you have over a 95% confidence level of understanding where the rates of returns of the portfolio come from.[50] That's a very high confidence level. In fact, very little of the additional return is unexplained.

Performance Paradox

"A paradox, a paradox, a most ingenious paradox…"

–The Pirates of Penzance

You may have observed a seeming contradiction in my earlier statements when I wrote that a manager's performance has zero correlation to future performance. In fact, I spent a great amount of time in showing you that track record investing is a dysfunctional way to invest; yet, I am talking about the past. How is this any different?

The simple answer is this: we are measuring two very different things. The past does have the ability to inform us of the predictability of various outcomes depending on what we are measuring. For example, if I measure the average temperature of Cincinnati, it is 55 degrees. That gives me a great statistical average to make inferences about the future weather, it does not tell me what the temperature is going to be on any given day. On the other hand, if I have a room full of people flipping coins instead of actually picking stocks to beat the market, there will be zero correlation to who flips heads the most in one test versus the next test. The job of academics studying the market is to parse out factors that have statistical relevance and those that are simply random noise—not an easy task, and one that requires a Ph.D.-level understanding of statistics. In this case, when we are measuring performance, we are examining market dimensions not random stock picking. This makes all the difference in the world. Paradox solved.

In a recent workshop with two hundred investment coaches, Professor Kenneth French posed the question, "How many years of quarterly data does it take to discern a meaningful scientific inference for rates of return?" Doctor Lyman Ott, who is on my Board of Advisors and who has authored books that are required material for Ph.D.- and masters-level statisticians, silently wrote in his notes "64 years." He was not going to blurt out the answer, but I was standing behind him and saw him write it down. I had heard this lecture before and knew he was right.

So let's just round that up to 70 years and call it the 70-Year Axiom. It means if you are attempting to analyze any data pertaining to portfolio design, you need at least seventy years of returns to have any statistical validity.

So it should be noted (and we'll look at this in future chapters) that these investment premiums are not risk free, meaning there are periods of time historically where these premiums do not show up. As a matter of fact, they wouldn't be called premiums if there *weren't some risk there.*

So anytime you hear someone come up with some statistical jargon, take it with a grain of salt. If they say gold has done well over the last 10 years or tech stocks have done well over the last 10 years, remember that it takes a high degree of scientific accuracy, lots of statistical analysis, and at least 70 years of data to know whether or not it's a real premium, or whether it's simply data mining.

We have seen by testing these premiums on a global basis that they consistently show up not only here at home in the good old U.S. of A., but also in Europe, Asia, Australia, and South America. If we examine these premiums globally, you can see that the largest premium in the market is the market premium itself, followed by the value premium, and then the small premium.

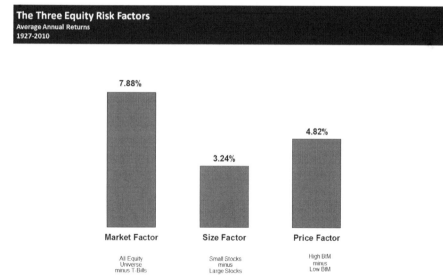

Graphing all stocks, with small stocks at the top of the vertical axis and large stocks at the bottom, with value stocks on the horizontal axis, with value to the right and growth to the left, you can easily observe that the highest return quadrant is the upper right quadrant. The further out you get in the upper right quadrant following the arrow, the higher the expected risk and future expected return. Which is exactly what you would expect to find if the Cost of Capital = the Return on Capital. It seems the markets are amazingly efficient at rewarding investors for taking the right kinds of risk.

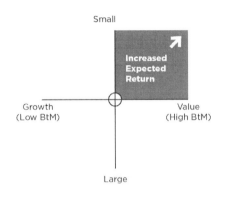

The Dimensions of Stock Return

Three Dimensions Around the World

- **Equity Market**
  (Complete value-weighted universe of stocks) Stocks have higher expected returns than fixed income.

- **Company Size**
  (Measured by market capitalization) Small company stocks have higher expected returns than large company stocks.

- **Company Price**
  (Measured by ratio of company book value to market equity) Lower-priced "value" stocks have higher expected returns than higher-priced "growth" stocks.

Source: Dimensional Fund Advisors. Past performance is no guarantee for future results.

Even the most novice investor has an intuitive grasp of the concept that risk and reward are somehow related, but statistics will show us that not all risks are equal. There are many investing risks that have no expected return. In fact, they simply reduce expected performance. Your job as an investor is to discern prudent risk from imprudent risk. Investors will often use this idea that risk and return are related to justify taking imprudent risks.

You can tell them that plowing a lot of money into one stock is very risky. They might say, "I know it's risky, but risk and return are related, so I should get higher rates of returns, right?" But not all risks are created equal. In other words there are some stupid risks. For example, if I play golf in a thunderstorm, and I take my nine-iron and hold it up in the air, am I taking risks? Well, obviously yes, I'm taking the risk that I'm going to be hit by lightning holding a nine-iron aloft.

The question would then be, "Is there any expected premium or rate of return for taking that risk?" I gain no benefit for such a reckless action. There are far more imprudent risks than prudent risks in the investment world.

Investors often take imprudent risk, and the investing world is full of imprudent risk and very few prudent risks. A prudent risk is a risk that has an expected historic premium and is academically sound; an imprudent risk has, well, none. So when I look and start to graph out prudent versus imprudent risk, I can take prudent risk and allocate my portfolio more toward small stocks and more toward value stocks and receive a premium in my portfolio—a historic premium—for owning those asset categories.

When I build my portfolio (and those of my clients), there are three crucial decisions in hooking into the greatest wealth creation tool on the planet, free markets.

- How much of my portfolio am I going to put in equities versus fixed income?
- How should I allocate between small stocks versus large stocks?
- How should I allocate to value stocks versus to growth stocks?

The Three Crucial Decisions account for 95% of portfolio returns (performance).[43] When properly educated, investors have the opportunity to productively apply these factors to their portfolios. Make no mistake, how I allocate my portfolio accounts for 95% of the performance of my portfolio over the long haul. So the three questions above signify the crucial decisions that most investors need to focus on, even though they usually don't.

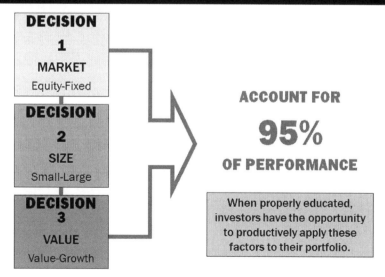

Three Crucial Decisions

DECISION 1
MARKET
Equity-Fixed

DECISION 2
SIZE
Small-Large

DECISION 3
VALUE
Value-Growth

ACCOUNT FOR
95%
OF PERFORMANCE

When properly educated, investors have the opportunity to productively apply these factors to their portfolio.

Dimensional Fund Advisors. Average explanatory power (R^2) is for the Fama/French equity benchmark universe. See Endnote 50

I was on CNBC one day, and the host asked me what would scare me from the financial markets, specifically because I am considered such a long-term investor. She was really asking what would cause stocks to fall in the short-term and make me panic and switch over to cash. I replied, "I don't get paid to panic, and the only thing I can think of that would change my mind about equities would be an extinction-level event—maybe an asteroid slamming into the planet, global thermo-nuclear war, aliens coming down and taking over the world. That could, you know, hurt equities." I was being sarcastic, but I was also trying to make the point that civilization as we know it depends on the functioning of all of the companies throughout the world.

For example, many people believe you can effectively avoid the "pain" of investing in companies by investing in the things that people think are safe, like government securities, or putting money in the bank, in insurance companies, or in annuities. Where do people think that the money that supports those institutions comes from? The reality is, if 12,000 companies globally go bankrupt simultaneously in a flash, it doesn't matter if you have your wealth in Treasury-bills. It doesn't matter if you have your money in some annuity or some insurance company or some bank. It's a bad day for everybody.

Ultimately, if 12,000 companies in 45 countries go simultaneously bankrupt, you're talking about an extinction-level events here, gang. As in, we're churning our own butter and hunting our own dinner, folks.

In the end, that's not going to happen. The world economy is too dynamic and flexible for any Armageddon scenario. So we have to be realistic. If you don't believe me and think the end times are nigh, there is nothing you can do about it. As a hedge, put your money in seeds, guns, and ammo—and don't forget the fallout shelter!

Putting It All Together

With these basics in mind, you can understand how to design a basic allocation, a mix of assets we will improve on significantly throughout the book. But now we can apply some basics with the Three Factor Model. Your first, and by far your most important decision, will be to determine what percentage of your portfolio will be allocated to equities versus fixed income. Your fixed income should be both high-quality and short-term to offset the short-term volatility of the equity portion of your mix. The following graph provides examples of how to do this based on your risk tolerance—from an aggressive mix of 95% equities (the greatest volatility) to the 25/75 mix with 75% fixed income and only 25% equity exposure.

Decision 1: Equity-Fixed

Chart 1: Equity Commitment: Free Market Standard Portfolios

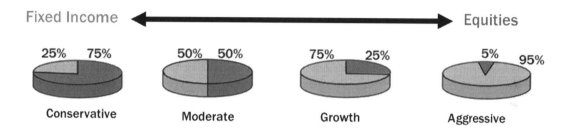

Fixed Income ◄────────────────────────────► Equities

| 25% 75% | 50% 50% | 75% 25% | 5% 95% |
| Conservative | Moderate | Growth | Aggressive |

Around eighteen years ago, I hosted a conference call for twenty advisors to discuss portfolio allocation and performance. On the call, one advisor said, "Over the last year I took the risk of putting some equities in my clients' portfolios and didn't get the return." Naturally frustrated, she added, "We took the risk, but we didn't get the reward." I paused momentarily and replied, "That is the nature of risk. Even when you take prudent risk, you can't get the reward in every period. That's the risk part." So as an investor, you must come to terms with the reality that even when you take "the right" risks, you will not receive rewards in all periods, especially in short blocks of time. If you expect to always win, you will surely lose. You will be an easy mark for the Wall Street conmen, prognosticators, and gurus.

If you allocate a portion of your portfolio to equities (almost every investor should have some), even if it is a small amount, what is the probability that you will experience the equity premium? In other words, given differing time periods, how often have stocks beaten fixed income?

Market Risk Premium

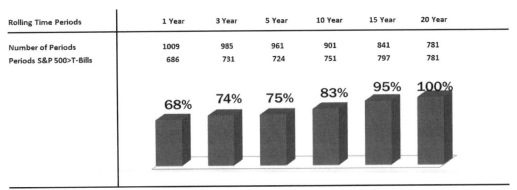

Equities (S&P 500) vs. Fixed Income (One-Month T-Bills)
Monthly Data: January 1926 – December 2010

Rolling Time Periods	1 Year	3 Year	5 Year	10 Year	15 Year	20 Year
Number of Periods	1009	985	961	901	841	781
Periods S&P 500>T-Bills	686	731	724	751	797	781
	68%	74%	75%	83%	95%	100%

**Percentage of all rolling time periods in which equities
(S&P 500) outperformed fixed income (T-Bills).**

2010 Dimensional Fund Advisors Returns Software. See Endnote 49.
Past performance is no guarantee of future results.

In roughly 68% of the previous one-year periods going back to 1926, stocks have outpaced fixed investments. In ten-year periods, that number moves to 83%, and over twenty-year periods since 1926, there's not a single two-decade span in which stocks have not outperformed fixed investments. These numbers are quite impressive and mean that, even in one-year periods, you are likely to do better with equities. As your holding periods increase in duration, the likelihood that you would be better off with fixed investments shrinks dramatically.

Once you have decided your fixed versus equity mix, you must decide how much small risk versus large risk to allocate to your portfolio. Keep in mind it is a small risk *premium*, not a small *guarantee*.

So, how often can you expect to receive the additional return?

Small Risk Premium

Small Stocks (CRSP 6-10) vs. Large Stocks (S&P 500)
Monthly Data: January 1926 – December 2010

Rolling Time Periods	1 Year	3 Year	5 Year	10 Year	15 Year	20 Year
Number of Periods	1009	985	961	901	841	781
Periods Small > Large	541	512	546	569	598	634

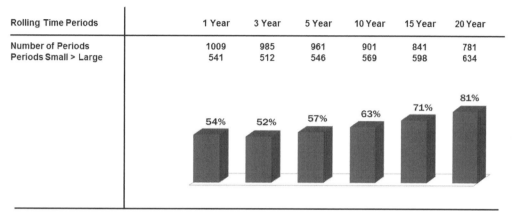

Percentage of all rolling time periods in which small outperformed large.

2010 Dimensional Fund Advisors Returns Software. See Endnote 49.

In one-year periods, the small premium historically outperformed a little over half the time. Over ten-year periods, they outperformed 63% of the time, and over 20-year periods, 81% of the time. So comparing the small premium to the equity premium you observe that it is both small (3% compared to 7%), and its probability is slightly less. As you will see later, not only does it have higher expected returns, it can reduce volatility when added to your mix. So, you must decide how much small versus large. Finally you must make your third decision, how much of your portfolio to allocate to value stocks (or distressed stocks) versus growth stocks.

Value Risk Premium

Value Stocks vs. Growth Stocks
Monthly Data: July 1926 – December 2010

Rolling Time Periods	1 Year	3 Year	5 Year	10 Year	15 Year	20 Year
Number of Periods	1003	979	955	895	835	775
Periods Value > Growth	574	655	718	736	738	752

1 Year	3 Year	5 Year	10 Year	15 Year	20 Year
57%	67%	76%	82%	88%	97%

**Percentage of all rolling time periods in
which value outperformed growth.**

2010 Dimensional Fund Advisors Returns Software. See Endnote 49.

Historically the value risk premium has been observed in 57% of the one-year periods, 83% of the 10-year periods, and 97% of the 20-year periods. This tells us that the value premium is both more dependable in the long run (97% versus 81%) compared to the small premium and larger than the small premium (in the ballpark of 5% for value stocks versus 3% for small).

In the case of all three premiums, the longer you hold them in your portfolio the greater the likelihood you are going to receive the rewards of adding them to your mix. The decisions of how much equity versus fixed, small versus large, and value versus growth are far more important than when to get in and out, what stocks to buy, and which manager has a five star rating.

In fact, a study conducted by Brinson, Beebower, and Hood confirmed that these types of allocation decisions explained up to 94% of a portfolio's return.[21] Even more importantly, the results imply that market timing and stock picking resulted in negative return, which means that asset allocation was responsible for 100% of the positive return in a portfolio. If all you understand from this book is this simple fact, you will already know more than 99% of all so-called financial planners and money managers. I tell you this based on my personal experience of training thousands of investment professionals over the last two decades. Rarely, if ever, have I observed an advisor who grasped these simple truths before taking my training. And even today, there is only an elite group of investor coaches with whom I personally partner who put these principles into practice with their clients.

In spite of these simple long-term truths about equities, many investors will still ask, "Should I be in the market? Should I wait until things get better and there is more certainty?" To which I retort, "Let me give you the facts. Then, you tell me."

The question is direct, "Should I be in the market with a portion of my money or be completely locked into a 'safe money' approach?" Let's look at these facts. Let's apply the approach I have just outlined and allocate 70% of our assets to equities and 30% to short-term government income. Let's also add small stocks and value stocks as outlined in the Three Factor Model. For simplicity's sake, we are only going to use U.S. stocks. Below is the pie chart of your portfolio. We use straight market indexes to represent returns, no stock picking or market timing.

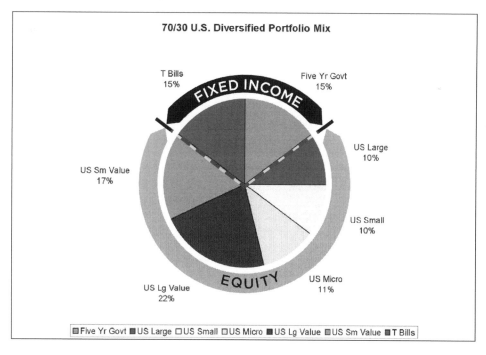

The following indices are being used for this model: Long Term Government Bonds, One Month U.S. Treasury Bills, Fama/French U.S. Small Value Index, Fama/French U.S. Large Value Index, CRSP Deciles 9-10 Index, Past performance is not indicative of future performance. See Endnote 49.

Now let's break it down into 10-year time periods and see what our return would have looked like. And let's go all the way back to 1929 before the Great Depression.

Year	Hypothetical	Year	Hypothetical
1929	2.17%	1965	4.78%
1930	4.28%	1966	6.39%
1931	7.51%	1967	10.20%
1932	12.24%	1968	7.60%
1933	13.65%	1969	6.40%
1934	10.69%	1970	10.50%
1935	13.17%	1971	12.09%
1936	13.30%	1972	11.82%
1937	8.88%	1973	13.58%
1938	13.77%	1974	18.00%
1939	11.43%	1975	20.69%
1940	12.88%	1976	19.33%
1941	16.50%	1977	17.23%
1942	18.16%	1978	16.15%
1943	16.74%	1979	16.90%
1944	12.29%	1980	16.29%
1945	13.44%	1981	12.92%
1946	11.47%	1982	14.68%
1947	12.59%	1983	13.89%
1948	10.92%	1984	13.07%
1949	14.89%	1985	12.12%
1950	14.68%	1986	12.22%
1951	11.34%	1987	12.35%
1952	12.38%	1988	14.84%
1953	10.72%	1989	13.80%
1954	12.90%	1990	13.01%
1955	10.37%	1991	15.16%
1956	10.67%	1992	13.36%
1957	9.69%	1993	10.18%
1958	14.59%	1994	11.62%
1959	13.04%	1995	13.24%
1960	9.98%	1996	11.26%
1961	10.65%	1997	11.33%
1962	9.92%	1998	9.07%
1963	11.45%	1999	5.03%
1964	7.94%	2000	6.32%
		2001	7.05%

Performance figures taken from DFA Returns Software Version: 2.0.
Past performance is not indicative of future performance. See Endnote 49

As you analyze the graph, how many negative ten year periods are there? You should quickly notice that the answer is none. There is not a single negative ten-year period, even starting at the Great Depression or World War II. While there is no guarantee that negative ten-year periods could not occur in the future, this is impressive indeed. A diversified, well-allocated portfolio is far less risky over the long-term than most people believe.

In keeping up with inflation, how does our sample portfolio perform? Inflation is bad for "safe money" investments in two ways: it reduces purchasing power, and it reduces the value of underlying bonds. Using the same rolling ten-year periods, we can graph inflation as measured by the Consumer Price Index versus so-called "safe" investments like short-term T-bills representing the essential risk-free rate.

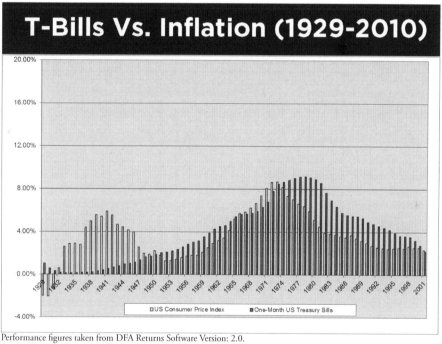

Performance figures taken from DFA Returns Software Version: 2.0.
Past performance is not indicative of future performance. See Endnote 49.

You will see many ten-year rolling periods in which T-bills are outstripped by inflation. In fact, just looking at the entire time 1929 to 2010, T-bills only average 3.92% and inflation clocks in at 3.68%. That means T-bills paid a pathetic 0.24% real rate of return, which would be wiped out by taxes, making the real after-tax returns negative. This is what I call going broke safely. The longer you hold large amounts of "safe money" in your portfolio, the greater the chances that you will lose to inflation.

Now let's compare the more diversified 70/30 portfolio.

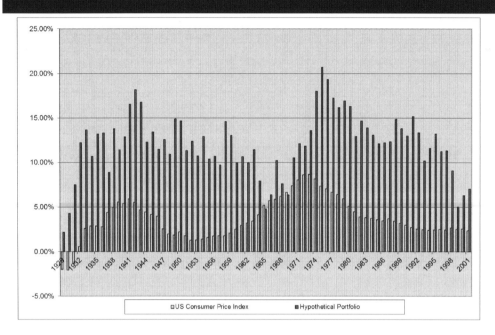

Diversified Portfolio¹ v. Inflation (1929-2010)

Performance figures taken from DFA Returns Software Version: 2.0.
Past performance is not indicative of future performance. See Endnote 49.

Visually, this graph is stunning. The additional return in excess of inflation for almost all periods is immediately obvious. In only one period does inflation surpass the returns of the diversified mix. Furthermore, if you look at the long-term returns, inflation is 3.68% and the equity/fixed mix is 12.06%. The average hypothetical return in excess of inflation is 8.38%. It should be crystal clear that if you have at least a ten-year time horizon and you are rightly concerned about the effects of inflation, equities are a no-brainer.[42]

Using an example of a $10,000 initial investment in T-bills (our risk-free proxy), you would have $1,863,000 at the end of the period in which the Consumer Price Index only grew to $1,285,000. That initial investment in the diversified mix—$377,991,030. [49]

1929-2010: $100,000 Grows To...

Diversified 70/30 US Portfolio	$ 377,991,030
One Month T-Bills	$ 1,863,000
Consumer Price Index	$ 1,285,000
Gold	$ 6,750,000

Performance figures taken from DFA Returns Software Version: 2.0.
Past performance is not indicative of future performance.
Gold prices obtained from Kitco.com See Endnotes 49 and 52.

And just for fun (and because so many people currently believe gold is such a stable investment), I put it in gold chart, too. It stumbles in at $6,750,000.[52] When compared to a diversified portfolio, gold is a clear loser.

The risk-free, safe money portfolio grows to $1.8 million just barley ahead of inflation at $1.2 million. The diversified portfolio growth to $377 million is vastly superior to inflation, the risk free return, and gold.

So should you own equities?
You tell me.

7

THREE SIMPLE RULES

October: This is one of the peculiarly dangerous months to speculate in stocks.
The others are July, January, September, April, November, May, March,
June, December, August and February.

—Mark Twain [53]

I AM GOING TO SHARE THE THREE SIMPLE RULES TO INVESTING with you in this chapter. Rules so simple that a third grader could easily understand them. During a recent appearance on Fox Business News the anchor said to me, "Wow, you just made it sound so simple," and it is. But don't confuse simple with easy. Knowing the rules and following them are two very different things.

It's not what you know that counts; it's what you actually do. And I can tell you very few investors or advisors can throughout years of investing actually apply these amazingly self-evident rules to successful investing. My guess is that you have already heard or read about them in the past. Nevertheless, we are going to focus on them intensely in this chapter. If you don't fully grasp the basics you will be lost later when I outline why they are so difficult to do with real money.

Every year, legendary coach Vince Lombardi started the season by holding up the old pig skin and saying, "This is a football." He drilled the basics over and over into his players' minds, bodies, and souls. Lombardi understood that if you cannot execute the "script" skills of blocking and tackling, you cannot and will not win games—no matter how sophisticated the player.

In investing terms, if you cannot grasp and execute these three simple rules, you will fail no matter how advanced the academics, statistics and science that have been applied to create your portfolio. Without these plain and simple rules the results can be dire.

Three Simple Rules to Investing

Ever think about the mouse trap?

I know, not normally—neither do I. But the mouse trap is a good way to open this chapter—which is all about investing in equities (and how to do it right).

John Mast invented the mouse trap back in 1899.

Over the years, many inventors have tried to come up with a "better mouse trap." In fact, there are about 4,400 registered patents on the mouse trap—with about 400 added each year. But John Mast's "snap trap" is still the one that most people buy. Sometimes straight forward, common sense action is the best path to take. In this case, simple really is better.

Equities are at the heart of my three rules of investing, each laid out as follows:

#1 Own Equities

#2 Diversify Globally

#3 Rebalance

Granted, it's not a glamorous three-pronged strategy for creating wealth, but it is a compelling and effective one. In previous chapters we talked about owning equities, the premiums for equities, the market factors involved in owning equities, and the related formulas for managing an equity-based portfolio.

In its purest form, this means you must hold at least a portion of your wealth in equity-based mutual funds, diversify by making sure your equities are not all in one type of stock or even in one country. If you cannot take 100% equity exposure to volatility, offset your investments with short-term high-quality bond funds, and finally rebalance your portfolio on a quarterly basis. After that, periodically sell off asset categories that are relatively high (over their portfolio targets) and buy categories that are low (under their targets).

There, see? Wasn't that simple to understand? Even to a casual observer these "investing truths" should be self-evident. Unfortunately, they are nearly impossible for people to consistently apply to their own portfolio. Let's break down each rule, see what it means, why it is so critical for your success, and look at some examples of how frustratingly hard it is for both Main Street and Wall Street investors to apply.

Rule #1: Own Equities

After the mountains of evidence I gave you in the last chapter about the long-term benefits of equities to compound your money and outpace inflation, holding them should be a no-brainer. But Dalbar research tells us that the average investor does not hold their equity mutual funds for anything close to a long-term period of twenty years or more. In fact, the average holding period is only approximately three years.[13] Why does this happen in spite of all the data? How can investors and advisors be so dumb?

First of all, understand that as long as you are trading, Wall Street keeps making money, whether as spreads, commissions or other fees. Getting in and out of equities may be bad for you, but it drives the bullies' trading profits. Don't go to Wall Street for advice on how to stop this problem. In other words, never ask for help in solving a problem if your abuser stands to profit by keeping you in it.

Most brokerage firms and so-called money managers don't get paid for helping you maintain discipline and abide by these rules. They get paid to forecast and predict and move money around. Never pay anyone to speculate and gamble with your money. The hard part, and the path that will help you grow your wealth, is to stay disciplined while others panic.

If we go all the way back to 1926, taking into account the Great Depression, wars, and recessions and you look at the following graph, historically equities perform well over long periods of time. Make no mistake; investing is always a long-term proposition. It's never a short-term gamble of speculating—a game of "get in and out," although many investors seem to think so, because that's what their financial advisors tell them. The fact is, that's exactly what people do - treat equities as a get-in/get-out type scenario. So it's crucial to expand to a long-term time horizon. But even over recessions, depressions, wars, long periods of time, equities have premiums, and it's your job as an investor to figure that out and internalize it so you will never be tempted to panic.

Growth of Wealth

Monthly: 07/1926-12/2010

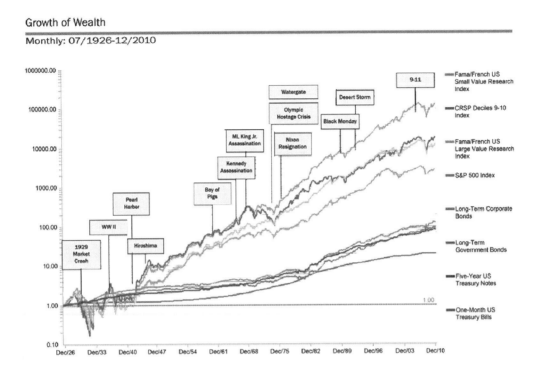

2010 Dimensional Fund Advisors Returns Software. See Endnote 49.

In the graph above, I have represented various market indices based on research conducted at the University of Chicago Booth School of Business at the Center for Research and Security Pricing. It should be noted that the Chicago Booth School is one of the most prestigious in the world and boasts 17 Nobel Prize Winners in its economics department. This is more than any other University. Much of the ground breaking research I am sharing with you was pioneered there. The graph has been scaled so that all categories can be demonstrated. Observe how the large value index, the 9-10 deciles (which represent micro-cap stocks) and the small value index far outpace inflation. I have also included boxes demonstrating some of the worst economic and global tragedies that equity markets have endured. The market has survived in every single situation, including the Great Depression and World War II. The market has always recovered long-term. When an anchor on CNBC recently asked if I was bullish or bearish I replied, "Long-term, the arrow is always green and up." Historically, the next one hundred percent movement is up.

In spite of this clear fact, you will never have any difficulty finding those pundits who believe "this time is different."

When markets drop in the short-term, a seasoned Main Street investor knows it is never the right time to panic and go to cash. You might find some comfort in the fact that many advisors make the exact same mistakes. Part of my job is to coach advisors and investors to follow these very simple rules of investing in equities, and to remind them to avoid panicking when the market turns down and unpredictably drags. In spite of my best efforts, advisors and investors often are their own worst enemies.

Case in point, from January 2008 to February 2009, the S&P 500 index dropped a total of -48%.[42] Most investors and advisors were stunned. "How could such a thing happen? This is the end of the world. It has never been this bad. It is never going back up." When I calmly reminded them that, it has always recovered losses and not to panic, they excused the impulse to imprudent behavior by throwing back at me, "Yeah, but this time it really IS different!"

I can recall in the spring of 2009, an advisor intent on moving his clients' assets of $20 million into cash. His message on my voicemail was, "I just can't ride this out. People are too afraid. I have to do something. I know you are going to say this is market timing, (here it comes) but this time it's different." Against our advice, he sold his clients out in the early spring of 2009, which subsequently turned out to be a disastrous result! From the period of March 2009 to April 2011, this asset class (large U.S. stocks) rose over 93%.[49] It was all too easy for the advisor to play on the fear of his clients and get them to move to cash.

This time it wasn't different—market losses and crashes are historically recouped by the market in a relatively short period. While I cannot predict the random daily movements of the market, I can predict how most advisors and investors will react. When a market crashes, they panic and sell. Not having any idea that their portfolio was this volatile, they thought they had a sure thing. When markets inevitably drop, they panic and go to cash. They wait on the sidelines while things eventually get better. They wait for "clear signs" that it is "safe." When it is back to an all-time high, they get a sense of deep confidence they are ready to jump and go "all in." A good investment coach earns his fees by helping investors remain disciplined when things are bad and keep their actions in check. Once you decide what percentage of your portfolio is right for equities, you should never change based on short-term market gyrations no matter what any Wall Street bully says.

Rule #2: Diversify Globally

Just like "Rule #1: Own Equities," it sounds easy, but it isn't. In theory this is basically, "Don't put all your eggs in one basket." It sounds very astute for any advisor who says,

"Well, you must remember diversification is very important." But how do you know how many "baskets" you need and if these baskets are really protecting your portfolio? One basic mistake investors make is believing that just owning a lot of "stuff" means that you are diversified—not true. Take the sample portfolio of stocks below. There are over 100 holdings. To the average investor it would appear diversified—it is not. All of them are tech-related companies. In the years 2000 through 2002, you would have lost over 60% of your money in a short period of time, just two years, if you invested in NYSE ARCA Tech 100 Index.[16]

Sample Brokerage Statement

Electronic Arts	Alcatel SA ADR A	Scientific-Atlanta	Mentor Graphics	Network Appliance
IBM	Motorola	Yahoo	Hewlett-Packard	Adobe Sys
Genentech	Xerox	Harris	Standard Microsystems	First Data
Synopsys	Siebel Sys	Dell	Cisco Sys	MedImmune
Amgen	Highmark Grp	Raytheon	Nextel Communications	Veritas Software
Boston Scientific	Corning	Xilinx		Unisys
KLA-Tencor	Adaptec	SAP AG ADR	Cypress Semicon	Oracle
Symantec	Vitesse Semicon	Biomet	PeopleSoft	EMC
St. Jude Medical	Tellabs	National Semiconductor	Teradyne	Applied Materials
Lockheed Martin	Ciena	NCR	Autodesk	Quantum Corp-Dlt & Storage
Chiron	Gateway Inc	Intel	American Power Conversion	Biogen
Medtronic	Solectron	SunGard Data Sys	Check Point Software Tech	Thermo Electron
Genzyme Corporation General Di	Compuware	Microsoft	Juniper Net	Symbol Tech
Millipore	3Com	Coherent	Sybase	Electronic Data Sys
Maxim Integrated Products	Novell	Goodrich	AOL Time Warner	DST Sys
Computer Sciences	Sun Microsystems	Lam Research	Nokia ADR	
Linear Tech	JDS Uniphase	Computer Assoc Intl	BMC Software	Apple Comp
Qualcomm	Nortel Networks	Storage Tech	Micron Tech	BEA Sys
Analog Devices	Kulicke and Soffa Industries	Agilent Tech	Cadence Design Sys	Applied Biosystems Group
Automatic Data Processing	LSI Logic	Tektronix	Network Assoc	
Novellus Sys	Advanced Micro Devices	Texas Instruments		

100 Holdings
All Tech Related

Clearly, holding a lot of stuff doesn't automatically produce diversification or reduce risk.

The Fine Art of Diversification

Let me tell you a story. It's about a man named Edward Noble, a guy who literally understood that variety is the spice of life.

In 1935, he approached Clarence Crane, the inventor of the peppermint Life Saver, with the idea of producing the candy in a variety of flavors. Crane didn't want any part of the plan, and he wound up selling the rights to Life Savers candy to Noble for $2,900.

Summary of Portfolio Performance

Time Period	Annualized Return
2000	-33.33
2001	-15.59
2002	-16.22
TOTAL RETURN	-65.14

See Endnote 18.

Today, Life Savers is a $1 billion business. The reason Noble—and not Crane—became wealthy was because he understood the power of diversification. He didn't base his success on just one flavor of candy. He understood that by offering a variety of flavors, he could appeal to more people with different tastes. At the same time, he protected his business should any one flavor fall out of favor with the public.

While this story is something most Main Street investors can relate to and demonstrates the value of choices, true diversification adds a much deeper dynamic. It actually tells us how to measure diversification and how likely various asset categories are to move together in a roller coaster fashion or offset each other and have dissimilar price movements. Dissimilar price movement is the Holy Grail of diversification and risk reduction, and, thanks to a Nobel-Prize Winning concept called Modern Portfolio Theory, we have an academic means of measuring just that—how well various assets combine to diversify your portfolio.

At the heart of this theory, developed by Dr. Harry Markowitz, is the central idea that by looking at a time-sensitive return you can get a feel for how similar the returns are of various investment categories when compared to each other. Do they move together? Or do they move independently, which tends to reduce risk?

To accomplish this task, statisticians compare the returns series of various asset categories with the hopes of identifying asset classes that have high expected historic returns but dissimilar price movement. They then create a correlation matrix, which visually displays all of the possible relationships of each category to every other category. You can think of this chart as the DNA that will determine the long-term success or failure of your portfolio mix.

After analyzing thousands of investors' portfolios over the last twenty years, it is obvious that investors have no idea how to effectively build diversification into their asset mix. They typically pick five to eight mutual funds that have impressive sounding names that claim to have "diversified" objectives. All too often, Main Street investors are horrified to learn that their chosen mutual funds are exact copies of each other, with little to no real diversification.

R2 Matrix
01/1999-12/2010

	S&P 500 Index	US Large Value	US Small Value	US Micro Cap	International Large	International Small	International Small Value	International Large Value	Emerging Markets	One Year Fixed	Five Year Fixed
S&P 500 Index	1.00										
US Large Value	0.71	1.00									
US Small Value	0.59	0.62	1.00								
US Micro Cap	0.59	0.44	0.79	1.00							
International Large	0.76	0.56	0.53	0.52	1.00						
International Small	0.56	0.44	0.53	0.52	0.83	1.00					
International Small Value	0.55	0.50	0.53	0.48	0.83	0.96	1.00				
International Large Value	0.74	0.62	0.53	0.48	0.96	0.81	0.85	1.00			
Emerging Markets	0.62	0.41	0.46	0.56	0.76	0.71	0.66	0.71	1.00		
One Year Fixed	0.07	0.05	0.05	0.06	0.07	0.08	0.06	0.05	0.08	1.00	
Five Year Fixed	0.10	0.10	0.09	0.13	0.07	0.06	0.04	0.07	0.10	0.40	1.00

See Endnotes 49 and 50.

The chart above demonstrates a simple correlation matrix. Although it may look intimidating, it is something every Main Street investor has the ability to understand. The vast majority of investors are weighted heavily toward U.S. large stocks. So as an investor, if you wanted to know if adding U.S. small companies to your portfolio would be advantageous, you could identify S&P 500 stocks at the top left-hand side of the graph and follow the column down to U.S. micro-cap to see that the correlation is .59. This means that roughly 59% of the return of these two asset categories is similar in nature, which also means that 41% of that return between the asset categories is dissimilar.

Therefore, by adding micro-caps to the portfolio you would be adding an asset category that has both a higher expected return than large stocks (remember the small premium from the previous chapter) plus adds diversification benefits versus a one hundred percent large U.S. stock portfolio. From a diversification perspective, the smaller the correlation is, the better the diversifier. A correlation of 0 means that there is no relationship, and a correlation of 1 means they move in complete lockstep unison. In this graph, you can see correlations of 1 in which academics measure an asset category against itself. You have to love scientists. Only they would think of measuring something against itself!

Using large cap U.S. stocks again as our starting point (top left-hand column), if I wanted to compare them to emerging market stocks, I would find a correlation of .62. This tells me that they exhibit roughly 38% uncorrelated movements. By filling out the graph, I can see the relationship to each and every asset in my sample portfolio. It is nearly impossible to be truly diversified without this type of matrix. If you do not have one for your personal portfolio, this should be a huge red flag for you.

Most investors just assume they are diversified until it is too late and they have lost more money than they could ever imagine. If you can't measure it, there is no way to properly apply it to your portfolio. In over a quarter-century of helping investors manage portfolios, three billion dollars under management, and 17,000 investors I have never seen a single investor produce this critical analytical tool before they first walked in our door—not a single one. The reality is that very few so-called "investment professionals" could provide such a tool.

Several other conclusions can be drawn from this graph. You can see as you add the asset categories that most Main Street investors lack, especially classes we discussed in the Three-Factor Model like small and value stocks, not only do they add additional risk premium, they also make excellent diversifiers when compared to the traditional large company portfolio. You can multiply their effect by adding international and emerging markets holdings to your mix.

You should also note that, although these are excellent diversifiers because the correlation is less than 1, they will not insulate your portfolio completely from dramatic equity swings. In other words, all equity asset classes are positively correlated.

Wall Street bullies mistakenly announce the death of Modern Portfolio Theory, stating falsely that it didn't work in 2008 and 2009 because all equity classes dropped at the same time. To that, I regretfully say in the voice of Homer Simpson, "D'oh!" Anyone who understands Modern Portfolio Theory knows that all stocks are likely to drop to some extent in large market swings, just like they are all likely to go up to some extent in huge market run ups.

To offset the risk of short-term losses in equity exposure as a whole, investors must be smart enough to look at the whole graph. Note, for example, the relationship of large S&P 500 stocks to five-year fixed. The correlation is .10, which means that this category of asset has an excellent opportunity to be positive when stocks are negative.

In similar fashion, note the relationship of international large stocks (top column) to one-year fixed income (bottom left). The relative .07 demonstrates that short-term fixed income greatly offsets the rest of equities. Even as equities dropped in 2008 and early 2009, short-term fixed income produced positive gains—perfectly in line with Modern Portfolio Theory.

When I first began my practice, I told my clients to just ignore the financial pornography that comes from newspapers, magazines, and television. But ignoring "the noise" is getting harder and harder. As an investor you will be constantly bombarded with messages urging imprudent action. Just as you are tempted by fast food commercials and messages to eat too much and gamble with your health, you will be constantly tempted to gamble with individual stocks and "hot sectors" that have nothing to do with real diversification.

For example, let's examine the "advice" (and I use the term loosely) of television investment guru Jim Cramer. Here's his sage recommendation on diversification: have at least five stocks in your portfolio, but own no more than ten. That is madness. Statements like this drive me crazy. This is a huge disservice to the Main Street investor. Can you say Wall Street bully?

Once you have prudently designed the right mix of equities and fixed income, how many stocks should you own? It is a great question, and one most investors never ask. When I told Liz Claman and Liz McDaniel live on Fox Business the answer, they said it blew their minds. The answer (drum roll please) is 12,000 individual holdings. Yes, I said it—because, dear Main Street Investor, you should have over 12,000 stocks in 45 different countries all over the world to be properly diversified.

Putting all of your assets into as little as five or ten stocks is playing Russian roulette with your portfolio. Recently I was asked to address the mutual fund trustees board for Dimensional Fund Advisors. It was a great honor. David Booth invited me to speak about how we use academic principles to help the Main Street investor. Most advisors only want the multi-million-dollar investors, and they don't focus on Main Street. So he wanted their committee to hear how we apply concepts to Main Street investors that are typically reserved for only the so-called elite or sophisticated investor.

On the board were a who's who of the academic investing community—legendary theorist Roger Ibbotson, Nobel-Prize winner Myron Scholes, economist and former Chief Economic Advisor to the White House Ed Lazier, and former Dean of the University of Chicago Booth School Of Business John P. Gould.

I am not easily intimidated, but I must admit I was a little nervous as I made my opening comments. I explained to the committee how we help the average American investor allocate a portfolio of as little as $10,000 into over 12,000 holdings in 45 countries, focusing on micro-caps, value, and short-term fixed income, and that it was my belief that one of our smallest clients was as diversified as a Fortune 500 pension plan with billions. As I relayed this concept, Nobel Prize-winner Myron Scholes somewhat gruffly interrupted with, "That's not accurate. They are *better diversified*."

Merton Miller, also a Nobel Prize winner in economics, put it this way, "Diversification is your buddy." When it comes to investing, no truer words were ever spoken. Not only can diversification increase expected return, it can also reduce the volatility of your portfolio at the same time. It is the closest thing to a free lunch that you will ever find in seeking to grow your wealth and reach your dreams.

It's not completely free because you have to spend the time to understand it and be smart enough to correctly apply it. Given its awesome power, it is perplexing that more people don't use diversification. The idea of increasing returns and reducing volatility begs another question. How exactly as an investor do you measure the risk of volatility in your portfolio? Here, too, we turn to the science of statistics for clues. The best way to calculate overall portfolio volatility is with a statistical measurement called standard deviation. We are not going to go in depth into how it is calculated. For our purposes, this is not important. All you need to know is that the number measures how much your portfolio "jumps around." A low standard deviation means lower volatility, a high number means more risk and more jumping around.

Low volatility is a kiddie roller coaster; high volatility is the biggest baddest coaster in the park. So your goal as an investor is to achieve the highest expected return for your personal risk tolerance. Academics call this means-variance investing. You can think of it as getting the biggest bang for your risk buck. After all, why would you take on additional volatility without the expected reward? When you have created a mix that delivers the highest expected return for your risk level, we call that creating an efficient portfolio. In all my years analyzing investors' portfolios, I have never observed an efficient portfolio mix from a new client—never. Like I said—it sounds simple, but it's not.

INCREASE RETURNS AND REDUCE VOLATILITY

Simplified Example Of Low Correlation Benefits
January 1971–December 2010 (in $U.S.)

	Large U.S. 100% S&P 500 Index	Large U.S. EAFE 70% S&P 500, 30% EAFE	Large U.S. EAFE Small Int'l 70% S&P 500, 20% EAFE, 10% Int'l Small
Return(%)	11.75	12.16	12.79
Standard Deviation	18.09	17.94	17.94

2010 Dimensional Fund Advisors Returns Software. See Endnote 49.

Consider the strategy found in this chart. Portfolio one represents a portfolio of 100% S&P 500 stocks. From 1971 to 2010, its return is 11.75% and its volatility is 18.09 (as measured by standard deviation). This would make for a fairly bumpy ride. Few investors can withstand that kind of volatility. So how can we make it a more efficient and comfortable portfolio ride?

First, let's add 30% into large international stocks as represented by the MSCI Europe, Australia, and Far East (EAFE) Index and lighten up on the U.S. portion, taking it down to 70%. What happens to risk and return? The return jumps to 12.16%, and the volatility actually decreases to 17.94%—the best of both worlds.

But let's not stop there! Now, let's substitute 10% of the large international for small international stocks. The return jumps again to 12.79%, and the volatility remains unchanged at 17.94%. In this simple example, by just adding two asset classes, we were able to raise the expected return by a full percent with no increase in volatility. Now we're cooking with gas.

If we continue this process to engineer a composite portfolio, what would that look like?

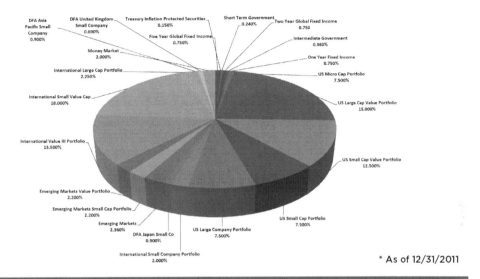

Aggressive Growth Portfolio (95% Eq/5% Fi)

DFA Asia Pacific Small Company 0.900%
DFA United Kingdom Small Company 0.690%
Treasury Inflation Protected Securities 0.150%
Short Term Government 0.240%
Two Year Global Fixed Income 0.750
Five Year Global Fixed Income 0.750%
Intermediate Government 0.360%
Money Market 2.000%
One Year Fixed Income 0.750%
International Large Cap Portfolio 2.250%
US Micro Cap Portfolio 7.500%
International Small Value Cap 18.000%
US Large Cap Value Portfolio 15.000%
International Value III Portfolio 13.500%
US Small Cap Value Portfolio 12.500%
Emerging Markets Value Portfolio 2.200%
Emerging Markets Small Cap Portfolio 2.200%
Emerging Markets 2.360%
DFA Japan Small Co 0.900%
US Large Company Portfolio 7.500%
US Small Cap Portfolio 7.500%
International Small Company Portfolio 2.000%

* As of 12/31/2011

12,977 Unique Holdings   13 Distinct Asset Categories   44 Total Countries

This is a sample portfolio applying the correlation matrix and Modern Portfolio Theory for an aggressive investor who can take a lot of portfolio swings. I recently took my kids to a local amusement park called Kings Island. One of the newest rides is the Diamond Back roller coaster. My son, Jonathan, had previously ridden the ride many times. He is a seasoned coaster rider.

I, on the other hand, was a first timer. I was somewhat taken aback taking my seat on the ride because there were no sides to the cart and no strap to pull down over my shoulders. I felt very vulnerable and exposed. I had just witnessed many of the cars return safely to the station without a mishap to the riders. Despite the evidence, I didn't "feel" safe. As the ride began to climb at a rapid rate up the first hill, my son lifted his arms over his head, while my hands clutched the lapbar in a death grip. The cars crested the first hill and rocketed down a nearly vertical slope. Fearing for the safety of myself and my son, I yelled at him to put his arms down and hang on to the bar. As kids are apt to do, he ignored me. He had complete confidence that he would not fall out of the ride, and he was loving every second of it. He was exhilarated and having fun. I was just plain scared.

If you have a very long time period to invest, understand volatility, and can remain disciplined, there is nothing wrong with an aggressive mix of pure equities. However, in my experience, very few people fit this bill. In most cases, it is necessary to add short-term fixed income into the mix to reduce volatility.

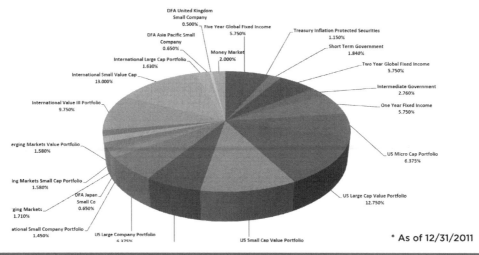

Long Term Growth Portfolio (75% Eq/25% Fi)

DFA United Kingdom Small Company 0.500%
Five Year Global Fixed Income 5.750%
DFA Asia Pacific Small Company 0.650%
Treasury Inflation Protected Securities 1.150%
Short Term Government 1.840%
International Large Cap Portfolio 1.630%
Money Market 2.000%
Two Year Global Fixed Income 5.750%
International Small Value Cap 13.000%
Intermediate Government 2.760%
International Value III Portfolio 9.750%
One Year Fixed Income 5.750%
erging Markets Value Portfolio 1.580%
US Micro Cap Portfolio 6.375%
ing Markets Small Cap Portfolio 1.580%
DFA Japan Small Co 0.650%
US Large Cap Value Portfolio 12.750%
ging Markets 1.710%
ational Small Company Portfolio 1.450%
US Large Company Portfolio 6.375%
US Small Cap Value Portfolio
* As of 12/31/2011

12,977 Unique Holdings   19 Distinct Asset Categories   44 Total Countries

This portfolio is tilted to 75% equities and 25% fixed income. You can observe the addition of Treasury-protected securities, one-year fixed income, two-year global bonds, five-year U.S. bonds and five-year global fixed income. This will significantly dampen volatility while maintaining a meaningful allocation of equities to offset inflation.

I firmly believe investors are capable of looking at the data and making the right decisions. On average, out of all the Main Street investors I have helped, the average portfolio mix is very close to this. It is approximately 70% equities and 30% fixed income. Given the right information, you are more than capable of making the right allocation decisions. My job is to arm you with the right data to make those decisions. This is the only way you will ever have true and lasting peace of mind, by making a purposeful and educated decision of exactly how to engineer your portfolio and why.

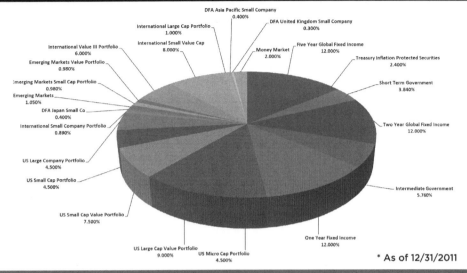

Balanced Growth Portfolio (50% Eq/50% Fi)

12,977 Unique Holdings   19 Distinct Asset Categories   44 Total Countries

This is a representation of a balanced portfolio of 50% equities, 50% fixed income. This portfolio is built on 19 distinct and separate asset categories. Few investors have large enough portfolios to achieve this type of diversification on their own.

Obviously, it would be impossible to produce over 12,000 holdings in 44 countries. Even with a million-dollar portfolio, there would not be enough money to make the required purchases. Even if you attempted to purchase retail no-load mutual funds to create this mix, you would find it almost impossible to recreate these portfolios.

An efficient method of capturing these dimensions is with an advanced concept called a fund of funds. In essence, you purchase several funds that are composed of multiple dimensions or categories. This allows you to capture as many as 19 distinct and separate classes while buying only several funds. These types of holdings are commonly referred to as structured market funds. They can prove indispensable when applying the third and final rule—rebalancing.

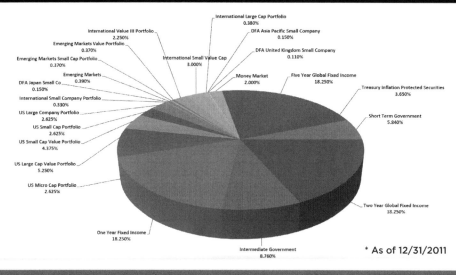

Income & Growth Portfolio (25% Eq/75% Fi)

International Large Cap Portfolio 0.380%
DFA Asia Pacific Small Company 0.150%
DFA United Kingdom Small Company 0.110%
International Value III Portfolio 2.250%
Emerging Markets Value Portfolio 0.370%
Emerging Markets Small Cap Portfolio 0.370%
Emerging Markets 0.390%
DFA Japan Small Co 0.150%
International Small Company Portfolio 0.330%
US Large Company Portfolio 2.625%
US Small Cap Portfolio 2.625%
US Small Cap Value Portfolio 4.375%
US Large Cap Value Portfolio 5.250%
US Micro Cap Portfolio 2.625%
International Small Value Cap 3.000%
Money Market 2.000%
Five Year Global Fixed Income 18.250%
Treasury Inflation Protected Securities 3.650%
Short Term Government 5.840%
Two Year Global Fixed Income 18.250%
One Year Fixed Income 18.250%
Intermediate Government 8.760%

* As of 12/31/2011

12,977 Unique Holdings   19 Distinct Asset Categories   44 Total Countries

The final portfolio represents 75% to fixed income and only 25% to equities. This mix drastically reduces short-term volatility while maintaining a minimum allocation to equities to drive at least some long-term growth. If you ask most people if they believe they are diversified, they will reply, "Yes, certainly," but they are not. Typically they have purchased seven or eight mutual funds or have a handful of stocks. They have no understanding of the correlations of their holdings or how similar or dissimilar are the movements of those assets over time. As you can see, there is a real science to diversifying your portfolio. Just buying a lot of stuff from a Wall Street bully or some five-star mutual funds will not cut it.

> "So be sure when you step, step with care and great tact.
> And remember that life's a great balancing act.
> And will you succeed? Yes! You will indeed! (98 and ¾ percent guaranteed)."
> —Dr. Seuss, Oh the Places You'll Go! [54]

Rebalancing

I recall recently staying up late at night, unable to sleep for whatever reason, and watching the rodeo on ESPN. It was a bull-riding event, and the color commentator said something interesting that I'll always remember.

"Do you know what separates the great riders from the mediocre ones?" he asked. "Great riders rely on balance. They wrap their hand around that rope and prepare for everything and anything—so they can hold on whichever way the bull turns."

Bad riders don't rely on balance; they try to anticipate the bull's moves. Of course, no one can really predict the way a bull will turn. So they go down fast and hard.

To me, that's a lot like investing. Successful investors don't try to predict which way the market will turn. They prepare for everything and anything by rebalancing their portfolios. As an advisor, that's what I want to do for you—help bring balance to your portfolio.

If your portfolio needs a forecast or prediction about the future to work, it is already broken. Your portfolio should put you in the best position to win no matter what happens.

Rebalancing means once you have decided on the proper percentages in your portfolio, you periodically and systematically measure your actual holdings in the portfolio and then make purchases and sales to keep your mix on target. This is much harder to do than it sounds, both emotionally and logistically, because you must constantly force yourself to sell a portion of the thing that has done well and buy more of the asset category that has recently lost money. In theory, most people will agree that this sounds like a prudent thing to do. After all, everyone knows you should "buy low, and sell high." But virtually no one can force himself to do it.

Instead, investors—and I'm including most investment advisors—want to do just the exact opposite, buy more of the thing that has recently skyrocketed and sell the category that is down. It sounds foolish, doesn't it? However, I can assure you, this is precisely what most Main Street investors and Wall Street investors do.

Perhaps a real example will help you to see just how hard this is to do and the dangers of failing to rebalance.

The year was 1997. We were in the midst of what would become the greatest five-year run for large cap U.S. stocks in the history of market. In 1995, these stocks made 37%, followed by 22% in 1996, 33% in 1997, 28% in 1998, and 21% in 1999. The combined compound average was 28.8% per year for a total return of 251%.[49] This is a truly astonishing series of returns! Toward the end of this period, news articles and programs began to proclaim "the death of diversification" and argued that you did not need to diversify. Diversification will just slow you down. Their advice: "Just buy large U.S. growth stocks because they are going up forever."

During this period, we owned large U.S. stocks in our portfolios, but by applying the Three-Factor Model and Modern Portfolio Theory to better diversify and raise long-term expected returns, we tracked significant differences when compared to one single asset class—the S&P 500. We were disciplined and prudent to sell off large U.S. stocks and buy international stocks and U.S. small stocks. The strategy is simple—own stocks, diversify, and rebalance back to targets.

Diversification can be a double-edged sword; it means that you will never be 100% allocated to the worst-performing asset category. It also means you will never be 100% in the top-performing asset category either. When one segment of your portfolio is skyrocketing, often greed and emotion can kick in.

In the middle part of 1997, there were three advisors who were supposed to understand all of this. After all, they had been through our training, seen the academic research, claimed to believe markets work, and expressed a desire to help investors eliminate stock-picking, market timing, and track-record investing. They were the advisors to a set of investors with assets totaling over $60 million. These advisors asked to have a meeting with me about the management of their accounts. For the sake of protecting their anonymity, we will call these three gentlemen Larry, Curly, and Moe. The following dialogue is an example of the kinds of conversations I had with them over a six-month period.

MM: "So gentlemen, how can I help you guys?" I could feel the anger in the boardroom growing. Stay calm and neutral. Reason and academics are on your side. "I got your email that said you had some concerns and…?"

Larry, the most aggressive of the three, interrupted. "Damn right we have concerns. We have more than concerns. We have some demands. We are not happy with returns, and we need to be all in U.S. stocks."

Curly: "We've done the research, and we believe that international stocks are going to be dead for years. I mean, we know they have been great for decades, but we just feel that the U.S. stocks, especially growth and tech, are the future." Curly paused as Moe jumped in. Larry sat to my left, fuming.

Moe: "You know, these times really are different. I mean that U.S. has a huge economic advantage over Europe and Asia. The Internet is the future. This is a new paradigm."

Larry: "And another thing…we also want to change our clients' models and lighten up on fixed income. We really don't see the market crashing for many years. We have been studying the demographics of the Baby Boomers, and we believe there is at least a decade of high returns to come before any crashes."

I sat calmly listening to their irrational ranting, feeling not unlike Alice having tea at the Mad Hatter's table.

Moe: "Not only that, but this is what our clients want. They don't want international or small stocks and they don't want any fixed. They just want tech and growth. And it's their money!"

Larry: "No doubt. We've got to do what they want. If we don't, they will move their money somewhere else."

Curly: "And Mark, we know what you are going to say—that this is market timing, and market timing doesn't work. But this is not market timing! This is just doing the right thing. These are our clients, and we have to do what is right."

Larry: "If you don't let us do this with your company, we are going to move all of our accounts. We did the math, and this will cost your company roughly $600,000 per year in revenue. We are a major portion of your assets, and we don't think you have any choice."

Moe sheepishly added, "Yeah, we aren't trying to be jerks, but it's just that we need to do this. We don't have a choice. Everybody else is doing this, too."

"We have you over a barrel here," Curly said as he slid a piece of paper across the table to me. "These are the mixes we want. We want all of the accounts switched by the end of the year."

Larry: "Or else we move it all."

There are times in life that define our character and shape our destiny. Many times these are the setbacks and breakdowns that seem tragic at the time, but in reality they give us the clarity to create an amazing future. This was one of those times for me. I took a deep breath and explained my position.

MM: "Gentlemen, they are certainly your clients. If you feel that the path you have outlined is best for them, you are morally obligated to implement it for them, but I can't be a part of this. What you've outlined violates all three of the simple rules of investing you claim to understand and believe. If you follow this path, you will be reducing the diversification of your clients' portfolios. You will be increasing their risk and volatility. You are not rebalancing. In fact, you are doing the opposite. You are selling assets that are relatively low and buying assets that are relatively high.

We exist to help investors eliminate dysfunctional behavior, and in this case you will be encouraging it. This violates every principle I have built this company on and every academic theory I have taught you. The risks you are preparing to take are not prudent or rational. Why should your clients pay you to chase markets and speculate with their money? They can do that on their own."

Larry sat fuming. Curly was looking like a scalded dog and Moe looked desperate and confused. He chimed in, "Yes, but it's their money. We have to give them what they want."

I knew I was wasting my breath. Larry was the ringleader, and he had made up his mind—the money was going to move. I had worked for three years training them, travelling to their offices, doing seminars with their clients. I had spent time away from my family on the road and poured my heart and soul into these relationships. I felt a deep sense of loss.

It would have been easy to give into their demands. With our management system in place, it would have only taken a couple of days to reallocate the accounts. I could have kept the revenue. I wouldn't have had to deal with the anger and animosity of the three advisors fighting me, and surely there would be more advisors who would take a similar view and would want to leave too.

Misery loves company, and I was sure the Three Stooges would call other advisors and attempt to stir up a mutiny. In their eyes, I was the bad guy standing in the way, and they were going to do everything within their power to exact revenge. In spite of all of this, I could not move the money because it was not the right thing to do, no matter how much it would set my company back. I founded our company to help the Main Street investor eliminate the dysfunctional behavior they felt compelled to implement. Their clients were the ones who would ultimately pay the price.

MM: "Guys, I know this seems like the easiest path right now and many investors are antsy for this, but it's our job to tell them the truth even when they do not want to hear it. It's their money, and they are free to do anything they want with it, but you and I do not have to be a party to this destructive behavior.

This is like a patient who goes to an oncologist who tells him that he absolutely must stop smoking. As the patient walks out of the office, there's a cigarette machine in the lobby because the doctor can make money off of encouraging patients to destroy their health. It's good for business, but this is not prudent for the patient or in his best interest.

I cannot be a party to anything that I believe is an imprudent behavior. So if you want to discuss how we can educate or coach your clients to stay disciplined, diversified, and rebalance, we can come up with a plan; but if you are hell bent on market timing and violating the simple rules of investing, I guess our meeting is over. You will have to move the money."

Market timing never feels like market timing, and it is never the right way to do things. A great coach will never be a party to dysfunctional behavior. If your advisor can't say "no" to you, he or she is worthless or—even worse—dangerous.

Aftermath

Investors who allowed themselves to chase performance and violate these rules would live to regret it. Large U.S. stocks suffered severe losses in future years: 2000, -9%; 2001, -11%; and 2002, -22%, for a combined loss of over 40%. While the market would eventually turn around, it would not be Large U.S. stocks that led the pack. From 2003 through 2006, U.S. large stocks made a respectable 14.79% annually for a total return of 63%. However, large international stocks (the very ones they wanted to sell), made 24.80% annually for a 142% total return, and small international stocks climbed an astonishing 34.5% annually for 227.9% accumulated return.[49]

In the end, I can be part of the problem or part of the solution, and violating the laws of rebalancing is always a problem.

Why Should You Rebalance Your Portfolio?

There are several reasons, actually.

- It controls your risk over time, so that asset categories that do extremely well don't become over-weighted.
- It prevents panicking and buying asset categories—or selling out of asset categories that are down and buying them when they're high.
- It ensures a systematic process of buying the asset category that is relatively low— relative being the key word here—and selling the asset category that is relatively

high, maintaining a standard deviation or volatility of the overall portfolio that is consistent with your investment objective. Investment risk can be controlled by curtailing overweighting and underweighting of funds in a portfolio.

When you build a diversified portfolio you always have something to rebalance against. In certain market conditions rebalancing can control risk and add return.

Rebalancing Study:
1/1/2007-12/31/2009

During one of the worst markets in history rebalancing mitigated losses by maintaining appropriate portfolio weightings.

	Conservative	Moderate	Growth	Aggressive
Rebalanced Portfolio	7.83%	1.76%	-6.77%	-13.21%
Non-Rebalanced Portfolio	6.47%	-1.03%	-8.94%	-14.63%
Rebalancing Premium	1.36%	2.79%	2.17%	1.42%

See Endnotes 49, 51.

This graph represents four sample portfolios we discussed previously ranging from aggressive 95% equities to conservative with only 25% equity exposure. From 2007 to 2009 (one of the worst three-year periods in market history), you can see the clear advantage of rebalancing as stock markets dropped throughout 2008 and the beginning of 2009.

Each mix benefitted from systematically buying more equity shares while they were low, so when the market began to recover investors would have more shares in each equity mix. In the Aggressive model, this would have resulted in an additional 1.42% return, Growth benefitted by 2.17%, Moderate to the tune of 2.79%, and our Conservative investor would have added 1.36% return versus taking no action and simply allowing the portfolio to remain static.

When you hear people talk about buy and hold, you should think instead—buy and rebalance. In precise terms, Rebalancing is an effective way to control your risk while continuously and systematically maintaining discipline and your investment policy.

- **Risk Management.** Building portfolios from low correlated asset classes and rebalancing allows for effective diversification and reduces volatility of the portfolio while achieving the desired returns.
- **Buy Low—Sell High.** Market movements provide opportunities to buy asset classes when they are underweighted and undervalued and to sell securities when they are over-weighted and over-valued.
- **Maintain a standard deviation** consistent with your investment objectives.

Rebalancing from a plan is crucial, as it is extremely difficult to do it on your own both emotionally and intellectually.

Make no mistake—rebalancing is crucial. It is also extremely difficult to do on your own because your emotions get in the way or it just seems intellectually counterintuitive. In fact, I haven't found a single investor who was ever able to do this consistently on his own, and I've met darn few advisors who have been able to do this for them. Like I said, putting these rules into practice is difficult.

Assessing the Health of Your Portfolio

Any meaningful discussion of how to create the best possible risk/return solution for your portfolio should always begin with an understanding of where you are today. In other words, how much risk and return does my portfolio already have? Here, I find it helpful to use a medical analogy. If you are reading this book, you probably feel like something is "wrong" with your portfolio. In your opinion, it is "sick" or not working up to its maximum capability.

In my experience, people can get sick, companies can get sick, and even portfolios can get "sick." You probably have a sense that you have lost too much money in down markets or perhaps have not made enough in up markets. If you have taken the time and effort to read this far, you are highly motivated and, odds are, you are not a happy camper.

When you are physically sick, doctors have many tools to analyze exactly what is causing the problem. One of the most advanced tools is MRI (Magnetic Resonance Imaging). It allows the doctor to "see" what is actually going on inside the patient. It is a modern miracle. Often it's impossible for the doctor to diagnose what is the real cause of a problem without it.

Until you can actually see what is going on inside of your portfolio, you will never know how to fix it. That is why I have invested over 20 years over a quarter of a million dollars in designing an analytical software program that allows investors to "see inside" their portfolio and diagnose the primary disease that is destroying their peace of mind.

In one study, we analyzed 3,600 investor accounts just like yours. Most investors assumed they were adequately diversified because they owned five to ten mutual funds all with different names and stated investment objectives. The portfolios we analyzed had over 8,400 unique funds with a total market value of $428 million. Any investor (and most advisors) would believe that with so many funds and so much money, this sample of real-world investor accounts would be adequately diversified. They would be sadly mistaken. In reality, there is very little real diversification. In effect, all of the fund managers are following each other in herds, and as a result they promote the same stocks or the same types of stocks.

Let's examine the average Main Street investor mix in greater detail (see column two). In our study, the average investor has over 19% of their portfolio in cash or cash equivalents like money markets. Before the crash of 2008, this number was much lower. In short, the crash made people afraid and made them turn to holding cash. They are literally paralyzed by fear. Many of them are even afraid to even open their quarterly investment reports.

You will also notice that they have only 1.7% in short-term fixed income, 16.2% in intermediate-term bond funds (bonds in the 5 to 10 year maturity range), and 1.8% in long-term bonds. That brings the total for fixed income investments to 38%.

Now let's examine the equities. Although there are over 8,000 different funds in the study, the vast majority of equity holdings are in large U.S. stocks—over 40%. This should be a huge red flag. This is far too much exposure to one asset class. This is not diversification. U.S. Large value stocks only have a 1.8% allocation; U.S. small stocks have 2.56% and U.S. small value have a .70% allocation. When we examine international allocations, you will find 15.15% in large international stocks and a pathetic .67% in small international stocks.[31]

The case study in the example is the result of analyzing over three thousand Main Street investors' accounts. For investors who had done their best to diversify without the aid of the academic research, their results are dismal. In spite of their best efforts, there is little to no real diversification, and the returns are desperately low for the amount of risk assumed. The first column on the left represents various asset categories that can be used to create an effective globally-diversified portfolio focused on small and value stocks.

ALLOCATION OF SAMPLE ASSET CLASS MIXES

ASSET CLASSES	HYPOTHETICAL MIX	SAMPLE ASSET CLASS MIXES Percent of Portfolio			
		CONSERVATIVE	MODERATE	GROWTH	AGGRESSIVE
FIXED INCOME					
Cash Equivalents	19.01%	2.00%	2.00%	2.00%	2.00%
Short Term Fixed	1.70%	36.50%	24.00%	11.50%	1.50%
Intermediate Term Bonds	16.12%	36.50%	24.00%	11.50%	1.50%
Long Term Bonds	1.80%	0.0%	0.0%	0.0%	0.0%
Sub Total Fixed Income	**36.63%**	**75.00%**	**50.00%**	**25.00%**	**5.00%**
U.S. EQUITY					
Large Stocks	40.42%	2.63%	4.50%	6.37%	7.50%
Large Value Stocks	1.89%	5.25%	9.00%	12.75%	15.00%
Small Stocks	2.56%	5.26%	9.00%	12.75%	15.00%
Small Value Stocks	0.70%	4.38%	7.50%	10.63%	12.50%
Sub Total U.S. Equity	**45.57%**	**17.50%**	**30.00%**	**42.50%**	**50.00%**
INTERNATIONAL EQUITY					
Large Stocks	15.15%	2.63%	7.00%	11.38%	15.75%
Small Stocks	0.67%	4.85%	13.00%	21.12%	29.25%
Sub Total Int'l Equity	**15.82%**	**7.50%**	**20.00%**	**32.50%**	**45.00%**
GRAND TOTAL	**100.00%**	**100%**	**100%**	**100%**	**100%**

See Endnote 31.

Average investors fail miserably when it comes to building real diversification into their portfolios. In short, there is not a significant allocation to small and value stocks in these portfolios and the fixed portions are focused on cash and intermediate bonds—in effect ignoring short-term fixed.

Over twenty years of examining and analyzing investors' portfolios, things have changed but little. Investors who believe Wall Street's lies of stock picking, market timing, and track record investing pay little attention to building academically sound diversification into their portfolio. But it doesn't have to be that way.

For comparison sake, examine the fourth column labeled Moderate. In this sample of a broadly diversified portfolio, you will see a much greater emphasis on short-term fixed income, U.S. large value stocks, and international small stocks. The moderate mix utilizes dissimilar price movements, small and value premiums, and offsets the risk of equity volatility with short-term fixed income. The moderate mix also has a 50% allocation to fixed versus the average investor with roughly 40%. The results in portfolio volatility and expected return premium are dramatic.

Now that we know what is actually in the mix of assets for the average investor (you must discover what your personal mix contains if you ever desire to have peace of mind), we can begin to examine the performance of this mix based on its underlying asset allocation. In the next chart, you can examine the year-to-year return of these asset mixes.

When I explain this chart to investors, I always start with the returns from 1973 and 1974. In these first two years, the average investor loses 6.98% in 1973 and 12.19% in 1974, for a grand total loss of 19.17%. Yikes! When I ask if their current advisor told them they could lose this much in a down market, not one single investor has ever told me yes. They were never told how risky or volatile their mix was. Truth be told, the advisor didn't know either. This is a case of the blind leading the blind.

You should never invest in a mix of assets for which you do not understand the historic worst-case scenario—never! However, this is not the only down period for this mix. For the period 2000-2002, the portfolio dumps another 17%, and in the single year of 2008, it crashes over 21%.

When average Main Street investors see this for the first time, they are aghast. They had no clue that their portfolios were so volatile. When I ask them if this meets their personal sleep-at-night factor, seldom am I told "yes." If you examine the last two years of this chart, you will see the overall expected returns and the volatility measure side by side.

HISTORICAL INVESTMENT MARKET PERFORMANCE OF SAMPLE ASSET CLASS MIXES

This illustration shows the annual rate of return for certain hypothetical asset class mixes based on the performance of various market indices and index mutual funds. The intent of this chart is to show the benefits of diversification into several asset classes with low or negative correlation among the selected asset classes.

SAMPLE ASSET CLASS MIXES					
YEAR	HYPOTHETICAL MIX	CONSERVATIVE	MODERATE	GROWTH	AGGRESSIVE
1973	-6.98%	0.23%	-5.91%	-12.07%	-16.79%
1974	-12.19%	1.52%	-7.25%	-16.02%	-23.11%
1975	26.80%	19.19%	30.04%	40.90%	49.30%
1976	16.43%	17.03%	21.40%	25.78%	28.30%
1977	2.64%	8.76%	16.14%	23.52%	30.51%
1978	11.39%	11.31%	18.27%	25.21%	31.79%
1979	14.09%	14.99%	15.58%	17.17%	17.67%
1980	21.93%	14.37%	19.01%	23.64%	27.50%
1981	5.08%	17.42%	13.32%	9.22%	5.69%
1982	18.10%	23.01%	210.73%	18.46%	15.88%
1983	17.75%	14.59%	20.62%	26.66%	31.46%
1984	7.70%	9.21%	8.58%	7.94%	7.57%
1985	29.63%	22.82%	30.45%	38.08%	44.99%
1986	23.60%	16.83%	23.28%	29.73%	36.10%
1987	7.42%	5.45%	8.02%	10.58%	13.63%
1988	15.12%	11.50%	16.26%	21.02%	24.88%
1989	19.19%	12.72%	16.02%	19.32%	22.02%
1990	-2.41%	2.91%	-4.23%	-11.38%	-17.15%
1991	20.25%	16.28%	18.96%	21.65%	23.06%
1992	4.56%	7.57%	6.85%	6.14%	4.52%
1993	12.69%	10.87%	16.12%	21.37%	25.89%
1994	1.82%	0.35%	1.71%	3.07%	4.52%
1995	22.00%	12.91%	15.61%	18.32%	19.74%
1996	13.33%	8.37%	9.78%	11.19%	11.93%
1997	17.55%	9.32%	10.48%	11.65%	11.61%
1998	17.09%	6.74%	8.18%	9.61%	10.88%
1999	15.11%	7.85%	12.25%	16.64%	20.52%
2000	-2.92%	5.31%	2.90%	0.49%	-1.94%
2001	-5.29%	5.39%	2.93%	0.47%	-2.24%
2002	-9.69%	2.03%	-3.11%	-8.25%	-12.10%
2003	21.35%	14.19%	26.43%	38.68%	48.56%
2004	9.58%	6.68%	12.05%	17.41%	21.95%
2005	5.54%	4.06%	7.14%	10.22%	12.97%
2006	13.43%	9.06%	13.78%	18.49%	22.42%
2007	5.84%	4.05%	3.63%	3.21%	3.17%
2008	-21.58%	-5.40%	-17.32%	-29.24%	-38.99%
2009	17.99%	10.49%	19.57%	28.65%	36.04%
2010	9.56%	7.01%	11.03%	15.04%	18.12%
Annualized Return	**9.47%**	**9.45%**	**11.06%**	**12.40%**	**13.22%**
Standard Deviation	**11.44%**	**6.35%**	**10.41%**	**15.27%**	**19.45%**

See Endnote 49.

For the investor's current mix, the historic return from 1973-2010 is 9.47%—not bad. But this represents a pure asset class return without management fees and internal commissions or costs. The volatility can be measured by something called standard deviation. For our purposes, all you have to know is that the higher the standard deviation number, the more volatile the portfolio, the lower the number, the less volatility. The average Main Street investor has a volatility factor of 11.44% over this sample time period.

Once you are armed with this type of information, you can make much better judgments. For example, the average investor could move to a moderate mix of assets, which had less volatility (standard deviation of 10.41% compared to 11.44%) and a higher expected return (11.06% versus 9.47%).

Why in the world would anyone stay in a portfolio with higher risk and lower return? The average investor has the worst of both worlds (high risk and low returns), and guess what, Wall Street doesn't care. It's time for you to stand up to the bullies and become 100% accountable for your portfolio allocation and long-term plan.

HISTORICAL INVESTMENT MARKET PERFORMANCE OF SAMPLE ASSET CLASS MIXES

This illustration shows the annual rate of return for certain hypothetical asset class mixes based on the performance of various market indices and index mutual funds. The intent of this chart is to show the benefits of diversification into several asset classes with low or negative correlation among the selected asset classes.

SAMPLE ASSET CLASS MIXES					
YEAR	HYPOTHETICAL MIX	CONSERVATIVE	MODERATE	GROWTH	AGGRESSIVE
$100,000 Invested would have grown to:	$3,117,000	$3,094,000	$5,392,000	$8,490,000	$11,200,000

Even a small increase in return can accumulate to a massive difference in wealth with compound interest. For example, for every $100,000 invested, the average investor accumulates $3,117,000 over this 38-year period. The same $100,000 grows to $5,392,000 with less volatility in the moderate mix.[49] Few investors will stick with an inefficient portfolio when they see how much is on the line.

In the end, every investor must come to terms with how much volatility he can handle and the expected returns on his mix. The goal is to get the highest expected return for your personal risk tolerance.

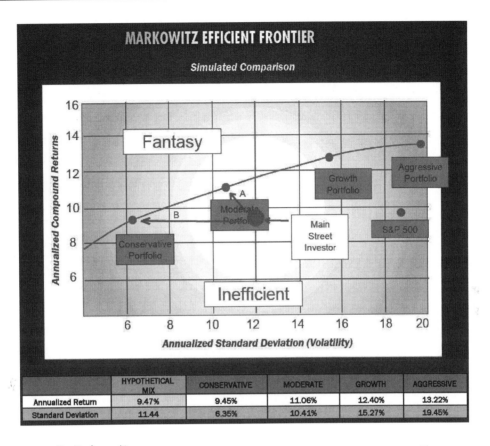

	HYPOTHETICAL MIX	CONSERVATIVE	MODERATE	GROWTH	AGGRESSIVE
Annualized Return	9.47%	9.45%	11.06%	12.40%	13.22%
Standard Deviation	11.44	6.35%	10.41%	15.27%	19.45%

See Endnote 49.

Dr. Harry Markowitz won the Nobel Prize in economics for helping investors focus in on this critical task. By using his hypothesis, we can construct a curve that gives us the highest expected return (based on market premiums) with the least amount of volatility (measured by standard deviation).

In the graph, you will see return along the vertical axis and risk along the horizontal axis, greater risk to the right and higher returns toward the top of the graph. Any point below the line represents an inefficient portfolio—one that has too much risk for the expected return. Portfolios that are above the line (for the same assets) are theoretically impossible because the line represents the highest return for a given level of risk. Therefore, the upper part of the chart represents Wall Street's lies and fantasies.

Now we can graph the average investor mix. Undoubtedly, you'll notice that it is below the efficient frontier line—it is an inefficient mix. If an investor who holds this mix is comfortable with the expected amount of volatility, he should move to the moderate mix of assets which has a significantly higher expected return and less volatility—the best of both worlds (see arrow A). If you are not comfortable with the expected volatility, then just slide along arrow B to the conservative mix with similar return and dramatically less risk.

The goal of every investor should be to become a means-variance investor, which simply means you get the highest expected return for the volatility or variance you are willing to personally accept. First, you must start by understanding where you are now.

I have five daughters and, as you can imagine, they love to shop. When I am at the mall with them, they instinctively know where they are at all times. I, on the other hand, am constantly lost. My only hope is to find one of those mall maps with the little red dot that says, "You are here." Knowing exactly where I am, I can successfully set my course and navigate the maze of the mall.

Your existing portfolio does have a risk-return structure, but unless you are a Ph.D. and Nobel Prize winner, you probably have no idea what it is. You are flying in the dark. By having an independent "MRI" of your portfolio, you can regain control and experience the empowerment that only educated investors can ever achieve. One final note—don't try to get this type of information or analysis from the Wall Street Bullies. They will laugh in your face and give you their most recent crystal ball prediction.

8

WHAT INVESTORS REALLY DO

"Greed, for lack of a better word, is good. Greed is right. Greed works.
Greed clarifies, cuts through, and captures the essence of the evolutionary spirit."
—Gordon Gekko, *Wall Street*

I GRADUATED FROM MIAMI UNIVERSITY IN 1986 with degrees in both accounting and finance with a heavy emphasis on economics. The movie Wall Street debuted in 1987, and it only seemed natural to me to buy several three piece suits from Men's Warehouse®, suspenders included, and slick my hair back just like the Wall Street magnate Gordon Gekko. Being young and naïve I took the "greed is good" speech to heart and set out to help investors grow their wealth, reduce taxes, and plan for their retirement. At the time, I had no idea just how much pain and suffering greed and avarice can cause everyday Main Street investors. Greed lies at the very heart of many of the worst investing decisions you can ever make.

What exactly is greed? According to Wikipedia, it's "an excessive desire to possess wealth, goods…with intent to keep for one's self. Greed is inappropriate expectations." Webster's puts it this way, "a selfish and excessive desire for more of something (as money) than is needed."

By definition, greed is an excess of desire. Don't get me wrong, it is only human nature to want things, even money. Who doesn't want a nice house and car, a well-paying job, enough money for their kids' educations and weddings, and money to travel? There is absolutely nothing wrong with that. I would call these healthy desires.

Greed causes pain and suffering for others and quite often for the person who is trapped in its clutches. Violence, manipulation, famine, murder, even war and genocide can all result from greed. Greed always ends badly. Greed also destroys those people caught up in it. Consider the pirate Hendrick Lucifer who captured a Cuban trading ship loaded with 1.2 million gold guilders but in return for acquiring them, got two gunshot wounds and forfeited his life.

Greed is perhaps the number one offender in causing devastating investing behavior. Greed is not good. Greed is always destructive.

In this chapter, we will examine common major mistakes so you can avoid them. Many of them are driven by greed, and if you are not aware of them you to can easily be sucked in. Greed is one of the weapons the Wall Street bullies will use against you. It is the proverbial carrot that tempts you into destructive behavior.

What Investors Really Do

"Wall Street never changes, the pockets change, the suckers change, the stocks change, but Wall Street never changes, because human nature never changes."
–Jesse Livermore

There's an old maxim attributed to former Boston Bruins goalie Gerry Cheevers, who summed up the lonely yet high-profile life of a professional hockey goalie.

"How would you like it," Cheevers once asked an interviewer, "if every time you made a mistake a big red light went on?"

The hockey great—who won two Stanley Cups during his career—has a great point, and one that I wish investors would heartily embrace.

The point is this: I actually wish a big red light would flash when investors do make mistakes.

Here's what I mean. In Chapter Seven, I detailed what investors should do with their portfolios. You know…invest in equities, diversify, and rebalance on a regular basis.

But is that what investors actually do? Unfortunately, not by a long shot. Most investors pay lip service to those things, but in reality, they let their emotions get the best of them. They chase hot markets, run after highly-touted stocks while frantically waving their checkbooks, and generally act like Las Vegas gamblers who hang their hats on "the next big thing."

Like most Las Vegas washouts, investors who adopt this strategy wind up just like the gambler who experiences the dark side of Sin City—the visit to the cardiologist and the Greyhound bus trip back home, penniless—when that next big thing doesn't pan out.

As an advisor, I can tell you that most of these investors were warned that chasing hot markets or "can't miss" stocks was a big mistake, but they rarely listen—until it's too late.

It's like tourists who go on a scuba diving excursion while on vacation. They go out on the sea when the sun is shining but after they hit the water, the ocean swells, the sky darkens, and it's tough to get back to the boat if you don't know what you're doing.

This once happened to a friend of mine, an experienced diver. He was out on the ocean in rough conditions, and he saw an inexperienced woman trying to get back on the boat. Concerned, he offered to help. Stubborn and not understanding the danger, she refused. Sure enough, the lady tried to climb back on the boat at the bottom of a swell. As she pulled herself up, the boat jumped four feet in the air and smacked her in the face, and she wound up breaking her nose and losing two teeth.

Why do I tell this story? So you can learn these lessons. First, in risky situations, always take advice from someone more experienced than you. Second, sometimes getting out can be more dangerous than getting in.

In other words, it's a lot like investing. Misguided, panicked investors try to get in and out of markets, and wind up in the financial equivalent of the emergency room after getting smashed in the face by volatile markets.

Is there any hard evidence that when investors systematically dump more money into asset categories when they are up, then panic and sell when they are down? You bet! When you look at this data, you'll also find that this is also what most financial planners and stock brokers do. It seems that, shockingly, no one is immune to greed.

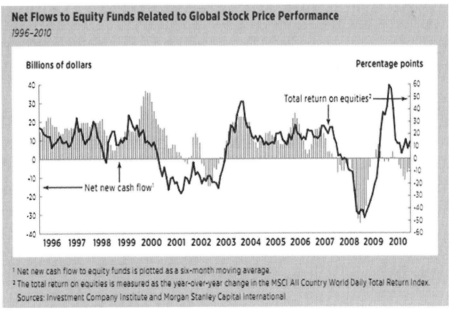

"2011 Investment Company Fact Book." See Endnote 2.

This graph demonstrates the return on equities (the stock market) versus the inflow or outflow of assets into equity-based mutual funds. You can observe that in up years, like 2004 when stocks were up 40%, there were massive inflows into mutual funds. At the highest point of the market, nearly $20 billion of new money came rolling in every month. The market's up, people, buy high! Of course, this is the opposite of rebalancing.

In 2008, you can see the market crashed—down 30%. (Ouch, that's gotta sting.) This situation provided an excellent opportunity to buy stocks "on sale" while they were distressed. For any long-term investor, this should have been a wonderful time to buy low. Is that what most investors did—did they see it as a great time to buy mutual funds? No way! During the worst part of 2008 when the market was down over 30%, net outflows were over $30 billion dollars for just one single month. Everyone was selling when they should have been rebalancing.

Rather than following the three simple rules of investing, people panic and go to cash when markets drop, and they chase hot sectors after huge run-ups. Sometimes they do both at the same time. Sadly, this is what most advisors do, too.

One of the biggest threats from greed is being sucked into an investing bubble. In an instant, a bubble can destroy decades of investing. A prudent investing strategy can protect your hard-earned money from this kind of danger.

Bubble, Bubble, Toil and Trouble...Understanding Market Corrections

Hey, let's face it. The stock market is a dynamic place, ebbing and flowing along on a tide of investor emotions, economic numbers, and big moves by Wall Street's heavy-hitters. Sometimes these factors can move the market dramatically, and they can sting you good if you're out on a limb, chasing a "hot market." If the market moves up significantly for a sustained period, Wall Street types call that a "Bull Market." When the market moves down significantly—10% is a good rule of thumb—then the experts say it's a "Bear Market," or what is more esoterically known as a "Market Correction."

In reality, it is not a correction at all. That implies the stocks in the market were mispriced to begin with. In reality, shift in the market simply reflect all knowable information.

The Power of Speculative Bubbles

U.S. investors have been "bubbled" to distraction in recent years. First there was the dot-com bubble of the early 2000s. Then, there were the housing bubble and the credit bubble that blew up in 2008.

But bubbles are not new—far from it. The South Sea Company was established in 1711 and generated a monopoly for England to trade in South America. It was the "can't miss" company of its time. The mania grew as more and more aristocrats dumped millions of British pounds into the stock. Tales of the ventures the company was pursuing were proclaimed loudly on the streets of London—they were called "bubbles" coining the term we now use today.

Even Issac Newton, arguably one of the greatest critical thinkers of his day and the inventor of calculus, was sucked into the mania. He lost his entire fortune, equivalent to $3 million in today's currency, in the crash. Stock prices for the company skyrocketed from 100 pounds to 1000 pounds per share in under a year. When it all came crashing down, stock prices plummeted from 1000 pounds to less than 100 pounds per share.[55] Massive amounts of wealth were destroyed overnight. Newton said, "I can calculate the movements of the stars, but not the madness of men."[56] I'd add to the list of things Newton didn't count on the effect of his own greed and overconfidence. Losing money in a bubble is not something that only happens to "dumb people" or "other people." It can happen to the most brilliant of people. It can happen to you. Maybe it has in the past, and you only now realize it. A bubble can literally destroy your life savings.

Gold, Japan, and Real Estate

Let's jump forward to modern times. Let's look at the 1980s.

I want to take a little walk down memory lane because this is not the first time people have speculated, gambled, and panicked. In the '80s, all we heard about was gold. I remember the International Investors Gold Fund. When I first got in the business, International Investors had made 13% a year during the 1980s, several times eclipsing 30% in a year.[57]

Let's look at Japan. Everybody was talking about Japan in the 1980s. Remember what everyone said about Japan? The Japanese work harder than Americans, they're smarter than we are, and they make their kids study harder than we do. The Japanese have a new system of management, they're brilliant, and they're going to take over the whole world.

People said Japan had the perfect government—you know, government working with business—because they have a ministry of finance and a ministry of manufacturing.

Then there was real estate, where prices really took off during the 1980s. Congress wrote tax laws that were beneficial to real estate, and everybody was building, speculating, gambling, and writing off tax credits and depreciation. I remember when California was hot, Texas was hot, Florida was hot. Everybody was getting rich.

Until it all failed. Gold crashed and actually lost value over a 20-year period.[52] Japan still hasn't recovered. Real estate crashed, recovered, and crashed again. People were shocked. Investors everywhere couldn't believe what had happened.

No one knows in advance where the next bubble is going to be, but you can protect yourself from it by following the three simple rules of investing.

The key is to remember that stock market bubbles can't hurt you as much when you are a buy-and-hold or long-term investor. By remaining disciplined and resisting the urge to sell when everyone else is selling, you can ride out market declines triggered by investment bubbles.

You can also recognize the warning signs that you are starting to gamble and speculate with your money. You avoid the seductive suggestion to add stocks to your portfolio that show recently skyrocketing performance. If it's wildly popular and on the cover of every magazine, chances are it is not a prudent investment but a bubble waiting to happen.

- If it has a "can't lose" story about how it has made tons of money and will continue to do so based on someone's forecast of the future, buyer beware!

- If it has received massive inflows of cash invested or has become the popular thing to do, avoid it.

- If it does not have a cost of capital story—meaning there is real risk associated with the expected return—avoid it like the plague.

- In other words, if it has a great five-year track record and seemingly no downside (the proverbial free lunch), be highly skeptical.

- And finally, if it does not have an expected risk premium as outlined in the previous chapters, run—do not walk—in the other direction.

When you hear your internal voice saying, "Wow! That is great. Everybody is making money, and this is a sure thing," recognize this as greed talking.

Today I see the tendency to chase hot sectors playing out in gold, commodities, and long bonds. Fear mongers, gold sellers, and our fear of inflation have convinced millions of Main Street investors to put large portions of their assets in physical gold, citing the recent 10-year run-up as evidence that gold is going up indefinitely. They preach the same nonsense about commodities. Don't fall for the gold and commodities trap. Historically, these assets have extreme volatility and low return when compared to equities, and they make terrible hedges against inflation. You don't hedge a risk that has historically low volatility, like inflation, with something with excessive standard deviation or volatility.

Gold—great for jewelry, bad for your portfolio.

And if you own a diversified portfolio you have exposure to companies that mine gold, distribute it, sell it and store it. The same thing goes for commodities. If you are diversified there is no need to "double down" by weighting your portfolio toward these speculative sectors just because they have had recently high returns.

I have observed many advisors recommend these and other so-called "alternatives" to investors in the name of diversifying their portfolio, claiming that they have a low correlation to equities. To be good diversifiers, assets must possess two attributes. First, the asset must have low correlation; second, it must add an expected premium to the portfolio.

Low correlation alone won't cut it. Let's say that you can choose to put a portion of your IRA into [gambling] futures, and every year you can bet on the outcome of the Super Bowl, buy a lottery ticket, go to Vegas and play craps or blackjack. You get the picture. Will the outcome of these events have a low correlation to the performance of stocks? The answer is the outcome should be completely uncorrelated to the stock market. So should you add them to your portfolio because they have dissimilar price movement? No! Why? Because these "investments" have no long-term expected return. They have a negative expected outcome, just like gold and commodities net of taxes, cost of investing and inflation.

As for long bonds, over the last twenty years interest rates have consistently dropped encouraging investors to seek higher returns by extending the maturities of their bonds, especially in recent years when stock markets have had lower returns. This is a dangerous move. If interest rates spike, investors in long-term government bonds who "felt safe" can lose massive amounts of their principal. Remember, bubbles can happen in bond markets, too.

What do people do when markets crash? Usually, they panic and move to cash. At the same time, investors tend to get greedy and buy things that are highly speculative in their portfolios, like gold, or commodities, or futures. That, to me, is mind-boggling. On the one hand, investors are trying to lighten up on risk. On the other hand, they're actually pursuing risk. Consequently, they get extremely confused and upset. Unfortunately, this is what many advisors do to their investors. As a matter of fact, I'm going to prove to you in future chapters that advisors are even worse culprits when it comes to exacerbating this problem.

But for now, take a look at this DALBAR study of investors and how their average investment returns barely beat the rate of inflation. As I said in the opening of this book, there's conventional wisdom and actual behavior, but the myth that advisors work in their clients' best interests is demolished by charts like this one:

The Result

CATEGORY	1991-2010 ANNUALIZED RETURN
S&P 500 INDEX	**9.14%**
AVERAGE EQUITY FUND INVESTOR	**3.83%**
INFLATION	**2.57%**

*DALBAR, Inc., *Quantitative Analysis of Investor Behavior*, 2011
Results are based on the twenty-year period from 1991-2010
See Endnote 13.

As this chart demonstrates, by simply investing in the S&P 500 Index, your rate of return from 1991-2010 should have been 9.14%. At this rate, your money would double nearly every 8 years, meaning a $10,000 initial investment would be worth over $40,000. This figure far exceeds inflation for this period, which clocked in at 2.57%. You needed at least the inflation level just to break even on your purchasing power.

How did average investors do investing in equity mutual funds? They made a measly 3.83% return. That means that they barely kept up with inflation, and it would take a staggering 22-year period to double their money. If you subtract taxes from this dismal 3.83%, you would certainly underperform both T-bills and inflation.[13]

Most investors want stock market returns with T-bill risk, but what they get is T-bill returns with stock market risk.

The problem is two-fold. First, investors trust a Wall Street Bully who says he can actively trade stocks that can beat the market (inevitably, they don't). Second, when the market drops, they panic, get greedy, and buy when prices are at an all-time high. The average holding period is just slightly over three years. Statistically speaking there are no long-term investors. This is what the typical pattern looks like:

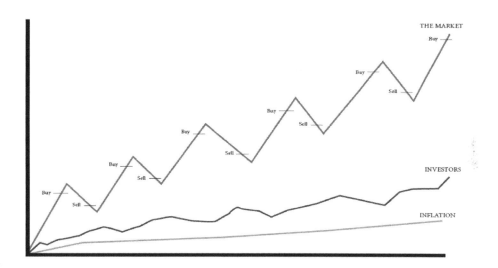

When Dalbar began their study, they included a section in which they showed the returns the average investor made when working with an advisor. They were hoping to see a longer holding period and higher returns. What better way to sell annual research at a thousand dollars a pop to advisors who can demonstrate to Main Street investors that they should trust them with their money? There was just one problem; the findings didn't bear this out. In fact, there was no significant difference between investors buying funds on their own and those using the typical financial planner or broker. Most advisors do not add discipline and prudence. They are part of the problem. There is an elite group of investor coaches who can help you counteract this problem, and I will talk more about how you can find one in later chapters. For now, know that most planners, investment managers, and brokers are *not* capable of helping you resolve this dilemma.

You should also know that most large financial organizations don't want you to solve these problems. It is simply not in their best interest. Their revenues and power base disseminate from stock picking, market timing, and track record investing. Your problems are their profits. When it became clear to me that free markets worked, that investors could eliminate speculating and gambling and achieve market returns while reducing volatility, and achieve peace of mind, I was elated. I felt like the little boy in Jack and the Beanstalk. I had the magic beans and I wanted to share them with everybody. For me it was an amazing breakthrough.

We could finally stop misleading investors and inadvertently victimizing investors. It would be a great awakening. Surely others would see the truth in this and want to join me in my crusade to save investors from the ravages of speculation. There was a better way! Others had to see it! I was quickly disillusioned. Consider the exchange I had with the head of a large broker-dealer. We were discussing the potential of bringing this system and process to his company's sales force so they could offer it to their clients.

I finished my presentation detailing the benefits to investors and asking for access to their sales force to present my solution. It was based on fees, not commissions, and it put advisors on the same side of the table as the investors by eliminating transaction-based commissions. It directly tied into Nobel Prize-winning research and offered true global diversification. After what I was sure was a great presentation and the beginning of a great relationship, I calmly waited for the president of the broker-dealer to make his comments.

President: "What's in it for us?"

MM: "What do you mean? The advisors can stop using funds that underperform the market. Your clients are happy, and you share in the fees that the advisor receives through your typical override. Win/win for everybody."

President: "I don't see it that way. We derive most of our income from the 'active' as you put it companies that you say underperform the market. They give us marketing assistance and money to run our conferences. They also run trades through our firm, so we make money when they trade. I don't see how this is good for us. You are basically saying they are full of crap. How do you think this makes us look?"

MM: "So, are you saying 'no'?"

President: "I'm saying what is in it for me?"

MM: I stammered, "What do you want?" He smiled.

President: "Well, first of all, I need $40,000 from you to sponsor our national conference. I'll give you a booth in the exhibit hall. For $60,000, you can do a presentation and address all of our reps, but I don't want you slamming on the other companies' investment management."

MM: "You want me to pay you to get access to your advisors?"

President: "Just think of it as a marketing expense. We use your money to pay for the conference and pay for our top reps to go for free. That's not all. How many trades can you run through us?"

MM: "There is very little trading because these are structured funds with less turnover, and I don't control that. The trading is done by another company."

President: "That is going to be a problem. Plus, if we do anything we are going to want at least 25 basis points in addition to the overrides on our reps."

MM: "Isn't that double-dipping? You are already getting paid."

President: "We do it with all our companies. That's just the way it is."

MM: "But I have cut my fees as low as they can go. If I give you additional fees, then they have to come out of the advisors' side, so they'll make less money but they are doing most of the work. Or it has to come out of the clients' side, which means they will make less money."

President: "I'm okay with that. I don't care if it comes out of the advisors' or the investors' side, but if you want to be a major player with this company, I need money for the conference, trades, and an additional 25 basis points."

MM: "And if we can't or won't do those things?"

President: "You can keep the handful of guys you are working with, you will certainly not get any promotion to our reps from us, and I will have to consider taking you off our platform. This is how we work it with all the major players. Take it, or leave it."

I didn't mind paying the marketing money. That just comes with the territory, but there was no way I would raise the fees to the investor or sell the advisors out to pay the borker-dealer more money. Running trades through them was not in my control, but if it had been, it was out of the question. Whether or not this was the best thing for the investor was never even considered in the equation.

All they wanted was another "product" to put on the shelf and additional ways to pump up profits. None of it was illegal, but it was far from ethical to my way of thinking, and it surely did not put the needs of the investor first. There would be no great awakening, no grand enlightenment. There was only resignation and resentment because I was upsetting the profitable bureaucracy they had so painstakingly created. My investment solution was not embraced with enthusiastic enlightenment and acceptance. Instead, I was to become an outcast, a pariah.

The President was confident I would take his deal. He controlled access to over one thousand financial planners and his broker-dealer endorsement would mean tens of millions of dollars under management, but it was a Faustian bargain I could not make. I would not sell my soul to them. I worked in the best interests of investors and the advisors who served them. If it was not in the best interests of investors, I wouldn't do it. It's a decision I have never regretted. Truly, you cannot serve two masters, and often what is good for the broker-dealer and institutional money manager is bad for Main Street investors.

Broad Asset Classes

Category	Ast-Wgt 3-yr Investor Return	Average 3-yr Total Return	Ast-Wgt 5-yr Investor Return	Average 5-yr Total Return	Ast-Wgt 10-yr Investor Return	Average 10-yr Total Return
US Equity Funds	-5.18	-4.96	0.64	0.91	0.22	1.59
Intl Equity Funds	-5.17	-4.55	3.27	5.23	2.64	3.15
Balanced	-2.15	-1.72	1.57	2.22	3.36	2.74
Alternative	2.36	-1.68	5.48	3.03	8.07	8.55
Taxable Bond	3.82	4.13	3.22	3.89	4.00	5.33
Municipal	1.01	2.50	1.45	3.02	2.96	4.57
All Funds	-2.71	-2.14	1.66	2.387	1.68	3.18

See Endnote 16.

As further evidence that investors allow greed to take over, above is a study by Morningstar. It shows that the average 10-year return for all mutual funds was 3.18% for the period ending December 2009, but the average investor return was 1.68%. It is clear that the average fund manager underperformed the market and the average investor underperformed the funds.

The fund loses returns through trading costs and excessive fees, and the investor loses from timing in and out of the market. All the while, the huge broker-dealers, fund companies, and Wall Street Bullies scrape up their fees and commissions.

Need more evidence? Consider the sad case of CGM Mutual Fund (ticker symbol LOMMX) managed by "guru" Ken Heebner. According to Morningstar for the 10-year period ending February 2010, the fund averaged a compound return of 18.72% per year. Who wouldn't want a little of that? Seeing this number, you might assume that the average investor made huge returns on any investment in the fund, but you would be wrong. According to Morningstar research based on actual money in and out of the fund, the average investor actually lost money to the tune of -11.56% each year.[16]

How is this possible? Think of it like an elevator. Start on the first floor of a 100-story building. On every floor three people get on (this is a really big elevator). On the first floor, there are only 3 people riding it; by floor fifty, there are 150 people; and by the time it hits the top, 300 passengers are on board. Then, tragedy!—the cable snaps and plunges 100 stories—but don't worry, this is a magical elevator and no one dies. However, this demonstrates how the fund can make money, but the average investor can lose. There are very few "riders" who actually are in for the complete 10-year returns. As the fund climbs, more and more investors jump on to ride, so there are many more people on board when it crashes!

CGM Focus Fund Returns vs. Actual Investor Returns

Trailing Returns (2/28/10)	10 Year	5 Year	3 Year
Investor Return%	-11.56	-14.04	-18.31
Total Return %	18.72	4.27	-1.09

Source: Morningstar. See Endnote 16.

Fund performance is irrelevant. The only thing that is important is the actual investor return. In this example, the penalty for "getting in late" or "getting in on the upper floor" was a staggering difference of -30.28%. The average investor underperformed the fund itself by over 30%. We can call this a behavior penalty. It is the return the investor gives away by violating the three simple rules of investing, and it is devastating.

Market Timing in Sheep's Clothing

Most investment professionals will tell you that market timing is the attempt to time the ins and outs between two asset categories—stocks and cash. But market timing comes in many different shapes, sizes, and derivations, and none of them work. Remember the Three Stooges? Although they wouldn't admit it, they were timing the market. Because the academic evidence is so clear that market timing is a failed method of investing, closet timers have developed a plethora of names to disguise their shenanigans.

Some will refer to it as *strategic* asset allocation. They claim to have the god-like ability to create a portfolio of multiple asset categories (for example, six different portfolio pieces) and then have the "analytical" tools to raise or lower percentages based on a forecast or prediction. So, instead of trying to time two classes, they claim to have the ability to time six. This is pure nonsense. By adding more classes you just made it more complex and problematic—not simpler. In a game of Russian roulette, it is worse to load the chamber with six bullets rather than two. However, I still contend this is a dangerous game you don't want to play at all.

Other names for market timing are trend analysis, demographics, and just plain research. Don't be fooled by any of these ploys. Anyone who tells you they know which way random markets are going in the short-term is either lying or delusional.

In any case, you don't want these folks anywhere near your money. Market timing by any other name still stinks.

Sure, it's tempting to try and time the market and get in on a good stock that's just beginning to take off. As study after study has demonstrated, it's impossible to time the markets. In fact, jumping in and out of the stock market may be the worst single thing you can do when building your own portfolio.

Why? If you're sitting on the sidelines waiting for the right time to get in again, you could easily miss the moment when momentum swings upward again. Yes, you could get back in later, but how much did you lose by being on the sidelines in the first place?

How Much Can You Lose by Getting In and Out?

The answer is "plenty." In a study published in the Financial Analyst Journal comparing the results between market timing and buy-and-hold strategies from 1926 through 1999, researchers found that buy-and-hold outperforms market timing a whopping 98.8% of the time. Those are pretty good odds.58

How good are your chances of making money in the stock market? The first few years of the 21st Century notwithstanding, they're great. To get a clear picture of why stocks are a good bet, take a look at the odds of making money in the stock market compared to the odds of some other life events (from the Forum for Investor Advice):[50]

- Odds that you'll win the lottery: 1 in 4,000,000
- Odds that you'll be dealt a royal flush: 1 in 650,000
- Odds that Earth will be struck by a meteor during your lifetime: 1 in 9,000
- Odds that you'll be robbed this year: 1 in 500
- Odds that the airlines will lose your luggage: 1 in 186
- Odds that you'll be audited by the IRS: 1 in 100
- Odds that you'll get snake eyes when rolling the dice: 1 in 36
- Odds that you'll go to Disney World this year: 1 in 10
- Odds that the next bottled water you buy is only tap water: 2 in 10
- Odds that you'll eat out today: 1 in 2
- Odds that an investment in stocks will make money in any given year: 7 in 10

As the chart indicates, you have a 70% chance of making money in the stock market in all one-year periods. As duration of your holding period increases, so does your likelihood of making money. Contrast that number to the odds of winning the lottery or being dealt a royal flush, and you will see why if there was a stock market game in Vegas you would never want to leave the table. As your holding period goes up, so too, do your odds of having positive returns and beating inflation.

Pitfalls of Market Timing (1982-1987)

There's no shortage of studies comparing buy-and-hold investing with market timing. One of the best studies I've seen is from the University of Michigan. Researchers there calculated the effect of being invested in the stock market 100% of the time (as a buy-and-hold investor would be) and being out of the market during days when the market rose. Their findings are below:

Period of Investment	% of Time Invested	Average Annual Return
Full 1,276 Trading Days	100%	26.3%
minus the 10 Best Days	99%	18.3%
minus the 20 Best Days	98%	13.1%
minus the 30 Best Days	98%	8.5%
minus the 40 Best Days	97%	4.3%

Source: University of Michigan Study, Bull Market of 1982-1987

Mistakes to Avoid

It was the philosopher-poet Homer who said that true reward was in the trying and not the succeeding. It was Homer Simpson who said trying was the first step to failure.

This is certainly true of all forms of market timing. It's a loser's game. Like gambling in Vegas or playing the lottery, the odds are stacked drastically against you, and the penalty far outweighs the rewards. Like in the movie *War Games*, the only way to win is not to play. The showman P.T. Barnum famously said, "There's a sucker born every minute," and he was right. Wall Street Bullies count on it. Just make sure that sucker isn't you.

Armed with the Dalbar research and the real-world knowledge of how investors actually behave, we can see a clear picture of the destruction these dysfunctional investing behaviors create. We will see that often we are our own worst enemies.

You may remember the Cost of Capital formula. In its simple form it basically says that all investors are entitled to a return on capital based on the cost of capital for any company they invest in. The investor's job is to not "mess it up." But most do mess it up—and badly.

Our original formula was:

The Cost of Capital = The Return on Capital

But now we add real world behavior and expenses:

Return on Capital = Cost of Capital - Investor Expense - Behavior Penalty

Let's start with the left side of the equation. We have in our example the S&P 500 Index, a proxy for the cost of capital for large U.S. companies, which was 9.14% from 1991 to 2010. In a perfect world where there are no active managers, expenses, or turnover costs and all investors are disciplined, long-term, seasoned pillars of restraint, this would also be the return for the investor. That is not the real world. In the real world, managers charge big fees. According to Morningstar, the average U.S. domestic fund charges 1.35% per year in a vain attempt to beat the market. In addition, they frequently buy and sell stocks, causing additional turnover and cost. Adding this cost to expenses can average 3% per year.[59] The vast majority of investors trust the Wall Street gurus to beat the market, so they reduce the 9.14% return to 6.14%. This is a heavy price to pay someone else to unnecessarily churn your portfolio. But Dalbar tells us the average investor only made

3.83%. Where did the rest of the return go? The additional 2.31% was lost to attempts at market timing. In other words, given this market segment, every investor is entitled to a market return of 9%, but loses 3% to bullies and 2.3% to getting in and out of the market, dropping their actual return to 3.83%.

Cost of Capital

$$9.14\% - 3\% - 2.31\% = 3.83\%$$

See Endnotes 13, 59.

This is what most investors do and what you must avoid at all costs. But why do we make these mistakes—chase bubbles, panic and go to cash—and repeat them over and over? How is it that we can unlock the secrets of deep space, physics, atomic energy, create things as advanced as iPhones and the Internet, but we can't discern when we are speculating and gambling with our own money?

To answer this question, we must start to learn a new field called "behavioral finance." Behavioral finance studies the intersection of psychology and finance, concentrating on behaviors that may affect investment decisions in ways that few can predict. These behaviors are, strictly speaking, not rational, in the sense that they will probably lead to losses rather than gains. Behavioral finance deals with mistakes. Not just the random kind of mistakes that are inevitable from time to time, but the systematic mistakes that investors tend to make again and again. The reason for these mistakes, it is proposed, is the nature of the human mind.

These are some of the psychological hurdles we must overcome:

Ego—Some may even say arrogance. It's human nature to think we know more than the next guy. Put it this way. You could gather every guy who had a hot stock tip that didn't pan out, and they'd fill every football stadium in America—and probably Europe, too.

Thinking Short Term—You're watching a football game. Your team's quarterback fumbles. Okay, short-term, you're not feeling so confident. But as the game develops, your team's quarterback makes a few key passes and leads his team to victory. That's a long-term gain, so to speak. Investing is the same way. Too often, we're focused on the short term at the expense of the long term. Focusing on the short term can lead to poorly thought out panicky moves. It can also increase your trading costs, since you're trading so much and so often to improve your portfolio position. Trading too often is not what you want to be doing with your money. Remember, it's all about picking the right investments in the first place and having the confidence to let them do their job over the long term.

Selling the Wrong Asset Categories—The stock market is a volatile environment. One moment you're up, and the next you're down. And people—being flesh and blood human beings—just can't stand seeing their stocks go down. So they sell them. The lesson here is that volatility happens, and you're not going to be able to escape it. If you want the return, you will have to find a way to stay disciplined long-term. The only way out is to hold long-term.

Not Having a Plan—You'd be amazed, but studies show that about half of all Americans don't have an investing plan. That's why advisors spend so much time on budgeting, goal setting, and knowing their clients' financial needs. After all, you plan for your vacation, you plan for your career, and you plan for your diet and health. Why should your finances be any different? If you don't have a proactive plan to rebalance in volatile periods you will react by market timing.

Choices Are the Enemy of Discipline

Dan Ariely, a behavioral economist at Duke University, conducted a study to determine the effect on prudent decision making by being overwhelmed by unproductive choices. Students from MIT were given a computer screen showing three doors—red, green, and blue. They were told that behind each door, they would be rewarded a number of points. The goal of the game was to get as many points as possible. They were only given a fixed number of clicks to choose the most "profitable" door. Each door was programmed with a variety of results. For example, the blue door would randomly give out 5-10 points, the red one, 1-5 and the green door 11-15.

The obvious strategy to maximize the points and win the game would be to find the door with the highest pay out, and then use every remaining click on that door. But there was a catch. For every time you clicked, let's say the green door, the other two doors became smaller and if you did not click on them, they would eventually disappear completely and no longer be available as a choice.

So did the majority of the MIT students play the right strategy and allow the "less productive" doors to shrink and disappear? The answer is no! When faced with the possibility of losing choices, most students clicked on the shrinking doors to keep them available as options despite the fact that they were wasting clicks that could have been building more points on a more profitable door.

To be a successful investor, it is critical to identify "doors" or asset categories that have a higher statistical likelihood of delivering premiums and eliminate those that do not. But just like the student's ability to say no to less productive shrinking doors, many investors and their advisors cannot say no. They crave choices even when they are less productive. Wall Street understands this, and they strive to create choice overload. In this case, more is clearly not better.

Mistaking Activity for Control

Most investors get a false sense of security by just making trades in their accounts. They feel that if they are doing something. They like the feeling of control, like pulling the arm on a Vegas slot machine. However, some activities create negative results and actually reduce your control. This is "out of control" behavior, think over-eating, drinking too much, or generating trades. These are all destructive behaviors that reduce your control. The only thing worse than doing nothing is doing the wrong thing over and over. More trading may "feel" like control, but it is dysfunctional.

As an investor, it is critical to understand that your brain is hardwired to seek choices, even when they are counterproductive. Wall Street is all too eager to provide thousands of choices to encourage you to trade in order to maintain the false sense of control that activity creates. The hardest thing for investors is to stay disciplined and "sit on their hands."

Blueprint for Success

What to do about behavioral investing, and investors chasing down "hot markets"?

Several useful suggestions have been made to help investors deal with behavioral impediments to investment success. Here's a list of habits to learn that can separate you from the herd:

1. Accept that investing is an art of probability.
2. Recognize and avoid the circumstances leading to undue confidence. Don't listen to the bullies.
3. Deliberately seek out the contrary view. If it is on the cover of a magazine, it is not prudent. Only hype and horror make the cover.
4. Have a written plan for each position.
5. Create feedback loops with your coach that allow for process analysis and improvement.

Also, try not to give too much weight to recent experience. Remember, nothing in life moves in a perfect straight line. Up market enthusiasm will eventually fade, and down markets will turn around eventually even if it feels like they never will. Recognize that your brain is lying to you. After all, you are only human. Recognizing the patterns and biases of your own mind is the first step to defeating them. Remember, when it comes to bull or bear markets, they didn't come to stay, they came to pass. Try some self-examination, too. People often see other people's decisions as the result of emotion, but they see their own choices as rational. Keep in mind that the stock market is a leading indicator. Everything you see and hear is already in the price.

Like I said before, adopting a long-term, diversified investment plan may be your best defense against many of the behavioral tendencies I discussed above. A properly-constructed portfolio will contain a number of different investments, each fulfilling a particular role or niche contained in the plan. While each piece may be more or less risky than the others, your primary consideration should be with the much larger and more important long-term objectives of your overall portfolio.

The right kind of behavior bypasses bubbles, eliminates useless chasing of hot and trendy markets, and in the end, creates true long-term wealth, the kind every Main Street investor wants.

MIND OVER MONEY

"Nothing has such power to broaden the mind as the ability to investigate systematically and truly all that comes under thy observation in life."

–Marcus Aurelius

ONE OF MY GREATEST PASSIONS IN LIFE IS CYCLING. I typically pedal 150 to 200 miles per week. It is incredible exercise. It keeps me fit, active, and energetic. It's also an amazing stress reliever. It is not uncommon for me to put in two or three hours in a day. I enjoy exploring the world, and I love to ride with my wife, Melissa, who is a fitness trainer. Cycling is all about weight-to-power ratios. To conquer mountain passes you need a ton of strength with as little body weight as possible.

When I am training, actually riding, I do a pretty good job at watching what I eat, but I am not as young as I once was, and I do get strains and pulls that can cause me to need rest time to heal an injury. Last year, I had a herniated disc that took me off my bike for six months. A rational, disciplined individual in these circumstances would reason, "Wow, I am injured and can't train. It is crucial to restrict my diet so that I do not get fat and make it even harder to get back in shape. In fact, I use approximately 1400 calories per day, so I need to cut down to at least that much. Train less, eat less."

This is what a prudent athlete would think—but is that what I did? Far from it. In fact, I started eating worse. Pizza, hamburgers, ice cream, chocolate-covered peanuts, and Hostess snack cakes became part of my daily fare.

I packed on twenty pounds nearly overnight. My clothes got tight, and I didn't like the way I looked. I felt shame and guilt and out of control every time I binged. My personal M.O. is that when I work out, I eat right; when I don't, I eat garbage. So what does my mind tell me? It says things like, "Hey, why me? Why do I have to be injured? All I want to do is work out and be fit. Why is this happening again? I am always hurt. Well, I know I should eat better but since I can't ride, I might as well really blow it and just eat whatever I want. After all, you deserve it, Mark. You deprive yourself most of the time, so go ahead and enjoy yourself. Once you feel better, you will work it off. You deserve a break. Go ahead, pig out!" Once I can train again, I get back on my bike feeling terrible and have to dig myself out of the hole I dug. It usually takes something like my wife beating me up a mountain climb for me to fully stop the negative behavior. I have repeated that pattern hundreds of times in my life. It is like that movie *Groundhog Day*. Same pattern, over and over again. Perhaps you can't relate, but maybe there is another area of your life where you know what to do, but you struggle at actually doing it.

In the strictest sense of the word, my behavior is dysfunctional. It is not giving me the desired result I am seeking, a fit and healthy body. Although I have a commitment to good health, there are times when my own human urges take over and I behave in ways that sabotage my own goals and commitments.

> *"The investor's chief problem—and even his worst enemy—is likely to be him or herself."*
> –Benjamin Graham

Recently, I ran into an academic study which reinforced a long-held notion of mine— that visceral, emotional, gut reactions drive investment decisions, and not intellect, research, and discipline.

The study came from the University of California's Haas School of Business in 2011 and was led by Professor Eduardo Andrade and Chan Jean Lee, a Ph.D. candidate, at the university.

Titled "Fear, Social Projection, and Financial Decision Making," the article explains that the "scared" investor's early decision to sell stocks happens through "social projection." In other words, investors tend to heavily rely on their own current feelings and inclinations when they estimate others' states of mind and preferences. As a result of social projection, an investor who is scared assumes that other investors are also afraid and that their fear will consequently drive the stock price down, prompting the one investor to sell early before the price sinks.[53]

"If I'm scared, I tend to project that you are scared," Andrade explains. "If I feel like selling, I assume or project that you are also going to sell, and that pushes me to sell earlier rather than later in anticipation of a drop in stock value."

According to data released by the university, Lee and Andrade set out to manipulate the participants' emotions in a way completely unrelated to the stock market. They created two random groups. One group watched clips from horror movies like *The Sixth Sense* and *The Ring*. The other test group watched documentaries about Benjamin Franklin and Vincent Van Gogh containing material not intended to illicit emotion. After the screenings, researchers told the participants that it was time to move on to another experiment, a stock market simulation.

In the stock market simulation, participants went through 25 rounds in which they had an opportunity to sell a $10 stock (part of their participation fee). The rules of the market stated that prices would decrease if any participant sold his or her stock, and prices would increase if every player held onto their stock. Each simulation involved approximately 26 anonymous participants; and therefore, prices could go up or down in any given round.

Selling patterns indicated that the scared players (that is, those who watched the horror movies in the previous task) were more likely to sell early in the game than those who watched the documentary films. Put simply, an incidental induction of fear triggered selling behavior. In order to test for the role of social projection, Lee and Andrade added a few twists. They reasoned that if social projection is a key mechanism during the decision-making process, the impact of fear should be reduced when people are less likely to try to project what others will do.

Consistent with this hypothesis, fear promoted early selling only when participants were told that the value of the stock was peer-generated. When participants were told that the stock value was randomly determined by a computer (where social projection is not a factor), the fearful experience derived from watching the horror movie had no impact on their decision.

The study also found that early sell-off occurred when the investor was told that others shared his or her risk attitude. At the same time, when the investor was told that his or her risk attitude was very unique in the market, the result tended to reverse.

Andrade says the study suggests that controlling the influence of fear in financial decisions can be profitable. "Generally speaking, those who made more money were those who decided to stay longer in the simulation game."

That's what I'm talking about. If investors can harness their "scared" side—and we all have one—they can make a lot more money in the financial markets.

You will often hear so-called investment experts say things like, "you have to eliminate feelings from the investment process." There is only one problem with that—it is impossible. No one can completely eliminate feelings and emotions from the investing process because we are all human. Pretending otherwise and insisting that your emotions won't come into play is a recipe for disaster. Instead, you must acknowledge that you do have feelings and emotions and that they will factor into your process. Your job is to put them to good use. There is an upside to every emotion. Even fear can have its place. For example, don't fear market drops; they are temporary and can provide long-term buying opportunities. You should fear panicking and trying to time the markets. Fear throwing your money away on stock picking and track record investing. Fear being taken advantage of by Wall Street Bullies. These are all healthy fears which will help you to find the courage to be disciplined.

How about anger? Can it be useful? You bet. If you have been sucked in by Wall Street's seductive lies, get good and mad. It just may give you the courage to take the action you will need to protect your family. There is a lot more at stake than your personal wealth. The success of your children and grandchildren also hangs in the balance. One thing I can guarantee is that they are not going to be taught these lessons in school. It's up to you to help them get in the game and learn these critical skills and mindsets. Wall Street is out to get their assets, too.

The HALT Rule

There is a rule of thumb that many people follow to keep their actions in check when emotions run high—the HALT Rule. The HALT Rule warns people to avoid saying or doing anything when they are:

- **Hungry** to get back money they lost. They become vulnerable.
- **Angry** over poor advice or returns. They may become overly cautious.
- **Lonely** and feeling abandoned by an advisor. They may listen to people whom they ought to ignore.
- **Tired** of the ups and downs. They may lock up their money and surrender flexibility with their assets. The best thing to do is wait until a more rational response arises.

Mind over Money

Thus, the name of this chapter, "Mind Over Money."

It's pretty simple when you think about it. It's just not enough to know that this is what investors do, and what many so-called advisors do. We have to actually know why investors and advisors make the decisions they make.

Look at it this way. If you've ever tried to lose weight, there are two simple rules, right? We all know that we should just follow two simple rules—eat less and move more. That's how you lose weight and get in shape. Most people will tell you that they have a commitment to good health, but the reality is that most of us could probably stand to lose a couple of pounds.

Let me ask you a few simple questions. Just so you know this includes you.

Do you have a commitment to good health? Most people say "yes" to this. You probably didn't wake up this morning and say "Man, I'm really going to trash my health today!" Now that we have established that you have made this commitment, do you wish you had eaten a little less in the last two weeks? Did you say no to that chocolate cake or pie—every time? Are you at your ideal weight? How about this, do you wish you had exercised just a little bit more over the last two weeks?

When I ask these questions in workshops, the vast majority of people will say they wish they had exercised more and eaten less. If you can say the same, it just proves that you are human.

In fact, if I gave you the perfect written eating and exercise plan with daily schedules for the next year that would put you at your ideal weight, how many people could follow it? The answer is, darn few and that includes me. In the same way, I could give you the allocation for an efficient portfolio and the instructions for how to rebalance and follow the rules for the next thirty years. How many people could follow it? In my experience, even less than could follow the fitness plan.

Investing really is like exercise. You can't get healthy with a few abdominal exercises. It takes discipline, a strict diet, and a variety of exercises over a meaningful and measurable amount of time.

The same is true of investing. Financial fitness can only happen with a disciplined investment process, diversification, and market appreciation over a meaningful period of time.

So, even though we know what the simple rules are, why don't we adhere to them?

The answer is multi-faceted (after all, we are talking about human beings here), but not all that difficult to absorb.

The battleground for your long-term peace of mind will be fought, not on a spreadsheet or a pie chart, but in the eight inches between your ears. That is why you must understand how your mind works.

There are three particular parts of the investor's mind that affect actual behavior:

- Cognitive, or what we know—logic, reason, and intelligence.
- Instinctual, or our gut—our reactions, intuition, and survival mechanisms.
- Emotional, or how we feel—things like pain, fear, love, passion, and joy.

So when we look at actual human behavior, what we've come to understand is that to be a successful investor, you must have the cognitive part of the mind sealed tight—with little room for error.

But that poses a big problem, because the vast majority of investors, including advisors, lack the Ph.D.- level knowledge to pull this off.

This process of decision-making is further complicated by our own lapses in human perception. In short, it is our perception that is flawed. What we think we see is not always reality, and what we miss is often right in front of our faces. Finally, we must take into consideration the media. We are being bombarded 24/7 by the media in all its forms—television, radio, magazines, books, smart phones, and the Internet. You cannot escape even if you tried. It is impossible to fully block out the media's effect on your peace of mind. Even if you take your family to a nice dinner or go to work out at the gym, there are ten 60" flat screens blaring out the latest tragic news story and flashing a market down arrow in your face. The media is here to stay, and it is only going to get worse.

It might help to think of this as a symbolic formula. To have any chance of being a successful investor, the cognitive mind must have a greater effect on behavior than instinct, emotion, and perceptions multiplied by the influence of the media. Unfortunately, for most investors and even many advisors, it is very difficult to insulate the cognitive part of the mind from the outside influences of instincts, emotions, and perceptions. Typically, the formula looks like this:

$$C < (I + E + P)M$$

Where C = cognitive, I = instincts, E = emotions, P = perceptions, and M = media. The cognitive side of the mind and the rules for prudent investing frequently lose to the combined effect of the forces that create the tendencies to speculate and gamble with your portfolio.

Let's examine the left side of the theoretical construct.

The Cognitive Mind

This is the part of the mind that processes facts, statistics and data. It is the rational and reasoning part of the mind. It is the part of the mind that unlocks the mysteries of the universe, like gravity and the theory of relativity. It is the part of the mind that makes reading this book possible. This is the part of the mind that most sets us apart from the animal kingdom. It is the seat of reason and intellect and when it comes to making important decisions, like how to invest your money, most of us like to think that this is the part of the mind that calls the shots. If only that were true.

To further complicate matters, most people lack the Ph.D. level knowledge to build a prudent long-term portfolio. If you do not understand the Nobel Prize-winning research that goes into building a globally diversified portfolio, the process is doomed from the start. In college, studying finance, economics, and accounting, I found it useful to create graphic representations of important concepts and theories that allowed me to pull them up quickly and burn them into the cognitive part of my brain. I also found, for some inexplicable reason, that they were easier to remember in sets of three—I call this the power of three. To aid you in anchoring these key concepts in your cognitive mind, I have taken the key concepts from previous chapters and organized them into easy reference points. These are the required concepts that every investor must integrate into a prudent investment process, or conversely eliminate, to be successful.

The Power of Three

Eliminate	Eliminate	Eliminate	Incorporate	Incorporate	Incorporate
Wall Street Bullies	Wall Street Lies	The Wrong Questions	Free Market Portfolio Theory	Dimensions of Equity Returns	Simple Rules
Con Men	Stock Picking	What stocks should I buy?	Efficient Market Theory	Market Factor	Own Equities
Prognosticators	Market Timing	What is the market going to do?	Modern Portfolio Theory	Small Factor	Diversify
Gurus	Track-Record Investing	Who is the best manager?	Three Factor Model	Distressed (Value) Factor	Rebalance

First of all, most people lack the doctoral level knowledge to be a successful investor, the things economists must learn to better understand the flow of money through the system. Yes, the rules are simple, but the actual math, scholarship, and the studies behind that the proper mix of assets are extremely difficult to calculate.

Once you have that knowledge, then you have to apply it to the portfolio. Most people just don't have that type of knowledge. Most people believe the myths that they've been taught by the industry—stock picking, market timing and track record investing. They don't have what I would call "rational" investing or logical investing because they don't have the analytical skills or statistical validation.

Once you have the cognitive part, then you must examine the right side of the equation, and that's where all the headaches begin. Most people are simply not wired to be successful long-term investors. Almost everything about being human is working against us. Our own human nature stands in the way of our being successful. Even the professors, the people that did the math behind the studies, find it extremely hard to actually follow the appropriate behaviors. They engage in the classical, "do as I say, not as I do"—as exemplified by some leading historical financial thinkers as I'll illustrate below.

I don't give these examples to belittle them, and I certainly hope that it doesn't discredit their actual studies, but what I want to do is establish in your mind that even the theorists, the people who did the science behind the studies, because of their own humanity find it extremely hard to implement their own theories without speculating and gambling.

Burton Malkiel, one of my heroes, wrote *A Random Walk Down Wall Street.* He said it's like giving up the belief in Santa Claus; even though you know Santa Claus doesn't exist, you kind of cling to that belief. Wall Street wants you to believe that they can do it. The evidence, however, is that they can't. I think he is absolutely right.

This from Burton Malkiel:

"The idea of a random walk is that the stock market doesn't have a memory, where it went the last day, last hour, last week, last month, doesn't tell you anything about where it's going to go in the future."[61]

What Malkiel is saying is pretty clear. The markets are random, so don't speculate and gamble with them. However, in his book, written with Charles Ellis, called *The Elements of Investing,* the author admits in the introduction that they delight in buying individual stocks and have a significant commitment to China. He enjoys the game of trying to pick winners and believes China is a major story for his grandchildren.[62] Major story? I think *The Velveteen Rabbit* is a major story for the grandkids—not "Grandpa Speculated and Gambled on China."

But that's where speculation leads you. Contrary to their stated goals of outperforming the market averages, investment managers don't beat the market, and the data bears that out. Malkiel knows it, but even he can't stop himself from speculating. Instead of role-modeling prudent behavior for his kids and grandkids, he is clearly saying one thing (the right thing) and doing another. Malkiel knows the market is random, but he's tempted to try to beat it, at least with part of his money. And he is not the only academic who finds it hard to maintain 100% discipline.

Yet, the market beats them. Still, most institutional investment managers continue to believe, or at least say they believe, that they can and will outperform the market. They won't, and they can't. Harry Markowitz said that, and we agree. He says asset allocation is the foundation upon which portfolios should be constructed and managed.

This from Markowitz: "Protecting against your own misunderstanding and ignorance is the least costly, most useful thing you can do to make sure that you don't get really hurt in your investing. So diversify would be rule number one."

And this: "If anybody tells you they know with any kind of precision which way the market will move, run, do not walk, in the other direction."

There's a good lesson for every investor in both those statements. But in an article entitled "The Big Bang," Nobel Prize-winner Harry Markowitz admits to both stock picking and market timing with his own money. Of course, in the article he only admits to instances when he "got it right" and fails to mention any portfolio moves that may have led to negative returns. Just like a gambler in Vegas who tends to only recall and discuss the nights he won and conveniently forgets the rest.

Rational investing has nothing to do with speculating and gambling, at least it shouldn't. In reality, returns should be based on careful academic analysis, theory and statistical validation. When it comes to breaking the prudent rules of investing, Malkiel and Ellis admit in their book *The Elements of Investing*—"Nobody's perfect. We certainly aren't."[62]

Even the scholars who discovered the theories cannot follow them, and they admit it.

> **Three Blocks**
> There are three mental blocks to rational investing behavior. I say this as the voice of experience. Even the proponents of market efficiency get trapped in stock picking, market timing, and track record investing.
> Given that, what chance do average advisors or investors have of ever doing it on their own?

For me, speculating and gambling is not a moral issue. Hey, if you want to gamble, knock yourself out, although I believe there are better ways to enjoy your money. But if you want to gamble, go to Vegas—at least you will get a free show out of it. But never gamble with your portfolio and investments—never. Those are the assets you need to fulfill your life's dreams. Why would you ever want to gamble that away?

Now let's examine the right side of the equation beginning with Instincts. Instincts are ingrained into all of us. They are hardwired to help us survive. We are all born with instincts.

It's no secret the world is a complicated place. It's very difficult to filter all the information coming in, so we have a simplified system of understanding what to move toward and what to shy away from. Most organisms instinctively avoid pain. You know, things like hunger, cold, heat, and being stabbed.

On the other hand, there's this other great stimulus (which I'm a big fan of) called pleasure. Things like eating, love, safety, warmth, comfort, and other things that provide pleasure.

By and large, things that are painful threaten our survival. If I hit my head over and over and over with a hammer, eventually it will kill me. If, on the other hand, I do things that are pleasant—like wearing clothes that keep me warm, finding caring relationships that help me to be happy, or eating a reasonable amount of food—that helps with my survival. However, our instincts are not perfect.

For example, can you think of an activity that's painful but actually helps your health? Most people come up with exercise. And that is absolutely correct. Now can you think of something pleasurable that can be bad for you? Most folks will answer: eating. Here they are also right on track. Eating three little peanut butter cups is pleasurable, and may even help my survival if I'm energy-depleted. But if I eat a whole bag of them, I get fat, my cholesterol goes up, and my risk increases for heart attack, diabetes, and all kinds of negative things.

From an investment standpoint, some things that are pleasurable can actually end up being painful situations, and our instincts get confused.

For a good illustration, let's look at 2008. Let's say that your portfolio statement shows that long-term government bonds were up 25.8%. Is that pain or pleasure when you see that number? For most people, that's pleasure. On the other hand, U.S. small stocks are down 38.67%. Pain or pleasure? Obviously that's pain. So what does the average investor want to do when they see their portfolio statement? I'll tell you what they want to do. They want to sell U.S. small stocks, and they want to buy long-term government bonds. That's mind over money for you.

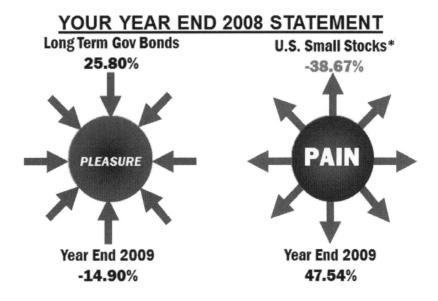

Source: 2010 Dimensional Fund Advisors Returns Software. See Endnote 49.

But in doing so, how many of the rules of prudent investing did they just violate? You know the rules: own equities, diversify, rebalance by systematically buying the investment vehicle that's low and selling the investment vehicle that's high. In the scenario above, our investor violated all three rules. He no longer owns equities, he is no longer diversified, and he bought the investment vehicle that was high and sold the investment vehicle that was low.

By now, I'm sure you can guess the result.

One year later, in 2009, long-term bonds were down 14.9%, small stocks up 47.54%.[49] To the extent our investor had actually owned these in his portfolio, he *should* have rebalanced his portfolio, and he *should* have sold off the excess bonds and bought more small stocks.

Actually, this is a very simple investment process—anyone can do it. The reality, however, is that our instincts are always pushing us in the wrong direction. Your instincts are your enemy, especially in the short-term, because we are all programmed for immediate present danger. This is your fight-or-flight response in action. Whether it's staying far away from a bad neighborhood at night or running from a sabertooth tiger, we're talking thousands of years of fear-based conditioning here.

We've only had a stock market for the past 200 years, and, believe me, our inexperience shows.

When instincts take over, we ignore the long-term and become hyper-focused on the next ten minutes. That strategy might have been great to get away from a sabertooth tiger, but it is disastrous when it comes to investing. Clearly, our instincts can lead us to self-destructive investing behavior.

Let's turn our attention to the "E" in our equation—emotions. Like instincts, emotions are part of being human, and we make many of our most important decisions based on them. For example, if you have ever been married, did you choose your partner and decide to get hitched based on a careful spreadsheet analysis of pros and cons of your prospective mate? If you did, you'd better burn it. Or did you marry your darling because you fell in love? Emotions make life more rich and fulfilling. If you understand how to use them prudently, they can help you become a better investor, but for most people they are at the very heart of destructive investing behavior.

Most folks don't want to admit they have this problem. They say the whole idea is to stay ahead of the curve and make money—and they'll do what it takes to "win." But when markets fall precipitously, like they did in 2008, all of a sudden those stable and secure investors aren't so stable and secure.

"Riding out" the steep decline all of a sudden doesn't seem to be such a great idea. When this occurs, a lot of people do what comes naturally and get the hell out—sell, sell, sell.

Sooner or later, the stock market stabilizes and even starts to grow in value. Wanting to get in on the action, investors edge back in and "buy at the high"—a classic blunder and a good way to lose money in the financial markets.

Think I'm kidding? The data bears out the "emotional mindset". A September 2005 study by the Stanford Graduate School of Business shows that "emotions can get in the way of making prudent financial decisions."[64]

Conducted by a team of researchers from Stanford University, Carnegie-Mellon University, and the University of Iowa, the study analyzed the investment decisions made by people who were unable to feel emotions due to brain lesions. The subjects' IQs were normal, and the parts of their brains responsible for logic and cognitive reasoning were unaffected.

Participants were given $20 at the beginning of a 20-round gambling game. At the beginning of each round, the participants were asked if they wanted to risk $1 on a coin toss. Those that said no kept their money. Those that agreed to participate earned $2.50 if they won the coin toss, but had to give up their $1 if they lost. Everyone then proceeded to the next round, in which the same steps were repeated.

Although the participants could decline to take part in any or all of the rounds, it made the most sense—financially speaking—to play each time because the potential return was so much greater than the potential loss.

"From a logical standpoint, the right thing to do was to invest in every round," said Baba Shiv, professor of marketing at the Stanford Graduate School of Business and co-author of the study. "With a 50-50 chance of winning, the expected value of playing each round was $1.25, while the expected value of not playing was just $1.00."

Of the 41 participants in the study, 15 had suffered damage in the areas of the brain that affected emotions, and these were the people who took the most profitable approach to the game. They invested in 84% of the rounds, earning an average of $25.70. In contrast, normal participants invested in just 58% of the rounds, earning an average of $22.80. To make sure that the study was not merely analyzing the difference between normal people and those with generic brain damage, the researchers also included control patients (participants with brain lesions, but not in areas of the brain involved in processing emotion). The control patients behaved in a manner similar to normal participants.

Fear seemed to play a large role in risk-avoidance behavior of the normal participants.

Interestingly, the study shows that all the players started out in roughly the same place: investing $1 rather than withholding it. But over time, the normal participants (and control patients) grew more cautious, declining to play almost as often as agreeing to risk $1 on the coin toss. "And what we found, through additional analysis, is that normal individuals were reacting emotionally to the outcome of the previous round," said Shiv. "If they lost money, they got scared and had the tendency to fall back and refuse to play further."

Researchers comment on the notion of an "equity premium puzzle" that has been the target of frequent studies by economists. The term refers to the large number of individuals who prefer to invest in bonds rather than stocks, even though stocks have historically provided a much higher rate of return. According to Shiv, there is widespread evidence that when the stock market starts to decline, people shift their retirement savings—that is, their long-term, not short-term, investments—from stocks to bonds. "Whereas all research suggests that, even after taking into account fluctuations in the market, overall people are better off investing in stocks in the long term," said Shiv. "Investors are not behaving in their own best financial interest. Something is going on that can't be explained logically."

Antoine Bechara, an associate professor of neurology at the University of Iowa, and a co-author of the study, theorizes that successful investors in the stock market might plausibly be called "functional psychopaths." These individuals are either much better at controlling their emotions, or perhaps they don't experience emotions with the same intensity that others do. "Many CEOs and many top lawyers might also share this trait," said Shiv. "Being less emotional can help you in certain situations."

Emotional investing isn't always a negative, study researchers say. The Stanford data shows that when people suffer a stroke or otherwise incur brain damage that affects the emotional side of the brain, it impacts their lives negatively in a number of significant ways: they typically lose their jobs and their friends, and they often experience bankruptcy. In general, they end up making social and financial decisions that are highly disadvantageous.

"True, the results of this study have serious implications for things like investing for retirement, something that is central to our lives," said Shiv. "At the same time, we want to qualify our findings, because by and large, if you look at most of the decisions we make in our lives, emotions are key to their success."

So here are some emotions that, as an investor, you might feel:

Mistrust

"It doesn't matter how sophisticated an advisor's charts are, or how much sense he makes, I just don't feel comfortable letting him handle my money."

Regret.

Another classic. "I'm not sure I should put my money in that fund. It has already lost 15%. Maybe I'll sell some of it tomorrow." That, obviously, is regret. Specifically, regretting having put money in the fund to begin with.

Envy.

"My boss made 25% on his money, and I only made 8%. Gosh, I wish I had that 25% too." Remember, portfolio envy can be very destructive.

Greed.

"I wish I'd known that stock was going up; I would have bought more." That's classic greed.

Loyalty.

Let's say that your dad worked at the same company all his life and left his money to you in his will. "It would be wrong to sell off my father's company stock just to diversify my portfolio and reallocate it to something more profitable." This is loyalty, however misplaced it may be.

Fear.

"What if the market drops tomorrow, and I lose it all?" That's the basic emotion of fear.

In the end, I'm a realist—and likely you are, too. That is also part of the human condition, although it can be buried deep down inside of us.

We all want the thing that will make us rich—right now. That's what emotions give us—these powerful realities that can change our bodies. Emotions aren't things that are just kind of up in our brain. They change our pulse, they change our sweat glands, and they actually make our heart race. Emotions are powerful, powerful things. Our emotions become a filter for the outside world. Now, some investment professionals will say, "Well, your job is to eliminate emotions from the investing process." Well, I've got bad news for you. You can't eliminate them from the process. You are human. It's not like you're Spock or Data from *Star Trek.* Emotions are going to be there no matter what we think or do.

The trick of becoming a successful investor is to turn those emotions into useful and powerful agents of change for the positive, and to eliminate and refrain from the negative emotions that are going to cause destruction.

As we examine the right side of the equation, it is easy to see that instincts combined with emotions make it extremely difficult for investors to remain disciplined even if they are cognitively aware of all the academic theories required for successful long-term investing. Unfortunately, it gets worse, much worse.

Perception is the way we use our senses to perceive the world we live in and the assumptions we make about the reality that surrounds us which just like instincts and emotions. Incorrect perception can destroy your portfolio.

The lens we look through.

In this picture, do you see two faces looking at each other, or do you see a goblet? It all depends on your perception. And in this example, you may be able to alter or switch your perception from seeing the glass to the faces. You have some control, but not all perception biases are so simple. Consider the case of the two tables. In the next picture,

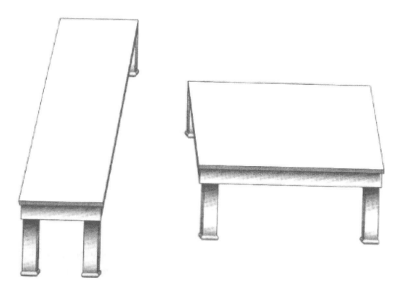

which is longer?

It appears that the table on the left is longer. In fact, both of the tables are the exact same length. If you don't believe me, measure them. But even when you know that the table on the left is the same, it is impossible to "see" it this way. Your eyes and your brain will not let you no matter how hard you try to "tell them" that they are the same. This is a visual illusion. We all see something that is not real, the first table being longer. Perception biases tend to make us "see things" that do not exist and "fail to see" things that do. In effect, our own senses and minds deceive and lie to us. Fortunately, our brains do this in "predictable" ways, meaning that we all tend to make the same mistakes and if you know what they are, you can guard against them.

"P" represents the perception factor in our formula. As we examine each one you should note that these are perception biases that affect investors, brokers, planners, and Wall Street Bullies. No one is exempt.

Hindsight Bias

The first distortion is Hindsight Bias. This is the tendency to believe you knew all along what was going to happen. In a recent workshop, an advisor told me that he knew the market was going to crash in 2008, in his words "It was obvious the market was overvalued, and I know it is not going to go up any time soon." This was April of 2010, just before a major market move up.

I pressed him, "Well, I'm wondering, if you knew it was going to crash, did you mortgage your house and borrow money from the bank and sell stocks short so you could make massive profits?" He was clearly frustrated with my question.

"Well, no" he replied. "That would have been a huge risk!" I dug deeper, "How could this be a risk if you knew it was going to crash? That would have been huge profit with no risk."

Only in hindsight did he know what would happen. But to him, it really felt like he knew all along. This false sense of certainty causes investors and advisors to speculate and gamble going forward. But if they had really known what was going to happen, they would have taken different actions.

Overconfidence Bias

In my seminars, I always play a game where I ask the audience to rate their own driving skills on a scale from one to ten with one being a terrible driver, ten being great, and five being average.

I then ask everybody to stand up who is above average. Typically, 90% of the room stands up. Statistically speaking, 40% of the room is delusional. Half should be below average. The next perception bias causes us to overestimate our own abilities. It is the Overconfidence Bias. From Wikipedia: the overconfidence effect is a well-established bias in which someone's subjective confidence in their judgment is greater than their objective accuracy. In some quizzes, people rate their answers as "99% certain," but they are wrong 40% of the time. Investors are overly-confident that they can beat the market and outsmart everyone else.

Familiarity Bias

One of the most frequent mistakes I see investors make is putting too much money into a single stock. I call this the Familiarity Bias. This is the tendency to believe that, because we know a great deal about someone or something, it is safe. Because of this bias, many people have a vast allocation of their own company's stock in their portfolio. Proctor and Gamble is a Fortune 500 company, and their headquarters is located in Cincinnati. Many P&G employees have huge holdings of their company stock. Over ten years ago, I met with a man who had approximately $5 million in this one stock. He was only six months away from retirement. I recommended that he sell the stock and keep the money in cash until he retired, and then prudently allocate it globally into over 12,000 stocks.

He told me that he had worked thirty years for the company, and he knew it wasn't a risk. I told him it wasn't prudent. Nobody should have all their money in any one stock, no matter how familiar they are with it. He blithely ignored my coaching. Six months later, the stock value had been cut in half. In six short months he lost $2.5 million—roughly

half of his life's savings.

Remember, familiarity does not equal safety. Never mistake the two. Just because you work at a company or recognize its logo or buy its products or services, does not make it a great investment. In fact, to be truly diversified you should not even recognize the vast majority of the company names in your equity allocation. The next time you are tempted to believe that familiarity equals good, recall these iconic companies and the losses investors faced who gambled on them.

Expertise Bias

Everybody likes to have a hero. I believe that is why super hero movies like *Spiderman*, *Iron Man*, *Captain America*, and *The Avengers* are so popular. We humans also like real world heroes like football quarterbacks or star baseball players and, of course, true heroes like firemen and policemen who risk their lives to save ours. It's nice to have someone to look up to who can save the day when things get tough. So, of course, it is only natural to have a desire to look to investing "superheroes" to help keep us safe and make us rich.

Some of our investing superheroes are the icons of Wall Street like Warren Buffet, Peter Lynch, John Paulson, or George Soros, even Donald Trump. Surely, these "masters of the universe" can flex their investing powers and help make us millions. I call this Expertise Bias, and it amounts to hero worship. You should remember that someone is always going to get lucky and beat the market. It doesn't make them a hero; it just makes them lucky.

Remember, there is zero correlation between a money manager's ability to pick the best stocks in one period and repeat that feat the next period. Like monkeys flipping coins, it is random. Deep within the prospectus of every active fund manager is the warning, "Past performance does not guarantee future results." This is an admission of guilt required by law, and you should heed its warning. Think of it this way, not even Peter Lynch can find the next Peter Lynch.

But Wall Street doesn't want you to know that and as soon as their hot streak runs out, they will proudly award a new expert and claim them supreme. Don't fall for Expertise Bias.

Anecdotal Evidence Bias

One of the most powerful tools Wall Street Bullies and the media use to manipulate investors is anecdotal evidence. I live in Ohio and we have the lottery here. Perhaps you have one in your state too. Ohio's lottery slogan is "Chances are you'll have fun." That is a complete lie. Chances are you'll lose your money. Perhaps a ticket buyer may experience a brief high as the neurons in his brain receive a shot of dopamine at the fantasy of winning; other than that, the expected return on lottery tickets is negative. In fact, if I gave you the opportunity to own a million dollars of large U.S. stocks versus a million dollars in lottery tickets, you would truly be delusional if you chose the tickets. Yet millions of people purchase them every day.

Consider this picture of the Judsons that I found on the Internet. They won ninety-

two million dollars. Nice work if you can get it. The lottery commissioners (and their highly-paid marketing arm) use pictures like this, pure anecdotal evidence, to seduce you into playing. They don't show you pictures of all the people who lost, all the people who have become gambling addicts, and all the people who squandered their life's savings. The lottery hopes that this convinces you to "play" and "play often." They don't want you to know that, statistically speaking, you would have a better chance of catching a ping-pong ball dropped out of an airplane. The investment industry is just as bad; they are all too eager to put lucky hedge fund managers who made billions on a "hot" sector that just made 100% on the cover of a magazine. Anytime you see those you should think— Anecdotal Evidence—which is no evidence at all.

Great Story Bias

Everybody loves a great story. But in the investing world "good stories" are dangerous. Remember that recent high returns and a good story do not a good investment make. Global Crossing had a "good story." Their stock was skyrocketing, the Internet was hot, and they were going to connect the world with fiber cables at the bottom of the ocean. It was a "can't lose" high-tech company. Many investors lost their life's savings "betting" on Global Crossing. It felt like a sure thing, and they had a great story.

Stories mesmerize us, and destroy critical thinking. Prudent long-term investing should be boring; it has nothing to do with glitz, glamour, and amazing tales of "can't lose" companies.

Control Bias

Control Bias is the false perception that if we "do something" we are in control. When it comes to investing, many people feel a sense of control when they are actively making trades. But this sense of control is completely false. When you trade, you are out of control. This behavior is destructive both to your peace of mind and your portfolio. Slot machines are a good example of this. Gamblers believe that the more they pull the arm on the machine, the higher their chances of getting the preferred outcome (winning money). The reality is that the more they pull that arm, the greater their chances of losing. Gambling, like frequent trading, is a loser's game. (And don't forget: the trading-house always wins.) Remember, activity does not equal control.

False Patterning

Perhaps the most destructive perception bias is False Patterning. Human beings are hard wired to see and find patterns. Prehistoric man "saw" the patterns of migrating animals and planned hunts around that pattern or observed the seasons and "saw" the pattern of planting and harvesting. We are so hard-wired to see patterns that we even see them when they don't exist. This is especially true when it comes to investing. Remember that it takes rigorous academic study to determine market premiums. It takes at least sixty-four years of data to discern anything meaningful about a returns series. Burn that number into your head, dear Main Street investor. But most people see a false pattern after just a few years of market data. This is how investors get seduced into bubbles. Consider just a few of the most recent false patterns, always accompanied by a "good story" by the way, that sucked in tons of investors. U.S. Growth Stocks from September 1998 to August 2000 made an astounding 35.4% rate of annualized return.[49] Wall Street Bullies and prognosticators deemed this the "New Paradigm." Suddenly, you only needed Growth stocks to be diversified. Note: this was only a short, random period of returns, and not nearly enough time to discern anything statistically meaningful.

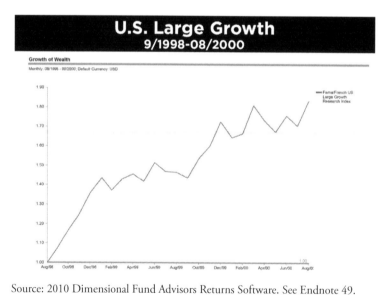

Source: 2010 Dimensional Fund Advisors Returns Software. See Endnote 49.

As the market raged, more and more people got in at the top. In the subsequent period, from September 2000 to July 2002, large U.S. growth stocks crashed and received a negative 26.3% annualized rate of return.

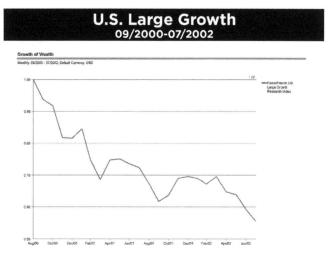

2010 Dimensional Fund Advisors Returns Software. Tech stocks are represented by the NASDAQ composite index. See Endnote 49.

But it got even worse. Tech Stocks raged from October 1998 to March 2000.

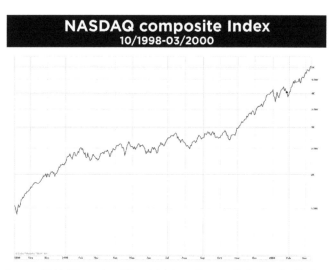

Source: 2010 Dimensional Fund Advisors Returns Software. See Endnote 49.

During that period, tech stocks produced an annualized rate of return of 94.21%.

And no, that's not a misprint. Everybody wanted tech! And it had a great story to go with the high performance. "Hey," people said, "the Internet is the future. These companies are on the ground floor. It's going to change everything. This is a can't-miss, once-in-a-lifetime opportunity." So in typical form most people got in at the top and—wait for it—lost an annualized -40.91% over the period of March 2000 to September 2002.[49]

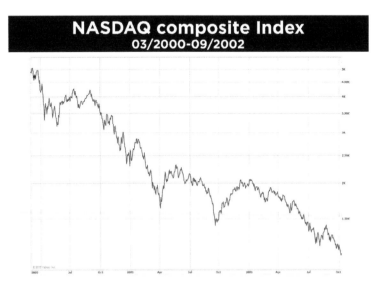

2010 Dimensional Fund Advisors Returns Software. Tech stocks are represented by the NASDAQ composite index. See Endnote 49.

Necessary Lie Syndrome

A necessary lie is a lie we tell ourselves just before we engage in an unhealthy or dysfunctional behavior. When it comes to drinking, for people who drink to excess, the lie is "I'll have just one." For overeating the lie is, "I'll start my diet tomorrow." For gamblers it's, "I'll stop when I get even." And for speculation masquerading as investing it is, "This time it will be different."

In other words, "I really do know what is going to happen this time, but what I am getting ready to do is not speculating, it's a sure thing." If you try, you can probably think of a time in your life when you have told yourself a lie just before you acted in a way that was self-destructive and you may be able to identify times when you have done it while investing. This is the brutal type of self-assessment that is required to be a successful investor. If you cannot be honest with yourself about your own mental biases, you will never be a successful investor.

Behavior Is the Most Important Factor of All

If you are hoping that seeing these perception problems on paper one time will free you from their effects—you are wrong. Perception dysfunctions are perpetual and persistent. Seeing them once does not solve the problem. Without the proper discipline and the ability to avoid these perception biases, instinct and emotions will call the shots—you will have little hope. Let's revisit our formula.

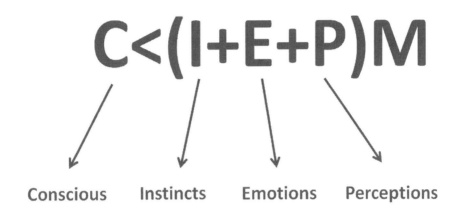

$$C<(I+E+P)M$$

Conscious   Instincts   Emotions   Perceptions

To be successful, the cognitive mind must have greater power than the instincts, emotions, and perceptions. This is a daunting task. But what does the "M" stand for? It represents the financial pornography of the investing media. Believe me, they do not have your best interest at heart and your peace of mind is not anywhere on the list of things they are concerned about. They need readers and viewers to sell advertising. It is all about profits and the way to keep you watching and reading is to tap into your emotions, instincts and perception biases. They magnify the urge to speculate and gamble. Many of them believe it is their job to help you forecast the future, a futile exercise. They believe the lies and perpetuate the myths. If it bleeds it leads, and if it is up 100% in the last year, everybody will be talking about it, no matter how imprudent it is. Think of this as financial pornography. Its job is to seduce and titillate.

Studies show that we are all poor judges of our own future actions. It is difficult for us to gauge our own actions in a "hot state." For example, I can show an investor whose portfolio mix could lose 10% in a down market. "Can you live with that?" I ask. In the calm of my office, the answer is, "Sure, I won't panic." But it is hard for them to imagine what it will really be like when the economy goes into recession, and every news story and talking head is hammering them about the pending financial Armageddon. In the heat of the moment, the deluge of doom and gloom can eventually take over and skew behavior.

Sex and investing have one thing in common, we make stupid decisions in a hot state; and unlike sexual pornography (that you must seek out)—financial pornography is everywhere, and it will come to you! Both are destructive. I have witnessed first-hand investors and advisors being seduced by the dark side and blow their life's savings. It is like Dr. Jekyll and Mr. Hyde. One moment, calm and reasonable; the next, inner nature takes control and wreaks havoc. Because of this problem, events are always viewed in the

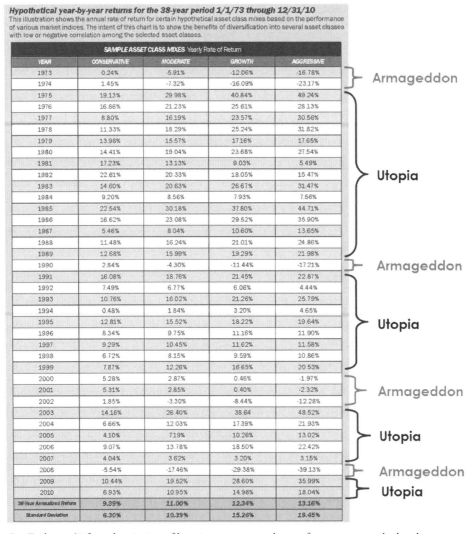

See Endnote 49 for a description of how investment market performance was calculated.

extremes. The media magnifies performance into Armageddon or Utopia based on recent returns.

When returns are positive, it is a new Utopia where everybody is getting rich; when returns are bad it's Armageddon, the end of the world and it's never going to get better. The reality is that nothing lasts forever. Remember, it didn't come to stay, it came to pass. Long-term investing is life-long investing.

The instinct, emotion, and perception biases are magnified by media biases, and their combined effect can be catastrophic. This is why their combined power to determine behavior outweighs the cognitive reasoning needed to navigate the fog of investing. To be prudent, you, the investor, must find a way to strengthen the left side of the equation so that your instincts, emotions, and false perceptions are not calling the shots. This is not an easy task, but it is achievable.

The Fourth (and Most Important) Factor

The fourth factor is behavior, which knowledge alone cannot overcome. In my experience, behavior trumps all other factors. Think about it:

- The market premium is useless.

- The small premium is useless.

- The value premium is useless.

Nothing works—nothing—without appropriate behavior. Fortunately, your behavior is within your power to control. Your behavior is the critical function, the critical factor, the fourth factor that is necessary to outwit, outsmart, and out-invest Wall Street. If you don't control your behavior, you'll become a victim of Wall Street.

Hey, the big money guys on Wall Street know it. It's about time you knew it, too.

10

FOLLOWING THE HERD TO SLAUGHTER

*"A truly strong person does not need the approval of others any more
than the lion needs the approval of sheep."*

—Vernon Howard

THE COMPLEXITY OF INVESTING and the overwhelming tendency to perpetuate self-
destructive investing behavior makes it seem only natural to seek professional help.
Many Americans turn to financial planners, brokers, or fee-based money managers. But
are planners as a whole any better than Main Street investors when it comes to following
the simple rules of investing, or are they part of the problem?

Are they true defenders and protectors of disciplined investing, or is this a classic case
of the fox guarding the chicken coop? As I will demonstrate, the average planner is not
any more seasoned and prudent than the average investor. In short, planners can be bullies
too.

*"A good financial advisor takes your money and his experience and turns
it into his money and your experience."*

—Anonymous

Maybe you've heard this joke.

The Wilsons invite their new neighbors over for dinner. During the meal, Mr. Wilson
is asked what he does for a living. Ten-year-old Tommy Wilson jumps in and declares,
"My dad is a fisherman! "

His mother immediately admonishes Tommy. "Son, why did you say that? Your daddy
is a financial advisor—not a fisherman."

"No way, Mom," says the boy. "Every time we visit dad at work and he hangs up the phone, he laughs, rubs his hands together, and says 'I just caught another fish.'"

Good joke, right? Or maybe you think that's too harsh toward financial advisors? Not by a long shot. If anything, I'm pulling my punches on the profession.

Let's face facts. Financial advisors are human too, and they're not immune from instincts, emotions, or perception distortions.

In fact they're more susceptible to them, and that makes them part of the Wall Street problem, not part of the solution.

Just how bad is that problem? Increasingly, the data shows investors are being ripped off by financial advisors. I'll spend the rest of this chapter showing you how and why that is so.

One Big Way Advisors Fail Their Clients

I see this one all the time—advisors not having enough respect for their clients (or themselves) to answer an investor's question clearly and thoroughly.

Rule #1 of client relationships is that the client has a right to know what the advisor is doing with his or her money. That means full disclosure. It's the advisor's responsibility to provide those answers.

Instead, I see advisors dodging and ducking those questions or giving incomplete answers.

This is the way the industry is purposely designed. There is a distinct separation of what happens behind the closed doors of broker dealers, fund companies, and planners and what they actually share with investors. For example, many planners hold themselves out to be wise and disciplined advocates for investors, but studies verify that planners who sell commission-based mutual funds are no more disciplined than investors trying to remain disciplined on their own.

In many cases it is hardly the advisor's fault. They are simply following the instructions and guidance of their broker-dealer or life insurance company employers. The grand architect of the investing schemes they use are created and packaged by the Wall Street type firms that employ them. They are just following orders. In addition, they have been taught by the industry to become a jack-of-all-trades but the master of none.

They futilely attempt to comprehend everything, a daunting task. Retirement planning, tax planning, estate planning, health insurance, life insurance, disability insurance, financial planning. The list goes on ad infinitum, including, of course, investment advice.

Early in my career, I fell into this business model. I was told by the companies I sold for that the more services I offered, the more I would sell, and the more money I would make. I was all things to all people. After a quarter of a century in the industry, I am convinced no one can effectively do it all. It's just too much. Don't get me wrong, all of these areas are important. I just don't believe that one person can do everything. That is why I have dedicated my life to only one part of the process—prudent investing.

Believe me when I say it is the most important piece of the planning pie! Why? Because if you are not capable of managing your portfolio, no amount of planning can save you. Mess up this piece and you are in trouble.

It's Academic

Let me kick things off with a Harvard University study that says financial advisors actually reinforce negative investor behavior, when they should be correcting them.

The study, led by Harvard economics professor Sendhil Mullainathan, says that financial advisors are merely "yes-men," a tendency that tends to keep cash in company stock and avoid portfolio diversification.[65]

The Harvard study commissioned actors to visit Boston-area financial advisors on nearly 300 occasions in 2008. Each actor played the role of an investor seeking sound advice.

The actors were split up into four groups, based on investment strategy. One group was invested mainly in index funds; a second told advisors they were interested in actively seeking a new, hot market sector; a third said 30% of their assets were tied to their employer's stock; and the last said they owned only cash assets.

Most often, the actors received advice that matched the slants of their current portfolios.

For example, cash-heavy investors were told to invest in index funds, seekers of hot stocks were pointed toward hands-on investments and those with company stock were usually told to hold on to their company shares. Only 40% of advisors told those with company stock to diversify their portfolios, despite the obvious benefit the investor (and the planner, due to commission) would have received from a better yield.

It's my belief that financial advisors don't want to upend the gravy boat, and thus tend to tell clients what they want to hear.

At the end of the day, planners need to get paid. They can't work for free. Instead of helping you fight your instincts, emotions and perception biases, they inadvertently use them against you. If you are afraid, well then, they sell you something "safe." If you just saw a gold commercial and you have fallen victim to false patterning and the good story bias, well then, chances are you are going to buy gold. The planners can even convince themselves, as you will see, that they are doing the right thing.

Another study—this one from the Employee Benefit Research Institute—concludes that advisors avoid conflict and confrontation for fear investors would not return if they did not hear what they wanted to hear. Investors share a lot of the blame, too. The EBRI report found that two-thirds of investors were interested in the services of an analyst only if the analyst's advice matched their own investing philosophy.[66]

Like I said, I don't want to place the entire burden of our dysfunctional individual investment system squarely on the shoulders of financial advisors. That wouldn't be fair.

After all, investment advisors are hardly immune to the instincts, emotions, or perception distortions that I described in Chapter Nine. In fact, they are even more susceptible to them than investors are. Most advisors are at least part of the problem, so what would be fair is to highlight the advisor biases. First, for the investors, so they'll know and be able to perceive them. Second, for the advisors who are truly coaches, so they understand the distinction of how they're different from everybody else.

I also want to help you distinguish what an investor coach will help you achieve that a simple planner never will. In other words, how to tell a true coach from a planner.

Another Way Advisors Fail Their Clients

Financial advisors like to show the world how smart they are—book-smart at least— and usually do that by using a lot of big words and exotic terms they learned in business school, but this stuff usually goes right over the client's head.

There's no law that says you have to sound like a Wharton finance professor to communicate with your clients. Or, more precisely, talk down to your clients.

Your coach's job is simply to clarify and cut through the complexity. If your coach doesn't use plain old everyday Main Street language, get a new coach.

Advisor Biases

These are perception biases that are specific to planners and money managers. Remember, they also fall prey to the perception biases outlined in chapter nine.

You can argue that financial advisors don't intentionally create various investment biases, and I'll buy that. It's probably not innate and likely not intentional. Advisors probably don't even realize they have the biases I'm about to point out.

But, believe me, their biases are there—just as prevalent as other human emotions like love, hate, jealousy or gratitude.

I'm no psychologist and I'll leave the psychoanalysis to the professionals, but I've been in the business long enough to know embedded attitudes about Wall Street and investing when I see them.

In that regard, these are some of the worst biases I see from financial advisors.

Confusion Bias

One of the most alarming drawbacks among financial advisors today is the culture of Confusion Bias.

By definition, Confusion Bias means taking financial information and confusing investors, so much so that those investors—who are understandably reluctant to reveal their alleged ignorance of financial matters—just sign off on whatever recommendation the financial advisor makes.

It's almost like a Jedi mind trick. The advisor unloads all the minutia and complexity they can on a given investment strategy in hopes that the client will have a problems separating reality from fiction.

In the end, the advisor pulls an Obi Wan Kenobi and says something to the effect of, "Pay no attention to my gold speculation advice. You will buy this commodity."

But what happens if the Confusion Bias results in a lousy investment result in which the client loses a ton of money?

The advisors I know try to pretend the issue never existed, like they have a magic eraser to wipe your memory clean. Do they really think we're that stupid? Do they think we're stupid enough to believe them when they say the market is going to 35,000 and when it doesn't, we won't notice? Unfortunately, the problem is most investors don't catch it because they don't keep track of all the myriad forecasts, outlooks, and advice that spew out of Wall Street and the advisory community.

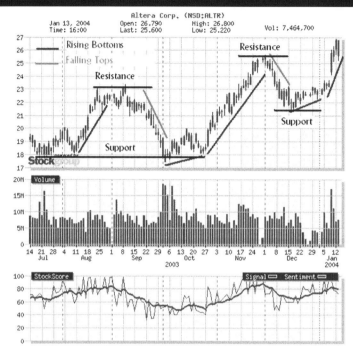

This graph shows an example of confusion bias. So-called traders will use stock charts and pretend to "read" them. When you see this, think of a palm reader or a tea leaf reader. This is all random data, but they will pretend to use it to predict short-term moves—Confusion Bias.

Fee Bias

Another problem with investment advisors is the Fee Bias. There's a myth that has taken hold that becoming a registered investment advisor and charging a fee eliminates conflicts of interest and assures the prudent fiduciary behavior of both advisor and investor.

Investors are often told that advising them to switch an individual retirement account to another investment vehicle and being charged a fee for that advice eliminates the conflicts of interest associated with commissions and insures fiduciary behavior by the advisor. The reality is that, while fees eliminate some conflicts of interest, there are other fees that advisors tend to keep a lid on. So fee-based advice only eliminates one form of conflict, which is trading on commissions.

Here's an example of what I call "bad mojo." Let's assume we have an investor with $1 million in assets, and she is working with an advisor who charges a 1% annual fee ($10,000 in fees goes to the advisor).

Well, if the advisor is doing a bang-up job, great—that $10,000 fee is well worth it. But let's say the investor panics, the stock market goes down, and she comes in and delivers the big ultimatum, "I want to move all my money to cash, or else I'm going somewhere else."

Now the advisor has a problem, with two possible outcomes (which I call "potential advisor behavior").

1. Go along to get along.

Wanting to keep the fees, the advisor agrees to move all of the client's assets to cash, thus enabling a dysfunctional investment process. Moving to cash is the last thing you want to do in a bear market.

2. Stand up to the client.

The other option is to refuse to comply with the request, and risk losing the client—and the $10,000 in annual fees. If the investor does take the money somewhere else, the advisor actually makes $0 in fees. If the advisor can convince the investor to sit tight and the market rebounds by 10%, then both the client and the advisor make out better with $100,000 more to the client and $1,000 more to the financial advisor.

What usually happens? The reality is that when advisors are faced with this dilemma, they choose Option #1 *nearly every time*. Chances are that more than one client will make the threat to cut and run—so the advisor is threatened with the loss of not just one client's fees, but several, which could represent a significant portion of the advisor's income.

Under that strain, it's much easier to give in to the client and move the assets to cash. That's the wrong move, of course, and it leads to encouraging more dysfunctional behavior. But advisors are people too, and they want to keep generating those fees.

A few years ago, I was talking to a reporter in New York City, and I explained that financial advisors should never enable dysfunctional behavior for the investor. To my surprise, the reporter was dumbfounded. She told me, with more than a hint of disapproval, "It's their money." I answered, "Yes, it's their money, and they have the right to move it anywhere they want. However, to give in to the investor's threat would be like a drug counselor scoring drugs for an addicted client just so they won't lose them. It's becoming an enabler." A coach gets paid not to be an enabler but to maintain discipline even when (heck, especially when) it's painful.

As an investment advisor, when someone wants to engage in dysfunctional behavior, the advisor, if truly a coach, will stand up to the client and say, "Even if it benefits me, I won't be a party to dysfunctional enabling behavior that hurts the investor." That's the difference between a garden-variety financial advisor and a true coach.

Yes, I understand the financial pressure a down market can have on an advisor. It impacts personal income, so it's easy to see the advisor's financial motivation, and the ultimate good of the investor is not always in alignment. I've seen many advisors actually cave in to this type of pressure.

This means that you must find a coach who will refuse to facilitate destructive behavior even when threatened with a loss of income. This is not an easy task, I assure you. In the crash of 2008 and early 2009, I fired over 300 investors who insisted on panicking. I refused to be part of the problem. Shortly after they moved their money, the market came raging back.

Rationalization Bias

When I talk to advisors, I ask them, "Why would you fold, and do the wrong thing for your client? You knew that it was dysfunctional and not in the clients' best interest." Invariably they say, "Well, I know it's really not what I should have done for them, but they're still better off with me instead of someone else." That's a wholesale rationalization. The advisor tries to rationalize that the client is somehow better off, even though the advisor's behavior is as misguided as the investors' behavior.

This, of course, is a lie advisors tell themselves in order to allow destructive behavior. You must find a coach that will help you stand up to the Wall Street Bullies and their lies, not facilitate the lies of speculating and gambling. The coach must truly put your welfare ahead of his and refuse to take part in dysfunctional gambling. Take it from me—that's a rare breed.

Herding Bias

In the animal world, many creatures have a herding bias to protect themselves from predators or negative situations. When threatened, most animals try to get as close to the middle of the herd as they can. Zoologists call it "safety in the center." The pressure to conform to group behavior is not compromised from within the group, but impacted from outside, by external threats. When the environment is uncertain (with predators around, or in dangerous situations), herding causes investors to move toward the center, too. There are two main reasons for this behavior:

1. Conventional advisors protect themselves from danger in a market environment in which everybody is predicting danger, and the vibe is negative.

Herd advisors think, "If the market goes down, I'll be correct for getting out." But if the market goes up, they can say, "Hey, I'm not the only one that got fooled; everybody was doing it."

In essence, they will have the typically adolescent excuse, "Don't blame me. Everybody was doing it." Even if it is not smart or prudent, they have the comfort of being in their peer group.

2. Another reason that conventional advisors "herd up" is because they really don't know what to do, so they look to the general consensus for clues.

They sincerely figure, "If everybody else is doing it, it must be the right thing to do."

Sociologists have a test in which one person is placed on the street in New York City looking up at the sky (they're not actually looking at anything). Researchers found that if you have one person looking up when pedestrians walk by, maybe 1 in 10 will actually look up to see what's up there. Usually, they find nothing; so they keep walking. But when three people are all looking up, then there's a mindset called "reality agreement" in which more people will stop and look up to the sky. If you put 15 people on the street looking up, virtually everyone passing by will stop and look up, too. Essentially, most people lack the analytical skills to determine the reality of the situation, so they just assume everybody else is right. The same thing goes with investing. When everybody is panicking, investors and advisors figure there must be a good reason—so they panic, too.

I see advisors make this mistake all the time. Just because everybody else is doing it, they do it too. To make matters worse, many of them are aware of the academic tenets of prudent investing and will invoke the appropriate language while simply following the herd. For example, they will talk about diversifying with gold to improve the portfolio. What they are really doing is following the crowd and chasing hot sectors. Gold is extremely volatile and (after taxes and inflation) has actually posted historical negative returns.[67] It is a terrible diversifier. In short, if everybody is dumping money into it, it is not prudent. Successful investing requires your coach to stay strong, be different, and stand up to the herd.

Guilt Bias

I saw Guilt Bias in 2008 and 2009, just when the Great Recession was hitting its stride. Financial advisors actually saw investors come in and knew they were frustrated, afraid, fearful, and losing money. Naturally, the advisor felt bad about the situation. In those situations, it's similar to a child that's going through hard times in school. Quite recently, my wife and I enrolled our children in a private school, which we figured would be better for them than the public school they attended. At the same time, we were very afraid because our kids were feeling pain and fear. Consequently, we were feeling some guilt, because they had to go through that anxious experience. But when a financial advisor takes on the guilt and the fear, it enables dysfunctional behavior on the investor's part. The problem? You can't have guilt when it comes to an investor's behavior, and it's a terrible thing for an advisor to do.

After several months of coaching our kids, they began to fit in at their new school. Their grades went up, they became more engaged in their extra-curricular events, and they made new friends. But the transition was not easy. To become a seasoned investor, you will need a coach who does not feel sorry for you when times are hard and give in to the fear and pain. They must stay strong and help you move through the economic chaos without taking the easy way out. You want to find a coach who has ruthless compassion and who will never cosign your own BS when you are experiencing some fear or doubt. You want them to be equally frank when markets are raging, and you're tempted to take too much risk. In my experience, prudence is never popular. A good coach doesn't need your money or your approval for their own selfish reasons. They should be willing to stay tough and stand up to you (in a caring way) when the going gets tough.

Lazy Bias

Speaking of kids, it's just easier to give them what they want. Hey, even I've been guilty of this behavior. Sometimes we give our kids an extra cookie to get them to calm down. Or adults may decide to pass on that healthy walk in the woods because the football game is on the tube.

This is the path of least resistance. Instead of having difficult conversations and addressing real issues, it is just easier to let things slide. After all, dealing with investors' feelings, emotions and flawed perceptions takes a lot of time and education. It is just easier to give them what they are seeing on TV and just "phone it in." Take the path of least resistance. Life is hard enough, why make it harder? Let's face it, prudent, long-term investing is hard work. It takes focus, time, energy and maturity. Many advisors just don't want to work this hard.

Value-Add Bias

The Value-Add Bias means that many advisors have difficulty communicating to their investors the true value of discipline, diversification, and market rates of return, so they fall back on selling past performance. Advisors may feel they have to jazz up the portfolio in some way to appeal to the investor or to attract them. It gets to be something of a feeding frenzy. So if gold is hot, they'll add gold. If options are hot, they'll add options. If futures are hot, they'll add futures, because they're trying to prove that they're doing something to add value, when in reality, they're just selling past performance. That's the fast lane to portfolio destruction.

These perception biases have real world effects on what advisors recommend to their clients and the positive or negative returns they receive. This is not just theoretical. These biases have destroyed massive amounts of wealth in the last two decades. I have listed them side by side. Note that the advisor biases are unique to them but advisors also suffer from the investor biases.

Investor Biases	Advisor Biases
Hindsight Bias	Confusion Bias
Overconfidence Bias	Fee Bias
Familiarity Bias	Rationalization Bias
Expertise Bias	Guilt Bias
Anecdotal Evidence Bias	Lazy Bias
Great Story Bias	Value-Add Bias
Control Bias	
False Patterning Bias	
Necessary Lie Syndrome	

If you really examine each of these investor biases—Hindsight Bias, Overconfidence Bias, Familiarity Bias, Expertise Bias, Anecdotal Evidence Bias, Great Story Bias, Control Bias, False Patterning Bias, and Necessary Lie Syndrome—today's financial advisor has some or even all of these traits. Advisors are human too and aren't immune to human frailties like guilt, laziness, or rationalization.

But very few of them take the steps needed to overcome these biases.

Let's say I'm an investor who only occasionally glances at the stock market—maybe they see something on CNBC, or pick up an investment brochure. But the so-called investment professional is different, they're looking at the financial markets and the investment world on a 24/7 basis.

As they immerse themselves in the morass of the money world, they are being hit by more information, more confusion, more herding bias, more guilt bias, and their whole life is determined (their whole future) by the profitability of their company. Consequently, there's more stress and anxiety for them than there is for the investor.

The more you examine the bias issue, you begin to understand that advisors are part of the problem; because any time there was a mass exodus it was inevitably advisor-driven.

The Pied Piper Effect

It's like these advisors are the pied piper, and they lead all of these clients at the same time into dysfunctional behavior. As I said, it's almost always driven by the advisor;

hardly ever by the investor. There's good news and bad news in that scenario. The bad news is, if you have the wrong advisor, who's not really a coach and falls prey to these biases, you're in danger. The good news, as an investor, is if you have the right coach and the right support group, you're probably going to do fine.

Coach versus Planner

First and foremost, almost all Main Street investors will need a good coach to educate, motivate, and help them to maintain the right behaviors. In my opinion, this is the single most important thing you can do for your financial future. A good coach will not tell you what to do, but will help you ask the right questions and allow you to find the right answers. Fixing your portfolio is likely your most pressing financial issue. No doubt financial planning is important, especially for investors with significant assets and tax issues; and there are many good technical planners. In my experience the investing piece of the puzzle is the most complex. Find a coach first, then a planner. Of the two, a coach is more important.

One More Way Advisors Are Failing Their Clients

Another big mistake I see from the advisory community is the quality (or lack of it) of their investment plans.

Way too often, I talk to advisors who are offering canned and pre-packaged portfolio construction ideas that I can spot a mile away. They probably got them from some industry conference or from one of the big financial institutions when those advisors were young and just starting out.

You can't use a one-size-fits-all approach with investors. Everyone has different income levels, different goals, and different risk levels.

Cookie-cutter plans just don't cut it.

The heart of the problem:

$$C<(I+E+P)M$$

Referring to our theoretical construct again, several things are clear:

1. What people know or think they know about investing is wrong.
2. Instincts and emotions cause us to act impulsively.
3. The lens through which we see the world is flawed.
4. The media magnifies our instincts, emotions, and perception biases.

Because of this, most investors and their planners violate the three simple rules of investing with tragic and disastrous results. If things are to change, investor coaches and their clients must find a way to strengthen the left side of the equation so that it can override the right side. The "less than" symbols must be flipped to a "greater than" symbol, and that is what the remainder of this book will focus on.

11

JOHN AND THE GENIE
AN INVESTING PARABLE

"A person often meets his destiny on the road he took to avoid it."

–Jean de la Fontaine

IT WAS THREE O'CLOCK IN THE MORNING and John told himself he should be asleep, but he wasn't. He was walking the pier alone in Santa Monica. The market wouldn't even open in New York for another three and a half hours. As you might expect, the pier was deserted except for a flock of seagulls and the occasional pelican sleeping on a piling. "Man those are ugly birds," he thought to himself. The rollercoaster stood silently and foreboding at the end of the pier. "A roller coaster on a pier, who the hell thought of that?" No one answered.

The air was chilly and his University of Berkeley sweatshirt was not enough to shelter him from the cold. It had been a terrible year. His father died after a long battle with Alzheimer's, and he buried him last January. It was November now. He was an only child, and his mother and father were divorced for ten years. He had visited his father a couple of times a month in the care facility. His mother remarried, collected $10,000 per month in spousal support payments, but frankly hated his father's guts and she was no help at all with the burden. He even suspected she took some perverse joy in his father's illness.

John's father had amassed a small fortune in the clothing and fashion industry as a designer. John admired his dedication and hard work, but fashion bored John to tears. His father had a long string of "woman friends," mostly models, but he never remarried. So when he died, he left his only son $3 million. At one point it had been $6 million, but when the market crashed in 2001, the fifty companies that his father owned in what he thought was a diversified portfolio lost half its value overnight.

After a short and angry call to his broker, his father sold it all and put it in CDs. Shortly after he sold, the market recovered, but John's father swore never to get in the market again. The losses were over a decade old.

Several years ago when John was appointed his father's guardian, he simply let the money sit in the bank. John was busy studying for his master's degree in economics from Berkeley. He had an amazing mind for mathematics, and he prided himself on the ability to solve sophisticated theorems and equations. The stress of watching his father deteriorate was taking its toll and his saving grace was his girlfriend, Harper. She was a fourth-year undergrad majoring in psychology.

While John could be negative and self-absorbed, Harper was kind, loving, and generous to a fault. When the stress of school and dealing with his father became too much, Harper always lifted him out of his self-pity and hyper-intellectualism. She had a good heart. John was lucky and he knew it. But he had lost Harper too, and over something as petty as money.

That spring, John finished his master's thesis, "The Inefficient Pricing of Market Sectors and Leveraged Arbitrage Trading." It revolved around several formulas, which depended on the systematic mispricing of market sectors that would "theoretically" allow an astute mathematician to make trades on margin with stop losses and extract major double-digit returns without taking any real risk. His professor at Berkeley loved his ideas and encouraged him to refine his research while he went for his doctorate. He met Harper at Starbucks for coffee between classes to tell her the good news.

"Well, they loved it. Three of the four professors actually clapped when I was done with my oral presentation."

"Honey, that is awesome. Congratulations. Now you can get your doctorate. We should go out tonight and celebrate!"

"That sounds great. How about sushi? My treat. And by the way, I am not sure about going for my doctorate. I think my formulas are sound enough that I can take huge profits from the market with little risk. All of my simulations prove it. Over the last twenty years, I would have made a killing trading on these formulas. Harper, it is literally a free lunch, and I'm the guy who cracked the code. I don't need a doctorate. My father left me three million bucks, and it's just sitting there in CDs. I can use that to start my own day-trading company. Gold, commodities, and hedge funds have been going through the roof, and with my formulas I can leverage that up and get out in the time if they fall. This is a no-brainer. I'll find the stocks that are mispriced. After all, not everybody has a master's from Berkeley, and then I can trade online."

"But, John, we had a plan. Two doctorates, finish college, get married—family, kids, little house, white picket fence… remember?" "Right, but this way we can get there faster. I still want all those things. I just want to put my math to work."

"Honey, I don't want to rain on your parade, but in my field, it is all but impossible to predict even one person's behavior. There is no formula known to mankind that will allow you to predict the behavior of billions of people all over the world. I'm not a math major or economist, but it defies common sense. Are you telling me you are the only person in the world who knows this formula? John, I love you and I have your back, but I just don't know about this."

"It's all going to work out. Hey, if the E-Trade baby can do it, I should have no problem. It will be all right." Harper kissed him and said, "I love you." "I love you, too," he said, and in that moment he truly meant it.

But it wasn't all right. It was a long way from all right. At first everything went according to plan. John opened an online trading account. Set up three screens, opened an account with $300,000 dollars and began trading. Quickly, he grew his account to $600,000. Based on three months of trading, he proved to himself that his math was flawless and transferred the rest of his inheritance into his trading account. He bragged to Harper.

"Just imagine, if I could double $300,000 in three months what could I do with the whole three million? I really can identify mispriced stocks. But not just that, it works on alternatives like oil and gas, commodities, gold, real estate, bonds. This is a license to steal."

For the next several months the market was flat, and John's account stayed at $3.3 million. It seemed his formula was not "identifying" the right stocks or sectors. But he was sure things would turn around. But over the next several months he lost the original $300,000 profits, plus an additional $400,000. He was down to $2.6 million.

He began shutting himself in his apartment for days at a time. He had to figure out what was going wrong. His stop losses were helping limit some of the downside, but there were days when the market triggered the sell but then went back up higher than the loss would have been. Harper begged him to come out and spend some time in the "real world," but he was sure if he did more research he could get the money back. One month when his indicators were telling him that the market was overvalued to sell it short, the market went up 20%.

He was becoming a hermit, totally obsessed with the market and proving he could beat it. After another quarter of trading he was down to $1.5 million. How could this be happening? He frequently talked to himself. *The market is up 30%, but I have managed to miss the "up days" because of stop losses. This is not supposed to work this way. What the hell is going on?* He buried himself even deeper in his work.

And that is when Harper sent him an e-mail. It was short and to the point:

> Dear John,
> I have not seen you in two weeks. You never answer the phone, and I don't even know you anymore. I know this is a crappy way to do this, but you have left me no alternative. This is not a healthy, loving relationship and because of that I cannot be in it. I deserve more. Please do not call me. I need time to think. Please respect my boundaries. I have respected yours.
>
>   –Harper

If he was being honest with himself, he knew this was coming. This was not an idle threat to get his attention. Both of her parents were alcoholics, and Harper had dedicated herself to a life of recovery to heal the scars of her childhood. That was part of why she had decided to major in psychology and work as a therapist. If anyone had healthy boundaries it was Harper, and he knew she wouldn't allow herself to be sucked into his obsession.

He hadn't shaved in days, and the pizza delivery guy knew him by his first name. He couldn't believe it wasn't working. *But I'll get her back. I'll get this to work, and then I'll get myself together and show up at her door.* But he knew it wouldn't work. She prided herself on making healthy decisions and having great, honest relationships. John knew he had destroyed the trust and safety of what they had.

He panicked and relentlessly harassed her with phone calls and text messages. He knew that would only make it worse and confirm that he was deep in a twisted obsession. First the trading and now stalking Harper, he didn't even know himself. "My God, I've lost my dad, half of his money, and the love of my life. I am losing my grip." After three days of blowing up her cell, he got a disconnected message from the phone service. She had changed her number.

He started having panic attacks and stopped eating. He dropped twenty pounds in three weeks. Insomnia was a nightly event. No matter how late he went to bed, he woke up every morning spontaneously at 4:00 a.m. Some nights he didn't sleep at all. He finally caved in and went to see a therapist. After describing his symptoms, the psychiatrist diagnosed him as being clinically depressed. The shrink recommended anti-depressants and weekly therapy sessions. "I am also going to prescribe something to help you sleep," he said.

"Am I going to be able to get out of this? I feel crazy. I can't seem to think my way out of this."

"Most people do get themselves out of this, but you have to do some work. You are also going to have to stop your dysfunctional behavior. First of all, leave that poor girl alone. What you are doing is making matters worse. You are also going to need to stop your obsession with beating the market—it's destroying you."

"I know. My father's account is down to $500,000. I feel terrible about it. I just keep thinking I can get it back. I don't understand how I can be wrong."

"Look, I don't understand squat about the market but I know dysfunction when I see it, and pal, what you are doing has disaster written all over it. You need to stop now. Even if it worked, it's not worth this. It's destroying your mental and physical health."

John committed to therapy once a week, and started taking the anti-depressants. He got the 'scripts for the sleeping meds filled, but hadn't used them yet. He didn't want to feel groggy. He would stop pursuing Harper, but believed he could get his father's fortune back and he believed the sleeping pills might make him too groggy to trade. But he also knew that was BS because he knew he couldn't trade on two hours sleep.

What the heck is that all about? If he was being honest with himself, he knew he was not done trading. He loved the thrill and excitement of it. Harper probably would have said, "You're addicted to the dopamine and adrenaline you get, and it pumps up your ego when you score a big win. You are getting your self-esteem from the market, but you are so much more than that. There is more to you than your intellect. You don't have to be smarter than other people and try to prove it by beating the market. No matter how much you win or how big your portfolio grows, it will never be enough. You are using your money like a drug."

That is what she would have said, if he hadn't destroyed the one true thing in his life. She was beautiful and loving and caring, and he had destroyed what they had together. "It must be brutal watching me destroy myself." But that thought was fleeting because it was followed by the idea that he would make millions, or billions and he would show her. Just like that crazy country song "How do you like me now?" and as he thought it, he knew it was a lie. Even if he made billions, she would never return. For that to happen he would have to have a purpose in life greater than ego, power, and control. He would have to focus on helping others and be a better person if he ever wanted her back. But this seemed an insurmountable feat.

And as he stared at the pier's railing, lost in morbid self-reflections and struggling with the depression and anxiety that was devouring him he caught a glint from the corner of his eye. There it was again. It wasn't just a reflection of light; it was actually a glowing object and it was buried in the sand.

John made his way back to the front of the pier and the beach itself being careful not to lose sight of the glowing object. As he approached the half-buried object in the sand he tried to imagine what could be shining so bright, but his mind drew a blank. This is nothing, who the heck cares what it is, just go home and try to get a couple hours of sleep before the market opens. But he couldn't. He was drawn to the object. He had no real control. It drew him to it.

When he freed the object, he instinctively began to wipe the sand away. It was glowing a bright blue-green and looked like an antique lamp. As he cleaned it off, he felt a finger tap him on the shoulder. Startled, he dropped the object, which was no longer glowing, and quickly turned around. He had not heard anyone come up behind him. The beach was deserted and for a brief moment he thought he was going to be mugged. He expected a homeless person or a gang member toting a gun, but instead there was a well-dressed man in what appeared to be a very expensive suit, pinstripes with a bright red tie. He was bald and had a single diamond earring in his left ear.

"Oh crap, you startled me. I thought you were a mugger."

"How can I help you?" replied the man in a calm, steely voice.

"Help me?" John asked, "Unless you can help me sleep, I don't think you can." He laughed nervously.

"Is that your wish?" came his reply.

"How did you come up behind me so fast? I didn't see anyone on the beach."

"You rubbed the lamp, so I came."

"The lamp? I rubbed the lamp?" John could feel fear grip him. Clearly, this guy is a nutjob. The instinct to run overcame him.

"Don't run, John. It's alright. I won't hurt you. I am actually here to help you. If you'll let me." John took two steps backwards. The guy looked harmless, but he was clearly crazy.

"Look, buddy, I don't want anything from you. Just back off and leave me alone."

The urge to run again pushed its way into his mind. He had been an all-state track star in high school, and if push came to shove, he was pretty sure he could outrun this guy as long as he didn't have a gun.

"No, John, I don't have a gun, and you don't need to run."

"What the hell? How'd you know what I was thinking ?How do you know my name?"

"I know a lot of things, John. I know you have lost most of your father's money. I know you have pushed away the love of your life, and I know that you are depressed and desperate."

I must be asleep or hallucinating, John thought. This is not real. So I have nothing to lose. I'll just play along and then I will wake up. No harm, no foul.

"Ok, I'll bite. How can you help me?"

"By giving you what you want."

"Why, because you are a Genie and you are going to grant me three wishes?"

This was not real anyway, so I might as well enjoy it and have some fun, he tried to convince himself. But it didn't feel like a dream. This felt real.

"John, you have been watching too many Disney movies. That is not how this works. Nobody gets three wishes. Nobody gets more than one. You better make it a good one."

"So, I get one wish? I can wish for anything?"

"No there are some ground rules. Some things I can't give you. For example, I can't bring people back to life. That is above my pay grade. You also cannot wish directly for money or its equivalent. That would be far too easy, take all the fun out of it."

"What about love? Can you wish for that?"

"John, I'm surprised. Still hoping that Harper will come back? No John, you can't wish for love. That is not my department."

"Ok," John said, playing along. "No money, no resurrections, no love. Can I wish for something that will help me make money?"

"As long as it is not a printing press, which is the same as wishing for money, that is not a problem."

"Even if it doesn't exist anywhere in the entire world?" John's mind was racing. He knew exactly what he wanted. He needed to know if it met all the rules.

"Sure, John, I can grant a wish for a magical object. That is not a problem. And I can see what you are thinking, John. I can have that on your desk instantly. But John, once you wish for it, that's it. No more wishes. That is how this works. So you need to be sure. I have been granting wishes for millennia and, fair warning, most wishes backfire on the grantee. So be sure, John. You only get one shot."

He knew what he wanted, and what the hell, this wasn't real anyway. "Okay, I want a—let's just call it magical—computer screen that shows me exactly what the prices of stocks should be. I want the screen to take into account all the knowable and predictable information about the future, and I want it to take into consideration the unknowable information like people's fears, hopes, greed and even their personal plans, and I want it to update instantly to show me what the 'right' price should be. Could you do that?"

"That is no problem. But John, what are going to use it for?"

"I am going to use the current market price screen on my desk to compare to the 'magic screen' price. If the 'magic screen' is high, I am going to buy the stock and cash in on the risk-free differential. If the 'magic screen' says it is less, I am going to sell the stock if I own it, or sell it short if I don't. This will be like shooting fish in a barrel."

"Are you sure that this is what you want?"

"I sure am. Make it happen, Genie!"

 "One last point, John. After I grant your wish, you throw the lamp back into the ocean. You won't see me again unless I want you to, so don't bother rubbing the lamp again. In fact, dear John, if you don't live up to your end of the contract this will be very bad for you."

"Ok, yeah, sure. No problem. Throw the lamp back. Got it."

In typical Disney style, the Genie said, "Your wish is my command!" The Genie snapped his fingers and then there was darkness.

John woke up in his own bed. It was the first time he had slept in months. He looked at the clock and it was 11:30 in the morning. He was famished. Miraculously, he had his appetite back, and for some inexplicable reason he felt the slightest glimmer of hope. "It must be because I finally slept." Then he remembered the Genie. "Not only did I sleep, I had the most amazing dream ever. I'll have to tell the shrink about that one. Must be some kind of childish wish fulfillment dream." John fixed himself a bowl of cereal and flipped on CNBC. The Dow was up 160 points. "Wow, I slept right through that. Better get crackin'."

He turned toward his desk, and a cold chill ran down his spine. There was an extra computer screen. There were four instead of three.

"That's not real," he told himself. But he knew that it was and although he was trying to talk his way out of believing it, he knew exactly where it came from. At first glance, it didn't look magical. It was a standard, flat-screen monitor. But on closer examination, it was different. There was no power source, no plug for the wall, and there was no manufacturer's identification of any kind. There was a post-it note on the middle of the screen. It said, "As you wish. Have fun trading." It did not have a signature, but sitting next to the computer was the lamp. It had lost its glow, but it was the same lamp from the beach.

"I have a master's in economics, magna cum laude from Berkeley—and this cannot be happening. This is not real." But there it was, sitting in front of him. In the background he could hear the news anchor exclaim that the market was up another 2%, one of the biggest trading days of the year!

His own computer screens were already on, he never turned them off. They were full of green arrows pointing up. "Maybe this is real. Maybe I am not losing my mind or maybe this a dream inside a dream like the movie Inception." He could feel the adrenaline hit his system as he thought about turning on the magic screen.

He examined the front of the screen and found the power button. He pushed it excitedly and the screen came alive with numbers and quotes. It contained prices for every stock, linked to all the other computers.

"It works! It really worked!" John set aside all disbelief and allowed himself to focus on the riches that would soon be his. There were always stocks with massive swings and now he could cash in at will. This was better than money. This meant unlimited wealth. He picked up the lamp and kissed it. He would keep his end of the deal but first a couple of trades just to see how his new screen worked.

"Let's take you for a spin," he said aloud.

He focused on one stock he had recently been following. Its bid price (or buying price) was $50 on his trading screens. He found the price listed on the screen the Genie gave him and he knew it had to be a mistake. It was the exact same price. "This can't be. The market price cannot be the best price. There has to be a difference in the market and the right price." After a closer examination, he found that all the prices were the same and that as his screens changed the magic screen changed at precisely the same moment.

John felt the excitement of trading being flooded out with the anger of being deceived. "This cannot be right! The only thing that was more insane than believing in a Genie was believing that the market reflected all knowable and predictable data instantly. If this were true, no one could systematically and predictably beat it. Beating the market would be pure luck. That is garbage. This cannot be about luck. "

What about all of his formulas and all of his heroes who had beaten the market in the past? Were they no better than monkeys throwing darts? "How am I ever going to get my father's money back? What if all that were true? I threw away the love of my life to speculate with random data strings. Harper, I miss you. What have I done?"

In a blind rage, with tears streaming down his face, he slammed his fists down against the desk and then shoved all of the monitors off of his desk. They went crashing onto the floor. They all shorted out, except the magic screen. It still flashed the prices up at him, mocking his arrogance and stupidity.

"I threw it all away for nothing," He fell to his knees and sobbed uncontrollably. "I give up. I can't do it. This is insanity. I can't beat the market. I can't see the future. I have to stop playing God. I am trying to control the uncontrollable. Who am I to believe that I am smarter than the collective knowledge of all the seven billion people in the world? I can't live my life like this. I don't want to live my life like this. I need help. I can't do this alone."

In that moment, John was beaten. He surrendered to the futility of trying to predict the future. "I don't want to live like this."

"What's the problem little buddy?" came a voice from the couch.

John whipped around, "I lost it all. This machine of yours, is it the truth?"

"Sorry pal, that screen is perfect. You asked for a screen that integrates all available information, stock market data, as well as all human emotions and that is exactly what I gave you. All the knowable and even the unknowable information is already in the price. The only thing that is not in the price is new, unpredictable news and events. Don't feel bad, only the Big Guy upstairs knows those. I could not have put them in the screen anyway. "

John was still on his knees wiping the tears from his eyes. "But what is the point of the market if you can't beat it?"

"The point is that returns come from the market, not the manager. You human beings are never satisfied with the miraculous gifts you have. Have you seen market returns, John? What makes you think you have to beat markets to live a wonderful life? And John, what makes you think money will make you happy anyway? You had three million dollars and you weren't happy or fulfilled. Money has become a curse for you. In fact, the more you have the more it will possess you. It's not entirely your fault. You are being bombarded with messages that more is better and even your so-called professors encouraged you to gamble with your money. Why is it so hard for mankind to accept all of the miracles around you without the lust for more money? Let me give you a little perspective—if you are on welfare today you have better access to literature, art, entertainment, food, spices, health care and travel than you would have had if you were the king of England three hundred years ago. King Henry VIII died because he didn't have penicillin for an infection in his leg. John, you spend so much time trying to get more money and beat the market and no time on the important questions. What is money really for? What is your true purpose for money? How can you empower people to have better lives? How can you be of service to others? How can you invest without speculating and take your own ego and need to speculate out of the equation? And John, how can you use money for good instead of evil? How can you make the world a better place and show love to the people who are important to you? John, why do you have to feel smarter than everyone else? Why do you have to be the Master of the Universe?"

"I have been around a long time, John, and I can assure you, you are just another bozo on the bus. Hell, John, you're not even driving the bus. You are no better or worse than any other person on the planet. No amount of money will make you better than anyone else. Are you ready to throw in the towel on this beating the market scam? Are you ready to surrender? Have you hit bottom yet?"

"I didn't want this. I just want my life back. I'm tired of having my money own me. I need help to change."

"That is the first step, brother. Without that, nothing gets better. You're going to be okay, John. I know it doesn't feel like it right now, but you are going to be just fine. I know you feel like what you are going through will never end, but it will. It didn't come to stay, it came to pass. And when everything is uncertain, anything is possible."

"What am I supposed to do now? How do I fix this mess? I want to feel better!"

"But you are feeling better. You are feeling fear better and pain better and guilt better. You have been running from those feelings for a very long time. The only way out is through. Love yourself enough to feel those feelings and heal them. It's okay; your feelings won't kill you. You need to let go of the outcome and work on yourself. Dude, listen up, I am giving you the wisdom of 10,000 years. Accept that your power is limited. You are not God. Stop pretending you are. Believe me when I say he doesn't like that. You have incredible abilities, but seeing into the future isn't one of them. That door will forever remain closed to you. Be grateful for what you have and the amazing wealth and prosperity around you."

"If I stop gambling and speculating, what do I do instead?"

"You keep it simple. You diversify, you make market returns for good, and you find ways to use your money to help other people. Stop thinking about yourself so much. It's not about you."

"What is it about?"

"It is about loving and being of service to others."

"That sounds like a Hallmark card. How can it be so basic?"

"All real truth is basic when you break it down into its simplest forms—even investing. It all breaks down to one simple formula: the cost of capital equals the return on capital. You humans love to complicate things. I guess it makes you feel important."

CNBC still blared in the background. The Dow was up another hundred points. "It seems like a long road ahead. How do I start?" asked John.

"It is simple, you just accept that you are not the highest power in the Universe and you pray for strength and wisdom and the will to carry it out. And you stop worshipping money. The rest will work itself out."

"You're not really a Genie, are you?"

"No, I'm not."

"Then, what are you?"

"I think you already know."

"Are you an angel?"

"Not just any angel—I am *your* angel."

"I don't really need to throw this silly lamp back into the water, do I?"

"No, it's just a silly prop." He snapped his fingers, and the lamp and the magic screen were gone. In their place were Johns restored computer screens.

John faced his desk, "I'm not going to need those anymore."

"You'll find some good use for them."

"Why didn't you just come to me in your real form?"

"Your mind couldn't conceive or handle my real form. John, our time is ending. Is there anything else?"

"No, I think I have everything I need to make a new beginning."

"I do too, John. God bless you."

And then he was gone. The news anchor said, "Gold is down 10% from its high only three months ago. Our next guest says get ready for new highs in 2012."

John said, "Really?" And began to laugh harder than he had in half a year.

John was true to his word. He gave two of his computer terminals to Big Brothers and Big Sisters, and he sponsored a ten-year-old boy named Gage who had lost his mother and father in a car accident with a drunk driver. They spent most weekends together hanging out, playing video games, going to the movies, or throwing a ball at the park. When Gage had math homework John helped him. He discovered he had a passion for teaching and coaching. He went back to college to get a teaching degree. He thought of Harper almost every day. But the pain of loving her was lessening in intensity. Now it had a bittersweet quality to it. Still more bitter than sweet. He missed her terribly but respected her boundaries and followed the coaching from his therapist. "Leave the woman alone," John knew he had screwed that up and had no one to blame but himself. He invested the remaining $500,000 into structured market funds and diversified globally. No more trying to beat the market. He allocated 75% to equities and 25% to fixed income. He peeled off $10,000 per year to give to charities like the cancer society, the Smile Train, Big

Brothers and Big Sisters, and Alzheimer's research in honor of his father. He also started to attend church on Sundays and a portion of his contributions supported his faith.

Instead of asking, "How can I pick the best stocks, get in and out at the right time, and crush the other traders," he focused on other, loftier goals. "How can I use my money to empower others? How can I create joy? How can I make the world a better place? How can I allocate my resources to help entrepreneurs create wealth on a global basis?" In his heart he knew these were the right questions. If he prayed, the answers always came to him. John was inspired with a new sense of direction and sense of passion. The way he viewed the world and his place in it shifted. His light and energy attracted other people; it lifted others up and empowered them to take actions of courage and strength. As John began to think more about others and less about himself, his mood was transformed. For the first time in his life he was truly happy. Several women in his classes asked him out for coffee, but he always politely declined. He was still healing. They seemed nice enough, but he just didn't feel any attraction, so he figured he just wasn't ready. He found himself lonely at times, but he didn't want to force the issue. Maybe he was keeping himself available with the hope that someday he would be with Harper again. His life was full and complete. If she ever made her way back to him, she would find a changed man. One that was capable of a loving and caring relationship. That much he knew. Would it ever happen? He had no idea. He had stopped trying to predict the future.

While John and the Genie is a fictional story, it represents the soul-searching process that every investor must eventually take on if they ever hope to alter their own behavior and experience around money and investing. The going will not be easy. It may be one of the hardest things you have ever done because it entails getting very honest with yourself and your investor coach. Which means you are going to take a thorough inventory of your own investing experiences and behaviors. And yes, you will need to see and admit where you have demonstrated negative or dysfunctional investing decisions. Until you are willing and able to look at this, there is little hope for real and lasting change.

Taking Your Investing Inventory

I've always equated long-term investing with a pilot getting ready to take an aircraft into flight.

Like that pilot, who always checks his gauges, goes through his flight plan, and runs his flight checklist, I want you do the same thing.

For example, before a good pilot hits those blue skies, there are three things he has to check before every flight, because neglecting even one of them can mean disaster:

Myself
Am I in good enough condition to fly?
(Am I emotionally, physically and intellectually flight ready?)
Plane
Is the plane structurally sound and well-maintained?
Flight Plan
Has the plan been developed to handle the weather conditions and stress of flying?
I believe these same rules apply to investors and investing.

- *Are you in the right frame of mind for healthy investing?*
- *Is your portfolio structured and sound enough to maximize your likelihood of success?*
- *Do you have a sound, well-thought-out plan to navigate volatile and turbulent conditions?*

Like the pilot getting ready for a safe, successful flight, it's obvious that you're going to need a team—especially a coach—to get your investment plan off the ground, into the air, and bring it home safely when you need to.

This is no hyperbole—you'll need a team to overthrow the myths and garbage perpetuated by Wall Street; and what's more, you'll really need to work like a team.

Just like it takes a team of scientists, engineers, air traffic controllers, pilots and co-pilots to design, manufacture and successfully fly an airplane, it will take a team approach to engineer, design, build and navigate a successful portfolio strategy. The basic principles are simple, but implementation can be complex and challenging. Without a total team approach, the investing process I have laid out is impossible.

It Takes a Team

My childhood dream was to be the captain of my varsity football team. While other 13-year-old kids went to the high school football games to socialize and "make out" under the bleachers (that's what we called kissing and hugging in the late seventies), I watched every single play and memorized them by heart. I wanted to lead that team to victory. My senior year, I got my chance and I became the team captain for the Greenhills Pioneers. Six years of hard work had finally paid off, and it became one of the most miserable experiences of my life.

The year before was amazing. As a junior, I played offensive guard and defensive end. I was one of the few players that played both offense and defense. It was an incredibly uplifting and inspiring experience. Our record at the end of the season was nine wins and one loss. We destroyed schools that were four time our own size. Most of the players were seniors and they had worked together as a dedicated fighting unit for over a decade. I was one of the few juniors who set foot on the playing field. They were an amazing team of the most dedicated, hard-working, spirited, emotionally and intellectually fit young men I would ever have the pleasure of knowing.

This all changed in my senior year. They all graduated and I inherited a team of juniors and sophomores who had never played football together. There was no cohesion. Most players were out for personal glory and prestige. The team was smaller, weaker, and frankly not as smart as the team the year before. Being the captain, I worked twice as hard as I did the prior year, but nothing I did seemed to help. The year I was team captain, we lost every single game. I was devastated. I cried after every game. I felt like a loser to the core of my soul. My self-esteem plummeted. I doubted my dedication, my strengths, and even my manhood.

I had known the thrill of victory and the uplifting experience of working with a dedicated, committed, and skilled team, but now I was learning the pain, doubts, and fear of losing. I began to doubt everything I thought I knew about myself. "Maybe it's all my fault. Maybe I am just not a winner. I must be a terrible leader. I'm a loser and a coward." These were the things I told myself after every game and practice. I went into a terrible shame spiral.

My dream of becoming the team captain turned into one of my worst nightmares, but it taught me something very important. Everything that makes a real difference takes amazing teamwork. It also showed me the critical importance of choosing the right players. I had no control over creating and designing the team or its players. No matter how hard

I tried, I was only as strong as the other people on my team. Additionally, determination and character are critically important.

It wasn't simply that this team was smaller or less gifted. It was that the players did not fully commit and sacrifice for the good of the team. I also saw that misery loves company. When one player complained that practices were too hard or the coach wasn't fair, they always found another player who would complain and moan and groan and eventually quit the team. I finished out the season and never gave up or quit, although there were many times I wanted to. I kept my head held high and kept fighting. Now I know the critical importance of building a great team and the power of coaching to change lives.

Make no mistake about it, you will make many if not most of the important decisions when it comes to building and creating a winning portfolio, but you will need a team to implement and maintain it. It is up to you to find and develop the team and to play your position with dedication and strength.

In my mind, beating Wall Street and establishing yourself as a successful investor is as much about problem solving as it is shedding the failed traditional methods of managing a portfolio. The best problem-solving techniques are the ones where you get help—from a team, a coach, or any knowledgeable small group.

That's the conclusion of a study from the University of Illinois that found groups of three to five people perform better than individuals when solving complex problems. Through their research, the study authors were able to prove that teams of three people were able to solve difficult problems better than even the best individuals working alone.[68]

In the study, the authors had over 700 collegians from the University of Illinois at Urbana-Champaign solve letters-to-numbers code problems, working either individually or as part of a group. Researchers found a surprisingly small amount of prior research on the effect of group size on problem solving. The researchers measured performance by comparing the number of trials needed to solve the problem as well as the number of errors made. The results demonstrated that groups of three, four, and five people performed better than individuals at solving the problems.

Lead researcher Patrick Laughlin attributed the improved performance of groups to, "the ability of people to work together to generate and adopt correct responses, reject erroneous responses, and effectively process information." He also noted that "the group members combined their abilities and resources to perform better than the best of an equivalent number of individuals on the highly intellective complementary group task."

The University of Illinois study translates well into our discussion of problem solving on Wall Street.

In the chaotic environment of the financial markets, dealing with any storm begins with problem solving.

That's especially true on Wall Street. The problem there is that a perfect storm, of sorts, includes the emotions, plus the instincts, plus the perceptions, magnified by the media. All combine to overwhelm the cognitive part of investing. How do you break through all that noise to solve that problem? What has to happen is this: the equation has to be flipped so that the left side of the equation is stronger than the right side of the equation. We must modify the left side, so that it's stronger.

Granted, this is not a scientific, academic three-factor model. What I'm proposing is a mental construct to help you think about, to know, and to visualize the process of investing. The end game here is that the cognitive side and the behavioral side have to line up equally. What we found over 20 years of practical experience is there are three critical things that must be added to the left side of the equation. We label them like so:

- Catharsis
- Focus
- Support

$$C(Ca+F+S)>(I+E+P)M$$

Catharsis

By and large, this is a process where you, as an investor, must hit bottom and admit at your very core that your behavior has been dysfunctional and that it's not just the portfolio that needs to be managed, but also that your behavior will continue to be dysfunctional into the future, absent any help. In other words, your own behavior is your own worst enemy here.

Let's face it, most people are willing to admit it when their portfolio is messed up, but very few people like to admit that their own behavior—which caused the portfolio malfunction—is messed up.

Maybe you can think of a time in your life in which a given behavior, or a specific relationship, or a situation on the job, finally caused you to arrive at the point of surrender.

In other words, the point where you said, "I can't take it anymore. I'm done, this is out of my control, and I need help."

What an investor must eventually come to, before they're willing to accept the free market, is this realization.

I am spiritually, intellectually, and emotionally incapable of managing my own behavior and my own portfolio.

This is a big pill for many people to swallow. Most people realize that, if left to their own devices, they eventually slip back into speculating and gambling with their portfolios. Ironically, by admitting our own humanity and frailty, we can gain new-found strength and accept a better investing solution.

This is a place that we don't like to get to. It's kind of like a boxer who just keeps getting beaten down and beaten down and beaten down, and finally just throws in the towel.

Usually, this situation only comes from a series of actual behavior, or better yet, actual failure in the real world. How do you get to the point where you're finally willing to say, "I've had enough?" It's usually when you've engaged in enough stock picking, market timing, and track record investing and lost enough money that you're willing to accept a better way. Normally when an investor says, "I'm not ready to accept a better way yet," I say, "Okay, go out and speculate and gamble some more until you are ready."

But no one can tell you when you have had enough. You must discover that for yourself. Of course, that starts with asking and having the courage to answer the right questions.

> *"I don't measure a man's success by how high he climbs but how high he bounces when he hits bottom."*
>
> —George S. Patton

You're Not Omniscient

I always have to remind investors to stop playing God.

Specifically, that means stop trying to predict the market, and stop trying to forecast the market. Above all, stop trying to find someone who promises these things because anyone who tells you they can do this is seriously delusional, uneducated, misinformed, or lying. So, don't ask anyone else to play God when advising you and building your portfolio—because no one can.

At the end of the day, once you come to terms with the limits of your own humanity and you recognize where your behavior and your portfolio has failed in the past, then you can ask for help. But as an investor, until you reach that point, you're pretty hopeless.

Let me give you an example.

When I first started investing, I hit that very same point about five years in, right down the list:

- I had graduated from Miami University.
- I had been listening to my broker-dealer.
- I had all these active mutual funds that I personally owned.
- I had real estate partnerships.
- I had annuities.
- I had active funds, with international and small cap mutual funds.

I was basically doing it all. After about five years, I noticed that year after year after year these brilliant fund managers, who had beaten the market in the past, failed to continue their performance, and that we were underperforming the benchmark by about 5% annually.

I would visit my brokerage houses, and I would see my broker-dealer, and I would go to the mutual fund companies, and I would say, "What is going on?" And they would say, "Well, don't sell that one anymore. Just sell this one." I couldn't take it. I couldn't, as an advisor, sit down and look at another client and tell them that I was doing the best thing for them. I had hit bottom and I knew it—I had become part of the problem. That was a sobering day, but until that day came, until I admitted that I needed help and asked for it, I was never going to make progress.

So as an investor, you might be tempted to think that's sad. Because who wants to admit failure? Who wants to admit that they can't do it alone? But until we, as investors, admit that we can't beat the market and we can't time it, we're not willing to accept what the market has to offer. I know this is a strong visceral image, but catharsis (Ca in our equation) looks like this:

My own behavior is my worst enemy.

And there is a sense of great release when you are able to admit that spiritually, intellectually, and emotionally you are incapable of managing your own behavior. Then and only then is real growth possible. This opens up the opportunity to accept a better way

Turning It Around

To be a successful investor, the first step is to turn inward.

It's probably the hardest step you're ever going to take as an investor, but it's also the most rewarding.

That's where focus, the second leg of that three-legged stool (that left-handed equation I mentioned earlier in the chapter) comes into the picture.

Focus

What are you going to focus on? The investment industry regularly targets what it wants you to focus on. We've heard it all before—five stars, forecasts, predictions, trend analysis, IPOs, stock picks—those are all shiny coins of the realm on Wall Street.

But what should you really be focused on? What are the right questions to ask to get going on your financial future? How can you raise your consciousness so that you're not sucked into this problem, this dysfunctional process, over and over and over again?

The answer, to me at least, is a simple one. We call them the 20 Must-Answer Questions for Investing Peace of Mind. While we believe that most investors are stuck in the investors' dilemma, we also believe that by answering these 20 must-answer questions, questions that any investor can answer with just a little bit of effort, that you can achieve peace of mind in your investment process.

So, how do you do that? First, you start by measuring the existing state of your portfolio. When you're feeling bad and exhibiting symptoms of some kind of physical ailment, you go to a doctor. The first thing the doctor does is order tests. The doctor doesn't just give you a prescription when you walk in the office. They want to check you out, and see what's ailing you first.

One of the tools they use is the magnetic resonance imaging (MRI) scanner. With the MRI, they can actually see what's going on inside of the human body. It's worth noting that MRIs are very expensive. The machines themselves can run into the millions of dollars, but they do a great job when you need to look under the hood.

In the investment world, once you know what the problem is (the MRI phase) then you can focus on those 20 Must-Answer Questions.

Useless Knowledge

Knowledge really is power, but to be effective, it has to be targeted knowledge. Take an old anecdote about auto industry legend Henry Ford.

One day, a man visiting the Ford factory in Dearborn, Michigan happened to encounter Henry Ford himself, who, pointing out a newly finished vehicle, proudly declared, "There are exactly 4,719 parts in that model!"

Impressed by Ford's apparent wealth of knowledge, the visitor sought out a company engineer and asked the man for confirmation, "Are there, in fact, exactly 4,719 parts in that model?" The engineer shrugged his shoulders. "I'm sure I don't know," he replied. "I can't think of a more useless piece of information."

The vast majority of investing information falls under the same classification—useless drivel. No, it is even worse than useless, it is dangerous financial pornography. However, if you know the right things, you don't have to know everything.

When you can answer "yes" to all the 20 Must-Answer Questions, you will be well on your way to creating investing peace of mind. The questions represent "F" on our equation, and they are the right things to focus on. As you take this test, you must be brutally honest with yourself. To get a "yes" answer, it must be 100% "yes." 99.9% won't cut it.

The 20-Must Answer Questions

1:   Have you discovered your true purpose for money? Your true purpose should be more important than money itself. Everybody knows money is not the most important thing in life. They know it so much, it's a cliché. What is your true purpose for money, and how is this purpose reflected in how you invest and how you live your life?

YES ☐   NO ☐

2:   Are you invested in the market? Do you own equities (or preferably structured funds that own equities throughout global markets)? Now that doesn't mean are you completely all in equities with 100% of your portfolio, but do you own some equities in your portfolio?

YES ☐   NO ☐

3:   Do you know how markets work? If you've been reading this book, you might have a pretty good glimpse into how markets work. That's part of my goal. To get a "yes" you must be able to clearly state where the return from markets come from and identify expected market premiums.

YES ☐   NO ☐

4:   Have you identified your investing philosophy? We all know that it is important to have a philosophy in religion, business, education, and life, but did you know that you can have a philosophy in investing? Can you clearly articulate your philosophy? (Quick hint: "make as much money as I can" is not a philosophy).

YES ☐   NO ☐

5:   Have you identified your personal risk tolerance? When I talk about risk tolerance, I talk about a specific scientifically derived number, not just a generality such as conservative or aggressive.

YES ☐   NO ☐

6:   Do you know how to measure diversification in your portfolio?

YES ☐   NO ☐

7:   Do you consistently and predictably achieve market rates of returns? Do you even know the meaning of market rates of return? It's hard to get market rates of returns if you don't even know what they are and how to track them in your portfolio.

YES ☐   NO ☐

8:   Have you measured the total amount of commissions and costs in your portfolio based on the investments you own and the turnover in your portfolio? Fees are an under-reported, but over-sized, problem for investors.

YES ☐   NO ☐

9:   Do you know where you fall on the Markowitz Efficient Frontier? Know the historically expected rate of return for your mix of assets and the volatility that you're prepared to accept in each part of your portfolio, or the portfolio as a whole. This is a huge factor in investing.

YES ☐   NO ☐

10:   When it comes to building your investment portfolio, do you know exactly what you are doing and why at all times? Or, are you a little bit like me when I go to the grocery store? I'm just picking groceries—you know, this looks good, that looks good—but I have no recipe. I have no plan or overall strategy. That's how most people build a portfolio. One year this bond looks good, one year this mutual fund looks good, one year that annuity looks good. There's no overall design to the plan itself.

YES ☐   NO ☐

11: Are you working with a financial coach rather than a financial planner? If you've been able to answer yes to all of these questions so far, rest assured you are working with a coach. Otherwise, you're probably working with a financial planner or some kind of money manager.

YES ☐   NO ☐

12: Do you have a customized lifelong game plan to guide all of your investing and spending decisions? Always think long-term in your financial present to build your financial future.

YES ☐   NO ☐

13: Do you have an investment policy statement? Is it written down? Do you have a process based on that investment policy statement to monitor your behavior and your asset allocations?

YES ☐   NO ☐

14: Have you devised a clear-cut method for measuring the success or failure of your portfolio once you've designed it? Engineers will tell you when you build a skyscraper; it doesn't just stand straight up. It actually has variance or tolerance of movement when it's built. Otherwise, the wind would push it over. So, that begs the question. "Do you know the tolerance level in your portfolio, and do you know if your portfolio is operating within your established measures?"

YES ☐   NO ☐

15: Do you fully understand the implications of diversification as far as it applies to your overall returns and your overall portfolio mix? Do you have a system to measure portfolio volatility? Do you have a scientifically derived number to which you can point that will tell you exactly what you're doing with that portfolio?

YES ☐   NO ☐

16: Do you have a system to measure portfolio volatility? This must be a specific statistical number that identifies the risk in your portfolio.

YES ☐   NO ☐

17: Are you aware of the cost associated with purchasing commission-based products, or are you kind of in the dark? Make no mistake—stockbrokers have their own interests in mind, not yours.

YES ☐   NO ☐

18: Do you know the three warning signs that you may be speculating with your money versus prudently investing it?

YES ☐   NO ☐

19: Can you identify the cultural messages and personal mind-sets about money that destroy your investing peace of mind? We call these money demons. Sometimes these are notions we formed about money, not when we were 55 or even 25, but sometimes when we were as little as 5 years old. These money demons can destroy our investing peace of mind.

YES ☐   NO ☐

20: Are you ready to shift your personal experience of money and investing from a scarcity mode to an abundance mode – where you can live your life rather than obsess about your assets? This is the only answer you need is "yes" to make progress today. This means escaping the Investors' Dilemma. You no longer feel money is a scarce commodity. You are now realizing that wealth is abundant.

YES ☐   NO ☐

So, how did you do? Don't feel defeated if you received a low score. This is only the beginning and it will show you what you need to know to make progress. Even industry experts seldom get a high score the first time they take the quiz. Why? Because the Wall Street Bullies don't want you to be focused on these questions. They know that you will no longer be a victim once you can successfully answer "yes" to all of them. With a little time and effort, every investor can get 100%. Let's reexamine our new equation for success.

$$C(Ca+F+S)>(I+E+P)M$$

In previous chapters, I explained how the Instinct, Emotion, and Perception Biases are magnified by the Media to overwhelm your cognitive mind and lead to destructive investing behaviors. To strengthen the left side of the equation, I have demonstrated how cognition is reinforced by personal catharsis and proper focus. The final piece of the left side of our equation is ongoing community support.

S = Support

Community Effort

As I've said repeatedly, investing is a community effort. That's where investment coaches and your support mechanism can help.

Coaches guide you to ask the right questions and find the right answers, but they do not tell you what to do. They give you education and guidance so you can determine what is best for you. They coach you through it. Your coach helps you develop a deeper understanding of markets and investing, and helps provide discipline when you are fearful.

When you feel that financial resources are abundant in your life, it's easier to go out there and take powerful actions to change the world. Having the mindset of community is absolutely key.

Most of us have been taught that investing is a solitary pursuit. We think we're supposed to meet alone with our financial planner or advisor, don't talk about money, don't share what's going on, and certainly don't share your fear, apprehension, goals, or your feelings. Those feelings could be joy, happiness, love—things that we hope our money creates for us, our families, and those we care about. But we're led to believe that we should do this in isolation.

All Dysfunction Loves Secrecy

Instincts, plus emotions, plus perception can get twisted and take over in isolation. Human beings are meant to live in community, in support of each other. It's the fear of sharing our own emotions and failed behavior that keeps us stuck. We gain strength through sharing our experiences, fears, and hopes. And we do that best in groups.

To be successful as an investor is to take strength and hope from others, to share our experiences, to know that we're not alone when the market goes down 30%, or when we see an advertisement for gold up 80%.

It helps us to know that there are other people wrestling with the same things, and we all experience the same fears—whether it's the economy, struggles at home, loss of a job, or health issues. All of these things can exacerbate your financial situation. When the market crashes or there's a bad period, and you combine that with health problems, family problems, or work problems, it magnifies the fear. It makes things worse. To be a successful investor, and even a coach, requires the support of a group.

Think of it this way. One of the only successful dieting programs in existence is Weight Watchers. The program is statistically, scientifically proven to help people keep weight off. They teach you the strategies, the intellectual parts of losing weight, but mostly they provide group support. Alcoholics Anonymous for people who have drinking problems, Gamblers Anonymous for people who have gambling problems—these are support groups.

The great part is there's a potential solution for these addictions, and it's forged in the spirit of community. Organizations like Alcoholics Anonymous work for people who admit that they have a problem and want help.

It's the same idea in the investment world. Confronting your humanity, working in a community, and coming to terms with these issues as an investor is a necessity, not a luxury. But it's not for people who need it. It's for people who want it. You have to want it with a deep, powerful passion to make it happen.

When we're in a group, when we share, we understand ourselves. It's hard to know yourself—who you really are at your core gut level—until you're willing to share yourself with others. The good parts, the bad parts, all the emotions; you learn from other people's experiences, and then you learn that you're really not so different after all.

If you cannot deal with your feelings, you cannot be a successful investor because, it's going to be all about how you handle your emotions and your feelings, your instincts, and your perceptions. What I've done with this book is to square the cognitive part of investing with the emotional part. The idea all along has been to teach you the cognitive part, and then to show you how to strengthen that left side of the equation, and we strengthen that with catharsis.

In this chapter, we strengthened that lesson with the focus of investing (those 20 Must-Answer Questions), with an emphasis on a successful lifelong investing process to be coached and share in a community, in a support group, all for the betterment of your investment success.

The greatest journey in investing is really a journey into the inner self. It's self-knowledge that pays the highest dividend.

That's really what makes investing interesting.

Community and Self-Knowledge
Community is at the heart of addiction-support groups (that's why they're called support groups) like Gambler's Anonymous and Alcoholics Anonymous. But support groups won't work, even in the investment world, if you don't have recognition of your emotional side, of your "inner self."

12

BECOMING A SEASONED INVESTOR

"Those who cannot remember the past are condemned to repeat it."[69]

—George Santayana

I LOVE THE SANTAYANA LINE, but this closing chapter of our book just as easily could have included another great line, this one from philosopher Georg Wilhelm Friedrich Hegel:

We learn from history that man can never learn anything from history.[70]

It really is a great quote, implying that no matter what we know cognitively about history or the past, we can never change our human nature and are therefore doomed to repeat the same mistakes ad infinitum.

Like Bill Murray's character in *Groundhog Day*, being forced to relive the same day over and over, seemingly forever, and repeating the same painful mistakes.

But as much as I love the line, I don't buy its premise. In fact, I don't believe we're incapable of learning from the past. While I believe it's hard, I don't believe it's impossible. In the end, just like the movie, the destructive pattern can be broken.

We Can Learn From the Past If:
- We care to look at it at all.
- We analyze it in a scientific way.
- We apply it to our own lives.
- We develop a system of communication and feedback.

The "possible" begins with certain requirements, for example, that we actually care to check the rear view mirror and look at the past at all, which many people don't do. If we do care to check the past, we need to analyze the past in a scientific way. Finally, you need change to occur; you must apply change to your life in a meaningful fashion to develop a system of communication and feedback to take into consideration intent and emotions so that they can become a useful and meaningful influence on your behavior.

Your goal as an investor should be to learn and grow by studying and analyzing the history and science of investing and your own personal behavior, experience, and feelings. I call this becoming a seasoned investor. Becoming a seasoned investor also means using your instincts and emotions in a positive and enriching way. How meaningless would life be without the gift of emotions?

When my daughter Amanda was five years old, she begged me ceaselessly for goldfish. After saying no for a solid month (I knew I was going to have to take care of them), I finally gave in and bought her a small bowl and two small fish. She named them Nala and Simba after the characters in The Lion King. Six months later, I took my kids to Florida for summer break and as we got ready to go to the plane, Amanda said, "Who is going to take care of Nala and Simba?" We had forgotten to arrange for them to be fed. Already running late for the plane, I suggested we let them go free in the pond on the golf course behind our house. She reluctantly agreed. In my right arm, I held fish bowl and in my left hand, I held her small hand. When we came to the pond, she bent down. I gave her the bowl and she slowly poured the water and fish out into the dark water of the pond. They swam by the edge for a moment and slowly disappeared into the deeper water. We were still hunched over the lake and I asked her if she wanted to say goodbye to Nala and Simba. She looked up at me with a tear rolling down her face and she said, "Daddy, I don't want them to have names anymore." Amanda was feeling pain and sadness for the loss of her fish. As I took her hand in mine to lead her back to the house, I tried to lessen her pain. "I am sure they will be okay. It is a great pond and they can be free." But as a fisherman, I know the danger for two small goldfish in a pond full of largemouth bass, and I felt the pain of guilt for not having planned better. But even deeper, I felt a sense of loss and pain and love for my daughter, who I knew would have to face deeper losses and defeats in life as we all do. I blinked away tears for her loss of innocence, and I felt connected and close to my beautiful little girl. But what does this have to do with money?

As you become a seasoned investor, you can learn to use money as a tool to create intimacy and connection and to learn about yourself and others. Money can be used to express love and appreciation, to reduce pain and suffering, and to express kindness.

Money, with the right amount of understanding, can make the world a better place. I know this is not a popular belief, but it is true. So, how can we manage our money in a prudent way and use money in a fashion to enrich our lives and the lives of others?

Seasoned means:
- Being able to withstand physical hardship, strain, or exposure.
- Being able to bear up under hard times.
- To become competent as with training skill or ability.
- When you are seasoned, you can see the truth about a situation. You're not naïve. Naïve means deficient in worldly wisdom or informed judgment, lacking in experience, or needing to learn from experience.

When you're a seasoned investor, you become prudent. Prudence is an important by-product of being seasoned. If you're prudent, you're imbued with wisdom or judiciousness, shrewd in your management of practical affairs in the world.

But here's the catch. Most investors are not mature or seasoned, nor are most advisors. They repeat the same mistakes ad infinitum without ever really learning. To mature and grow as an investor means to give careful consideration to what you're doing and why. Maturation, or growth, is the emergence of personal and behavioral characteristics through a growth process. Growth includes pain.

Most investment professionals are similarly immature. They do not learn from history, because they believe they are inoculated against following the rules of prudence. They might figure, "sure, it's good to be prudent. But I don't have to—because I know what I'm doing."

Those advisors "feel" like the rules don't apply to them.

They're somehow above the rules, just like a 12-year-old thinks he can climb a tree without falling down, or a driver who thinks he can guzzle cocktails and get behind the wheel.

The sad fact is that most investors, including professionals, are immature and even worse, naïve. In other words, they're unseasoned.

Let's see how that concept plays out. Unseasoned investors chase markets. They'll see data that shows technology stocks rise by 250% over a five-year period, then jump in at the end of those five years, and wind up losing 60% of the value of their portfolio. Like I said, immature.

Unseasoned investors also panic in down markets. They stock-pick, they invest in track records, and they market time like crazy. That last type of investment behavior really ticks me off, and I see it all the time.

Here's the thing about market timing—it never feels like market timing. Very few financial professionals who resort (and there's really no better term for it) to market timing will ever admit attempting to do so. Instead, they say, "We're not market timing; we're simply adjusting our portfolio to a new reality. It's different this time." Talk about whistling past the graveyard.

The Aim/Dent Story

Let me give you a good example of an immature investment strategy.

Let's look at the Aim/Dent Demographics Trends Fund, led by alleged Wall Street guru and Wall Street bully, Harry Dent.

In 1999, the AIM Dent Demographics Trends Fund was launched, based on the demographic economic and lifestyle trends identified by Dent. Unfortunately, the fund's results were miserable. From 2000 through 2004, the fund lost more than 11% per year and underperformed the S&P 500 Index by almost 9% per year. In 2005, its sponsor put investors out of their misery by merging it into the AIM Weingarten Fund.[16]

In 1999, the fund made 42% based on Dent's forecast. Then it lost 17%, lost 32%, lost 32%, made 36%, made 7%, and lost 58%, for a total period rate of return of -21% a year—before it shut down. Dent was kidding himself. He didn't realize that being a successful investor requires facing the truth, growing up, and becoming mature. As I've said all along in this book, capitalism and free markets are the greatest wealth creation tool known to mankind.

Dent's fund wandered away from the facts, turning to fads and trends that had no business in a market serious as Wall Street.

Yes, with capitalism, there will be ups and downs along the way, but the long-term prognosis is bullish.

For instance, from 1926 to 2010, we had a regular occurrence of historical events, huge in magnitude, and loaded with supposedly capital-killing scenarios of war, death, and destruction.

The list includes:

World War II, India-Pakistani War, Arab-Israeli War, The Cold War, Korean War Indochina War, Algerian War, Suez Crisis, Vietnam War, Bay of Pigs, Six-Day War, Central American War, Regular bouts of international terrorism, Soviet-Afghan War, Iran-Iraq War, Falklands War, Invasion of Grenada, Invasion of Panama, The Gulf War, Bosnia Conflict, the War on Terror (Iraq War, Afghanistan War)

Yet, alongside all of those nasty military conflicts, you also have the progress of capitalism. As you can see from the accompanying chart, over the long haul the Standard & Poor's 500 Index has more than weathered the storm. It has grown, alongside a capitalist economy, steadily over the past 80+ years.

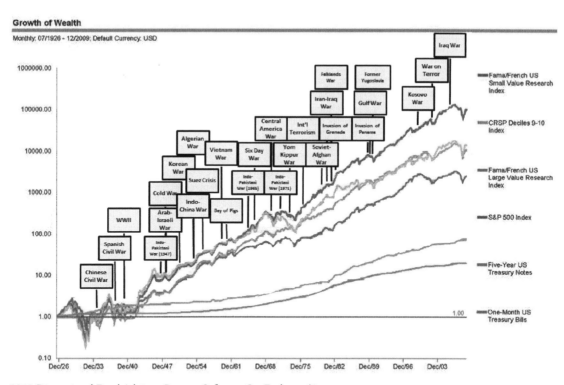

2010 Dimensional Fund Advisors Returns Software. See Endnote 49.

That chart tells you everything you need to know about capitalism and the stock market. Sure, there are myriad swings in the economy and in the financial markets. This is nothing new. It's called market volatility, and it's always been with us (and always will be). Market prices are random and unpredictable. No one knows where the next 20% move will be in the market, but we do know that the next 100% move is always upward. There's never been a time period in which we've had a 100% downward move in the market.

So remember that the next time you're talking with your stockbroker or financial advisor. Encouraging you to sell when prices are down is going to destroy your long-term potential for success, but it is what the Wall Street bullies want you to do, so they can earn a commission and increase their profits and destroy your wealth. Stocks are a long-term investment, and short-term fluctuations are, quite frankly, meaningless. The wisdom of the ages (and the S&P 500 performance chart), say this too shall pass, and only those who panic and sell on a down market are the long-term losers.

S& P 500 Performance: 1926–2010

Year	S&P 500	Average Annual Return	5-Year Avg. Annual Return	10-Year Avg. Annual Return	15-Year Avg. Annual Return	20-Year Avg. Annual Return	25-Year Avg. Annual Return
1926	11.62%	11.62%					
1927	37.49%	23.88%					
1928	43.61%	30.14%					
1929	-8.42%	19.19%					
1930	-24.90%	8.67%					
1931	-43.34%	-2.50%	-5.11%				
1932	-8.19%	-3.34%	-12.47%				
1933	53.99%	2.46%	-11.24%				
1934	-1.44%	2.02%	-9.93%				
1935	47.67%	5.86%	3.12%				
1936	33.92%	8.15%	22.47%	7.81%			
1937	-35.03%	3.65%	14.29%	0.02%			
1938	31.12%	5.54%	10.67%	-0.89%			
1939	-0.41%	5.11%	10.90%	-0.05%			
1940	-9.78%	4.04%	0.50%	1.80%			
1941	-11.59%	2.99%	-7.51%	6.43%	2.44%		
1942	20.34%	3.93%	4.62%	9.35%	1.53%		
1943	25.90%	5.05%	3.77%	7.17%	0.64%		
1944	19.75%	5.77%	7.67%	9.28%	2.46%		
1945	36.44%	7.13%	16.96%	8.42%	6.62%		
1946	-8.07%	6.35%	17.88%	4.41%	10.12%	6.10%	
1947	5.71%	6.32%	14.86%	9.62%	11.16%	4.71%	
1948	5.50%	6.29%	10.87%	7.26%	8.39%	3.11%	
1949	18.79%	6.78%	10.69%	9.17%	9.75%	4.46%	
1950	31.71%	7.68%	9.91%	13.38%	8.91%	7.43%	
1951	24.02%	8.27%	16.69%	17.28%	8.36%	11.72%	8.14%
1952	18.37%	8.63%	19.36%	17.09%	12.78%	13.15%	7.49%
1953	-0.99%	8.27%	17.86%	14.31%	10.68%	10.68%	5.90%
1954	52.62%	9.56%	23.92%	17.12%	13.88%	13.13%	8.09%
1955	31.56%	10.23%	23.89%	16.69%	16.78%	12.48%	10.54%
1956	6.56%	10.11%	20.18%	18.43%	18.24%	11.20%	13.37%
1957	-10.78%	9.38%	13.58%	16.44%	15.91%	12.98%	13.24%
1958	43.36%	10.29%	22.30%	20.06%	16.92%	13.48%	12.91%
1959	11.96%	10.33%	14.96%	19.35%	16.39%	14.15%	13.49%
1960	0.47%	10.04%	8.92%	16.16%	14.04%	14.76%	11.76%
1961	26.89%	10.48%	12.79%	16.43%	16.52%	16.86%	11.52%
1962	-8.73%	9.91%	13.31%	13.44%	15.38%	15.25%	13.04%
1963	22.08%	10.23%	9.85%	15.91%	16.56%	15.11%	12.75%
1964	16.48%	10.36%	10.73%	12.82%	16.40%	14.95%	13.46%
1965	12.45%	10.44%	13.25%	11.06%	15.18%	13.84%	14.46%
1966	-10.66%	9.88%	5.72%	9.20%	12.74%	13.72%	14.54%
1967	23.98%	10.20%	12.39%	12.85%	13.09%	14.63%	14.67%

Year	S&P 500	Average Annual Return	5-Year Avg. Annual Return	10-Year Avg. Annual Return	15-Year Avg. Annual Return	20-Year Avg. Annual Return	25-Year Avg. Annual Return
1968	11.06%	10.22%	10.16%	10.01%	13.96%	14.92%	14.10%
1969	-8.50%	9.75%	4.97%	7.81%	10.14%	13.43%	12.88%
1970	4.01%	9.62%	3.34%	8.18%	8.43%	12.10%	11.66%
1971	14.31%	9.72%	8.42%	7.06%	8.94%	11.65%	12.64%
1972	18.98%	9.91%	7.53%	9.93%	11.05%	11.67%	13.17%
1973	-14.66%	9.33%	2.01%	6.01%	7.27%	10.85%	12.22%
1974	-26.47%	8.45%	-2.35%	1.24%	4.31%	6.87%	10.08%
1975	37.20%	8.96%	3.21%	3.27%	6.50%	7.10%	10.26%
1976	23.84%	9.24%	4.87%	6.63%	6.32%	7.91%	10.26%
1977	-7.18%	8.90%	-0.21%	3.59%	6.44%	8.12%	9.19%
1978	6.56%	8.85%	4.32%	3.16%	5.44%	6.53%	9.51%
1979	18.44%	9.02%	14.76%	5.86%	5.56%	6.83%	8.41%
1980	32.50%	9.41%	13.96%	8.45%	6.72%	8.32%	8.44%
1981	-4.92%	9.14%	8.10%	6.47%	7.12%	6.76%	7.94%
1982	21.55%	9.34%	14.09%	6.70%	6.98%	8.30%	9.29%
1983	22.56%	9.56%	17.32%	10.63%	7.68%	8.29%	8.60%
1984	6.27%	9.50%	14.81%	14.78%	8.76%	7.80%	8.38%
1985	31.73%	9.84%	14.67%	14.32%	10.49%	8.65%	9.56%
1986	18.67%	9.98%	19.87%	13.83%	10.76%	10.17%	9.27%
1987	5.25%	9.90%	16.47%	15.27%	9.86%	9.27%	9.89%
1988	16.61%	10.00%	15.31%	16.31%	12.17%	9.54%	9.66%
1989	31.69%	10.31%	20.37%	17.55%	16.61%	11.55%	10.20%
1990	-3.11%	10.09%	13.19%	13.93%	13.94%	11.16%	9.55%
1991	30.47%	10.38%	15.36%	17.59%	14.34%	11.89%	11.19%
1992	7.62%	10.34%	15.88%	16.17%	15.47%	11.33%	10.56%
1993	10.08%	10.33%	14.56%	14.93%	15.72%	12.76%	10.52%
1994	1.32%	10.20%	8.70%	14.38%	14.52%	14.58%	10.98%
1995	37.58%	10.55%	16.59%	14.88%	14.81%	14.60%	12.22%
1996	22.96%	10.71%	15.22%	15.29%	16.80%	14.56%	12.55%
1997	33.36%	11.00%	20.27%	18.05%	17.52%	16.65%	13.07%
1998	28.58%	11.22%	24.06%	19.21%	17.90%	17.75%	14.94%
1999	21.04%	11.35%	28.56%	18.21%	18.92%	17.88%	17.25%
2000	-9.11%	11.05%	18.33%	17.46%	16.02%	15.68%	15.33%
2001	-11.89%	10.71%	10.70%	12.93%	13.74%	15.24%	13.77%
2002	-22.10%	10.21%	-0.59%	9.34%	11.48%	12.71%	12.96%
2003	26.68%	10.43%	-0.57%	11.06%	12.21%	12.98%	13.84%
2004	10.88%	10.43%	-2.30%	12.07%	10.93%	13.22%	13.54%
2005	4.91%	10.36%	0.54%	9.07%	11.52%	11.94%	12.48%
2006	15.79%	10.43%	6.19%	8.42%	10.64%	11.80%	13.37%
2007	6.49%	10.36%	12.83%	5.91%	10.49%	11.81%	12.73%
2008	-37.00%	9.62%	-2.19%	-1.39%	6.46%	8.42%	9.77%
2009	26.46%	9.81%	0.41%	-0.95%	8.04%	8.21%	10.54%

See Endnote 49.

We Are the Champions
Remember this—Capitalism and free markets are the greatest wealth creation tools known to mankind.

A Word on Faith

Discipline does require some faith.

I'm talking about faith not just in the construction of your portfolio, but faith in capitalism and faith in free markets. Also, the most successful investors I know have faith in a higher power. They have faith in God. And why? Because they have humility. Instead of playing God and pretending that they can figure everything out, and forecast and predict everything, they know that's God territory. That's omniscience and omnipotence, which no mere mortal possesses. They have faith that, through all of this, it's going to be okay. This is not an irrational blind faith. It's a faith based on rational optimism.

So here's to having faith in markets, a belief in free markets, a belief in capitalism, and a belief in that higher power! Here's to the humility to stand back and say, "Look, I don't know which companies are going to be the best, I don't know which markets are going to be up and down at which time. I know it's my job to allocate resources on a global basis, stay disciplined, not chase markets, and do use academic research to help allocate my portfolio assets." Here's to understanding your own humanness and realizing that, no matter how brilliant you are, you're going to have dark moments. You're going to have moments when it's going to feel like the right thing to do is get out.

I once talked with an advisor who had, at one time, understood these concepts, and who had successfully grown his business—a very large business, and a very successful one at that.

This advisor shared a remarkable story with us. When the market crashed in 2008, his company caved and gave into the panic knowing that it wasn't the right thing to do, but feeling helpless. They sold their clients to cash. When the market bounced back, big-time, in 2009, the firm's clients were left in the dust, and they lost about 50% of the value of their investment portfolios.

Now, I know there will be moments where the fear will be all-consuming because that's part of being human. There will also be times when the exuberance will be so high—when there will be some high-flying stock, fund, or ETF that's returning 50%.

And there will be times when despair sets in, and those same investments lose 50% of their value.

This is where discipline and faith must be brought to bear.

I've experience times in my own life when I tried to take over and exert my will on the world. Having that faith and discipline, I realize there are some things completely out of my control, including which way the stock market goes today.

Trying to play God with the financial markets is highly destructive. So don't do it. In the end, you will guess wrong. Instead, have the long-term courage to take the long view and stick to your plan. Know that courage doesn't mean the absence of fear. Courage means feeling the fear and doing the right thing anyway. Courage is staying with fear one minute more than the situation calls for.

In a way, courage is merely having patience in the middle of fearful situations—a true attribute for investors.

Patience means time. I must endure things, and I must experience them over time. Remember, there is no quick fix as an investor.

You have to be able to endure down markets to be a successful investor. You have to be able to endure stress and anxiety out in the world of uncertainty. You have to be able to focus on the next 20 years, not the next 20 minutes.

To be a successful investor means to be part of a community and to come to terms with your own humanity. That's what we're finding thousands of investors are doing. They're giving themselves the opportunity to achieve market returns, to be successful, and to get the peace of mind that they truly deserve. After working with hundreds of advisors and literally thousands of investors, over twenty years of hard-won experience, I know this is what you need to do.

Now, it's up to you to do it.

ACKNOWLEDGEMENTS

Writing any book is a team effort, and never more so than with *Main Street Money*. This book is the culmination of academic research and real world applications. No one person could have developed the critical research to make it possible.

Of course, without the love and support of my wife, Melissa, and our children this book would never have happened. Not only did they put up with my isolation in penning the piece, but also selflessly supported me in promoting this project on the road. As any "road warrior" knows, being away from your family is a heavy price to pay. Melissa was also a wonderful sounding board for key concepts and stories.

This book would not be possible if not for the strength, wisdom, and knowledge of my life long mentor and coach, my Dad, Joe Matson. Thank you for teaching me that the best security is in my own shoes.

To my sister-in-law, Michelle Matson, Zack Shepard, Dan List, Steve Miller, Kenny Gatliff, Donn Burrows, and Kim Pfeifer. Each of you could have easily been viewed as co-authors. Your unwavering support, strength and courage made this book a reality. You were always there for me with research, analysis, editing, theories, conceptualization, and faith.

I would also like to thank the entire Matson Money staff: Alex Ash, Matt Baechle, Mike Bowler, Amy Goldston, Judi Henderson, Bethany Wellman, Bridget Hughes, Linda Lotz, Megan Miller, Amanda Pardol, Joe Pegram, Ashley Pope, Alaine Schoening, Brad Skoog, Jeb Snyder, Kindra Walpole, Dana Weinstein, Patience Welch, Rick Wiehe, Sabrina Williams, Rebecca Kuhlmann, Diana Wulfeck, Zach Pfeifer, Kailee Cornell. You ran the company flawlessly while I was sequestered.

A special thank you to the visionaries at Dimensional Fund Advisors – David Booth and his leadership and drive; and Rex Sinquefield who first taught me the simple truth that free markets work; Michael Lane who has fought the good fight with me for nearly two decades, you are a true friend; Dan Wheeler who fought in the trenches with me and mentored me and who first saw that advisors could apply this to investors. I am grateful to Eugene Fama and Kenneth French for their ground-breaking research into efficient market theory and the three factor model, which makes up much of the investment theory in this book. Also, to Hunt Cairns from Dimensional who has provided stellar resources any time we needed them.

Brian O'Connell, my editor helped me structure and find the right tone—your help and guidance was indispensable.

Kim McShane, thank you for helping bring these pages to life with your vision, talent, and superior proofing and editing skills.

Jimmy Moock, Joe Anthony, and Doug Rose at FCA Gregory, the world's greatest media consultants, for helping us find out voice and finally get on the radar—you rock!

To George Veras who produced a killer public television special to get the message out there; and Lee Zeidman who helped fine tune the Main Street Money message and ruthlessly coached me on how best to present it – kudos. I would also like to thank Gustavo—and Maya— at International Media for your guidance and support getting the message to the world.

I'd like to give special thanks to all of the journalists and media professionals who have given me the opportunity to share this message on a national scale through television and print coverage: Larry Kudlow at CNBC; Dave Asman, Cheryl Casone, and Liz Claman at Fox Business; Jenna Lee at Fox News; Matt Miller at Bloomberg; Veronica Dagher at Dow Jones (WSJ); and Charles Passy at Independent (Smart Money).

I am eternally grateful for the faith, love, and support of the Matson Money Coaches who call themselves the Wolf Pack. It is your courage and hard work that turns the theories in this book into coaching sessions, workshops and one-on-one meetings that truly save the investor from speculating and gambling with their money. Although it is a long list, I have listed every coach who has saved even one investor, who truly takes a stand against speculating. Each of you is a hero and your investors are so lucky to have you. I will forever be indebted to you for your faith and support. I am grateful to U.S. Public Television for presenting Main Street Money and helping us get the message out.

Nabil Abdelhamid, Len Abrams, William Acuff, Matt Adams, Charlotte Adams, Doug Alden, Sam Badgley, Kent Balch, Carl Balestrieri, Vicki Balhoff, Richard Balhoff, Evan Barnard, Janet Bates, Randall Baxter, John Bean, William Beavers, Marc Becker, Christopher Bell, Trent Benedetti, Craig Berger, J. Robert Berry, John Berzellini, Daniel Betzel, Jim Bevins, Bryan Binkholder, Jerry Black, Christopher Blais, Anthony Bonanno,

John Borger, Shawn Bragdon, Mike Breedlove, David Breedlove, Mitchell Brill, William Brooks, Greg Brown, Eldon Brown, Scott Buchanan, Lawrence "Buck" Buchholz, Jeremy Burri, Bill Cantrell, Donald Cash, Chad Castle, Steve Casto, Thomas Cates, Robert Cerrito, John Choi, Mark Cieslak, Kasey Claytor, R. Douglas Cobb, Saul Cohen, Curtis Dean Cone, Mark Connely, Jamie Cooke, Linda Corujo-Ramsey, Bryan Cothran, Douglas Crosby, Rey Cruz, Daniel Cuprill, Vincent D'Addona, Kevin Daniel, Robbie Davis, Brian Dawahare, David Day, Joseph DeLisi, Matthew Deller, Anthony DeSantis, Anthony DeStefano, Tim DeVries, David Diehl, Thomas Diem, Howard L. Dingle, Joseph D'Intino, Marty Donnelly, James Dortch, Paul Drinkhahn, James Dubbert, Dennis Duffy, Michael Dum, Thomas Dundorf, George Ellis, Lawrence Epple, Curtis Erickson, Tim Estes, Michael Evans, Ross B. Feldman, Kenneth Feyers, Brad Fike, Eric Fischesser, Cathy Fitzgerald, Mayo FitzHugh, Christian FitzHugh, R. Michael Flanders, Clark Forward, Jeffrey Furest, Bill Furest, Dennis Gagnon, Philip Gallant, Gerald Gambatese, Robert Gardner, Reich Gardner, Scott Gartner, Jack Gelnak, Pamela Gilmour, Jason Giorgio, William Goan, Daniel Goodwin, William Greenfield, Christy Gregory, Marcia A. Grier, Jason Griffith, Elwyn Guernsey, Douglas Guernsey, Philip Guske, Alan Halka, Jim Hancock, Francis Hanley, MariJo Harding, Joseph Hassin, Tommy Hatfield, Tom Hatfield, Bill Hazlett, Greg Heaton, John Heinze, Dr. Josh Helman, William Helms, William Helms Jr, Jane Heron, Chris Herring, Barry Herrlinger, Michael Herron, Dan Hill, Gordon Hillegas, Dan Hoelscher, Ross Hoffman, Steven L Holland, James Hollon, Kurt Holzhueter, Karl Holzhueter, Steve Hoover, John Hutchinson, Lee Hyder, Brian Irving, Steve Irwin, Marty Jaras, Scott Jarred, Brendon Jenks, Gavin Jensen, Johnny Johnson, Guinevere Johnson, Drew Jones, Emma Kalaidjian, Allen Kampf, Steve Keeton, William Kelly, Bryon Kibildis, Myron Kidd, Karl Kim, Peter Kitzerow, James Koester, Theodore Kolman, Bob Korljan, Anthony Krance, Maria Kuitula, Chau Lai, Keith Laibson, Damon Lane, Barb Lane, Mike Lanway, Stan Lawhon, David Lazzaro, Eric Lee, Marc Lesser, Robert Lettin, Mitch Levin, Harry Lewis, Garry Liday, John Limongelli, Mark Lloyd, Geoff Lombard, Darrell W. Long, Mark Lund, Trevor Lyke, Jerry Lyke, Robert D Lyons, Robert H Lyons, Brendan Magee, Andre Markusfeld, Robert Marshall, Don Martin, Raymond Martin, Sam Martinez, Jeff Mathies, Joe Matson, Michael Matteoni, Roy McBryar, Richard McCool, Gary McGovern, Jim McGovern, Terrence McMullen, John Mears, Robert Miller, Charles Miller, Robert Mills, Frank Minitello, Frank Mokosak, Jeff Montgomery, Bob Morales, David Morgan, Evan Morrison, Edwin Morrow, William R. Muench, Bill Mullen, Nick Naseman, Bob Nash, Ryan Neff, Allen Neuenschwander, Michael Neuenschwander, Paul Nichols, Nathan OBryant, Tim O'Connor, Gene Offredi, John Okorowski, Jill O'Roark,

Frank Orzel, Liebe Ostrow, Daniel O'Toole, Eddie Overdyke, David Palmer, John Palmer III, Hank Parrott, Jerome Pasichow, Richard Pasick, G Thomas Pate, Richard Paul, Omar Pereira, Michael Peterson, Tammy Pick, John Pollock, Joseph Pombriant, Daniel Price, Eugene Pusczek, Thomas Quilici, Jose Quinones, Blake Rainey, Steve Rainey, Leonard Raskin, Richard Ray, W. Wesley Reed, Daniel Reese, Con Reha, Don Reichert, Louis Rendemonti, Richard Reyes, Steve Rice, William Riley, Michael Ringel, Tim Rosen, Don Ross, John Rossitto, Eric Rothman, Kelly Ruggles, Michael Sarcheck, Peter Schanck, Joe Schofield, Aaron Schroeder, Derick Schuhart, Earl Schultz, Chet Schwartz, Sandra Scolari, Debra Seaward, Mark Shelby, Harry Shepler, John Shipley, Marvin Shiue, Howard Shores II, Clayton Shum, Eddy Shum, Douglas Simmang, John Sklenar, Craig Slayen, Steven Smartt, Craig Smith, Keith Snyder, Mansell Spedding, Dan Spickard, Roland Stadelmann, Gretchen Stangier, Matt Starke, Mark Stoecker, Michael Stokes, Edward Storer, John Strasburger, Chris Strehle, Stephen Stricklin, Scott Sullivan, Ken Sutherland, Fred Taylor, Thomas Taylor, Jeff Teach, Ron Tetley, J'Neanne Theus, David Tolley, Dale Tondryk, Stephen Tosi, Alfie Tounjian, Robert Troyano, Danton Troyer, Michelle Tucker, J Douglas Umphress, Carole Upson, Thomas VanderHeiden, Rich VanderSande, Evan Vanderwey, Steven Vanderwey, Richard Villers, Wayne von Borstel, John Vucicevic, Aaron Wade, Richard Walen, Becky Walker, Jonathan Walker, Bessann Watson, Steve Weber, Steve Wegner, John Weider, Garth Weil, Michael Weinberg, Bryan Weiss, George Wells, Josh Wheeler, Roy Wiley, Paul Wills MD, Paul Winkler, Mark Witt, David Witter, Margaret Wittkopp, Jim Wood, James Woodworth, Phyllis Wordhouse, Ira Work, Kevin Wray, John Yates, Joe Yocavitch, Paul Young, Robert Young, and Henry Zupko.

ENDNOTES

1. Stossel, John, dir. "Do Managed Funds Lead to Big Earnings or Wasted Money?" Stossel. Fox Business: 17122010. Television. (1.3)

2. "2011 Investment Company Fact Book." Investment Company Institute. Investment Company Institute, 02052011. Web. 5 Jan 2012. <www.ici.org>. (1.8)

3. "U.S Millionaire Population Grows by 600,000 in 2010 to 8.4 Million." Spectrem Group. Spectrem Group, n.d. Web. 5 Jan 2012. (1.8)

4. "Securities Industry Financial Results." Securities Industry Association (http://www.sla.com/ressearch)

5. Van Caspel, Venita. *The Power of Money Dynamics*. 2nd edition. Reston Publishing Co., 1983. Print.

6. Lowenstein, Roger. "Long-Term Capital Management: It's a short-term memory." *New York Times*. NY Times, 07092008. Web. 5 Jan 2012.

7. August 21, 1990, Federal Reserve Chairman Alan Greenspan, Policy Meeting. Fed periodical.

8. "National Economic Accounts." Bureau of Economic Analysis. U.S Department of Commerce, n.d. Web. 5 Jan 2012. (1.13)

9. "Labor Force Statistics." Bureau of Labor Statistics. United States Department of Labor, n.d. Web. 5 Jan 2012. (1.13)

10. Kritzman, Mark. *Economics & Portfolio Strategy*. (2009): n. page. Print. (1.15)

11. Hulbert, Mark. "The Index Funds Win Again." The New York Times. NY Times,

21022009. Web. 5 Jan 2012. (1.15)

12. David, Rynecki. "In Search Of The Last Honest Analyst Our quest wasn't easy. But we did find a few standouts you can trust. Here, our third annual All-Stars." *CNN Money*. CNN Money, 10062002. Web. 5 Jan 2012. (1.17)

13. *Quantitative Analysis of Investor Behavior, 2011.* DALBAR, Inc. www.dalbar.com. Equity benchmark performance and systematic equity investing examples are represented by the Standard & Poor's 500 Composite Index, an unmanaged index of 500 common stocks generally considered representative of the U.S. stock market. Indexes do not take into account the fees and expenses associated with investing, and individuals cannot invest directly in any index. Past performance cannot guarantee future results.Average stock investor, average bond investor and average asset allocation investor performance results are based on a DALBAR study, "Quantitative Analysis of Investor Behavior (QAIB), 2011." DALBAR is an independent, Boston-based financial research firm. Using monthly fund data supplied by the Investment Company Institute, QAIB calculates investor returns as the change in assets after excluding sales, redemptions and exchanges. This method of calculation captures realized and unrealized capital gains, dividends, interest, trading costs, sales charges, fees, expenses and any other costs. After calculating investor returns in dollar terms, two percentages are calculated for the period examined: Total investor return rate and annualized investor return rate. Total return rate is determined by calculating the investor return dollars as a percentage of the net of the sales, redemptions, and exchanges for the period. (1.18)

14. Average of all US Equity funds available in the CRSP Survivor- Bias Free US Mutual Fund Database, data ending Dec. 2010. S&P 500 Index and CRSP Market Index data obtained from DFA Returns software 12/10. PAST PERFORMANCE IS NOT A GUARANTEE OF FUTURE RESULTS AND INVESTORS MAY EXPERIENCE A LOSS. (1.20), (2.8-10)

15. Source: Standard & Poor's, CRSP. For periods ending December 31, 2010. Outperformance is based upon equal weight fund counts. Charts are provided for illustrative purposes only. Index returns do not include payment of any sales charges or fees an investor would pay to purchase the securities they represent. Such costs would lower performance. Past performance is not an indication of future results (1.20), (2.2)

16. Morningstar Research. 28022010. n.pag. Morningstar Principia. Web. 5 Jan 2012. Top 100 Tech holding represented by the NYSE ARCA fund. AIM Dent

fund represented by AIM Dent Demographic Trends Fund (ADDAX)

17. "What the Experts Say About the Failure of Active Management." *Savant*. Web. 5 Jan 2012. www.savantcapital.com

18. "The Truth About Top-Performing Money Managers," RW Baird. Baird's Advisory Services Research, 01032011. Web. 5 Jan 2012. <http://www.rwbaird.com/bolimages/Media/PDF/Whitepapers/Truth-About-Top-Performing-Money-Managers.pdf>. (2.5)

19. Stewart, Will. "Lusha the chimpanzee outperforms 94% of Russia bankers with her investment portfolio." *Daily Mail Online*. 13012010. Web. 5 Jan 2012. <http://www.dailymail.co.uk/news/article-1242575/Lusha-monkey-outperforms-94-Russia-bankers-investment-portfolio.html>. (2.7)

20. Armstrong, David. "Why Active Management Stinks." *Money*. US News, 14012011. Web. 5 Jan 2012. http://money.usnews.com/money/blogs/the-smarter-mutual-fund-investor/2011/01/14/why-active-equity-management-stinks (2.7)

21. Brinson, G.P, L.R. Hood, and G.L. Beebower. "Determinants of Portfolio Performance." Financial Analysts Journal, July/August 1986, pp. 39-48 (2.8)

22. Bogle, John, *The Little Book of Common Sense Investing*, 209, John Wiley and Sons, Inc.

23. Historical time period represented by 07/1926—06/2011. Ranges of Stocks growing 10-12% represented by the S&P 500, with an annualized return of 10%, and the CRSP Deciles 9-10 Index. Ranges of Bonds growing 5-8% represented by One-Month US Treasury Bills with an annualized return of 5.4% and Five-Year US Treasury Notes with an annualized return of 8%.

24. ChartSource, McGraw-Hill Financial Communications. Based on total returns of Standard & Poor's Composite Index of 500 Stocks, an unmanaged index that in generally considered representative of the U.S. stock market. It is not possible to invest directly in an index. Past performance is not a guarantee of future results. Copyright © 2011, McGraw-Hill Financial Communications. All rights reserved. Not responsible for any errors or omissions.

25. Domoghue, William. "Low stock prices pay off." Wilmington Morning Star [Wilmington] 24 08 1991, 6C. Print.ChartSource®, McGraw-Hill Financial Communications. For the period from October 1, 1990, through September 30, 2010. Based on total returns of Standard & Poor's Composite Index of 500

Stocks, an unmanaged index that in generally considered representative of the U.S. stock market. It is not possible to invest directly in an index. Past performance is not a guarantee of future results. Copyright © 2011, McGraw-Hill Financial Communications. All rights reserved. Not responsible for any errors or omissions. Based on initial investment of $10,000. (2.14)

26. Maranjian, Selena. "The Worst Fund Ever Finally Dies." *The Motley Fool*, 27012010. Web. 5 Jan 2012. (2.14)

27. Sharpe, William. "The Arithmetic of Active Management" *The Financial Analysts' Journal*. Vol. 47, No. 1, January/February 1991. pp. 7-9 Copyright, 1991, Association for Investment Management and Research Charlottesville, VA

28. Cronqvist, Henrik. "Investors Lose When They Choose Mutual Funds Based on Ads." *Ohio State Research News*. The Ohio State University, 22032007. Web. 5 Jan 2012. <http://researchnews.osu.edu/archive/fundadv connect.htm>. (2.16)

29. Statman, Meir. "Odds Say You Can't Beat Index Funds." Money Central Investing, 29 May 2001

30. "Google Search." Google, 05012012. Web. 5 Jan 2012. (3.5)

31. Independent research done by Matson Money Inc. using prospective investor's asset holdings as entered by unaffiliated co-advisors via proprietary website database.

32. J.M. Keynes, *The General Theory of Employment, Interest, and Money*. (London, 1936) Pp. 383-84

33. Sinquefield, Rex. Opening Statement in debate with Donald Yacktman. Schwab International Conference in San Francisco, October 12, 1991.

34. Reagan, Ronald. Speech to members of IMF and World Bank. 29 Sepetember 1981.

35. Beinhocker, Eric. *The Origin of Wealth*. Harvard Business School Press, 2006. Print. (4.1)

36. Rand, Ayn. *Atlas Shrugged*. 1957(1992), New York, Dutton

37. Fischer, Ronald, and Diana Boer. "What is more important for national well-being: Money or autonomy?" *Journal of Personality and Social Psychology*. 101.1 (2011): 164-184. Print. (4.8)

38. "Government Spending." US Government Spending. Web.17 Jan 2012. http://www.usgovernmentspending.com/us_20th_century_chart.html

39. "Dutch East India Company." Wikipedia. Wikipedia, 21 December 2011. Web. 17 Jan 2012.

40. Frankl, Viktor. *Man's Search For Meaning*. 1. Pocket, 1997. Print. (5.5)

41. Churchill, Winston. Statement given when he left office as Prime Minister. 1945

42. . "World Development Report 2008." The World Bank. The World Bank, n.d. Web. 6 Jan 2012. (5.16)

43. Louis Johnston and Samuel H. Williamson, "What Was the U.S. GDP Then?" MeasuringWorth, 2011. URL: http://www.measuringworth.org/usgdp/ (5.18)

44. U.S. National Center for Health Statistics, Vital Statistics of the United States, annual, and National Vital Statistics Reports (NVSR) (formerly Monthly Vital Statistics Reports) (5.18)

45. "The World Fact Book." CIA Publication. CIA, 2011. Web. 9 Jan 2012. (5.18)

46. Gilder, George. *Wealth and Poverty.* 1981 (1993). Basic Books.

47. Source: "US Gross Public Debt." US Government Debt. US Government Debt, 06012012.

48. da Costa, Polyana . "QE1: Financial Crisis Timeline."Bankrate. Bankrate.com, n.d. Web. 17 Jan 2012."Consumer Price Index." Bureau of Labor Statistics. United States Department of Labor, n.d. Web. 5 Jan 2012. (6.9)

49. 2010 Dimensional Fund Advisors Returns Software. US long-term bonds, bills, inflation, and fixed income factor data © Stocks, Bonds, Bills, and Inflation Yearbook", Ibbotson Associates, Chicago (annually updated work by Roger G. Ibbotson and Rex A. Sinquefield). The S&P data are provided by Standard & Poor's IndexServices Group. Fama/French and multifactor data provided by Fama/French. Some data provided to DFA by the Center for Research & Security Pricing (CRSP), University of Chicago. Asset Classes defined as: Consumer Price Index for inflation, CRSP 30 day treasury bill index for Treasury Bills, CRSP Long-Term U.S. Government Bond index for Long-Term Government Bonds, S&P 500 Index for U.S. large stocks, CRSP 6-10 index for U.S. small stocks, , CRSP 9-10 index for U.S. micro-cap stocks, Morgan Stanley Europe, Australia, Far East (EAFE) Index for international large stocks, and the international small stock index created by DFA using CRSP data for international small stocks. US

Growth Stocks represented by Fama/French US Large Growth Research Index ,
and Tech stocks are represented by the NASDAQ composite index. Hypothetical
asset class mixes created using the allocations provided in this table

	70/30 Hypothetical	Aggressive	Conservative	Moderate	Growth
TBILL: One-Month US Treasury Bills	14.75%	2%	2%	2%	2%
FFBGH: Fama/French US Large Value Research Index	21.50%	15%	5.25%	9%	12.75%
S&P500: S&P 500 Index	10.50%	7.50%	2.63%	4.50%	6.37%
C9-10: CRSP Deciles 9-10 Index	10.50%	7.50%	2.63%	4.50%	6.38%
C6-10: CRSP Deciles 6-10 Index	10.50%	7.50%	2.63%	4.50%	6.37%
INTBN: Five-Year US Treasury Notes	14.75%	0%	0%	0%	0%
FFSMH: Fama/French US Small Value Research Index	17.50%	12.50%	4.38%	7.50%	10.63%
EAFE: MSCI EAFE Index (gross div.)	0%	15.75%	2.63%	7%	11.38%
INTIX: Dimensional International Small Cap Index	0%	29.25%	4.85%	13%	21.12%
DFIHX: DFA One-Year Fixed Income Portfolio (USD)	0%	1.50%	36.50%	24%	11.50%
DFFGX: DFA Five-Year Government Portfolio (USD)	0%	1.50%	36.50%	24%	11.50%
Total	100%	100%	100%	100%	100%

50. Dimensional Fund Advisors. Average explanatory power (R2) is for the Fama/
French equity benchmark universe. www.dimensional.com

51. Matson Money, Inc. *Rebalancing Research 2010.* Study done using DFA returns
software. Non rebalanced portfolio shows total return of hypothetical portfolio
beginning 1/1/2007 and ending 12/31/2009. Rebalanced portfolio took the same
hypothetical portfolio, and reset the asset classes back to the original allocation
each quarter. The return shown is the total return from 1/1/2007—12/31/2009
using this method. Hypothetical asset class mixes created using the allocations
provided in this table:

	Conservative	Moderate	Growth	Aggressive
Russell Microcap Index	5.00%	5.00%	10.00%	12.50%
Fama/French US Small Value Research Index	5.00%	10.00%	12.50%	12.50%
Fama/French US Large Cap Index	7.50%	10.00%	10.00%	12.50%
MSCI EAFE Value Index (net div.)	7.50%	7.50%	10.00%	12.50%
Cash	10.00%	10.00%	5.00%	5.00%
Citigroup World Gov't Bond Index 3-5 Yr. (hedged)	20.00%	10.00%	5.00%	0.00%
Merrill Lynch 1-Year US T-Note Index	20.00%	20.00%	10.00%	0.00%
Five-Year US Treasury Notes	25.00%	10.00%	5.00%	0.00%
MSCI Emerging Markets Index (net div.)	0.00%	5.00%	5.00%	7.50%
DFA Developed International Large Company Composite Index	0.00%	0.00%	5.00%	5.00%
Fama/French US Large Value Research Index	0.00%	5.00%	10.00%	12.50%
Dimensional Int'l Small Cap Value Index	0.00%	7.50%	12.50%	20.00%

52. "Historical Gold Charts." *Kitco*. Kitco, n.d. Web. 10 Jan 2012. <www.kitco.com>. 20 Year period indicated ranges from 1981-2000.

53. Twain, Mark. *Pudd'nhead Wilson*. 1894, Charles L. Webster & Co.

54. Dr., Seuss. *Oh, the Places You'll Go*. Random House, 1990. Print. (7.16)

55. Faber, Marc. "The South Sea Bubble and Law's Mississippi Scheme." Gold Eagle. N.p., 21102004. Web. 11 Jan 2012. <http://www.gold-eagle.com/editorials_04/faber102004.html>.

56. Murch, Walter, and Lawrence Weschler. "Economy: The Trouble with Bubbles." *Los Angeles Times*. N.p., 23032010. Web. 11 Jan 2012.

57. 28022010. n.pag. Morningstar Principia. Web. 5 Jan 2012. Fund symbol referenced is INIVX (8.5)

58. Edelman, Ric. "Does Buy-and-Hold Beat Market Timing." *Inside Personal Finance*. N.p., 2001. Web. 11 Jan 2012.

59. Morningstar Research. 28022010. n.pag. Morningstar Principia. Web. 5 Jan 2012. Average expenses of 3% is based on Morningstar Principia data updated through December 31, 2009, the average net expense ratio for the Morningstar Category of Domestic Equity funds (1.34%) plus taking the average turnover for the same Morningstar Category of funds (81%) times a total implementation cost (commission+ bid/ask spread +Market Impact +Delay +Missed Trades) of 1% (the 1% one way trading cost is also quoted in Charles Ellis's book Winning the Loser's Game, Fourth Edition, on page 7) times two for both sides of the trade. This equals approximately 3%. The 2.03% attributed to investor behavior is calculated by taking the S&P 500 Index return from 1991 to 2009 of 9.14% subtracting the above expense of 3% and also subtracting the Dalbar QAIB 2011 Average Equity Investors 20 year return of 3.83% (as found on page 8 of the Dalbar Study). This equals 2.31%.

60. Lee, Chan Jean and Andrade, Eduardo B. "Fear, Social Projection, and Financial Decision Making" (June 18, 2011). *Journal of Marketing Research*, Forthcoming. Available at SSRN: http://ssrn.com/abstract=1866568

61. Malkiel, Burton. *A Random Walk Down Wall Street*. 6th. W. W. Norton & Company, 1996.

62. Malkiel, Burton, and Charles Ellis. *The Elements of Investing*. 1st. Wiley, 2009. Print.

63. "Navigating The Fog." McGriff Publishing. Matson Money. 10/1996

64. "Emotions Can Negatively Impact Investment Decisions."Stanford Knowledge Base. Stanford Graduate School Of Business, 15092005. Web. 12 Jan 2012.

65. "Study: Financial Advisors Reinforce Bad Investment Behaviors." MyBankTracker. N.p., 28052010. Web. 12 Jan 2012.

66. McNamara, Kristen. "Financial Advisers Enable Bad Investor Behavior." *Wall Street Journal*. N.p., 11032010. Web. 12 Jan 2012.

67. "Historical Gold Charts." Kitco. Kitco, n.d. Web. 10 Jan 2012. <www.kitco. com>. Inflation represented as CPI, assumed tax rate of 35%. Data time period of 1926-2010.

68. Laughlin, P., Hatch, E., Silver, J., & Boh, L. (2006) "Groups Perform Better Than the Best Individuals on Letters-to-Numbers Problems: Effects of Group Size." *Journal of Personality and Social Psychology*, Vol. 90, No. 4. (11.15)

69. "George Santayana." BrainyQuote.com. Xplore Inc, 2012. 16 January. 2012. http://www.brainyquote.com/quotes/quotes/g/georgesant101521.html

70. "Georg Wilhelm Friedriich Hegel." iwise.com. Xplore Inc, 2012. 16 January. 2012. http://www.iwise.com/dYGo6

MARK MATSON is CEO and founder of Matson Money Inc., a registered investment advisor company that manages in excess of $5 billion*. With over twenty years of experience in the financial industry, Mark is a regular contributor in the national media, both in print and on television. His optimistic outlook on finance, investing, and economic issues makes him a frequently sought expert on CNBC, Fox News, BNN, Fox Business News, and publications such as the *Wall Street Journal, The New York Times,* and *Investment News.*

As a dynamic public speaker, Mark has shared his message of free markets and global investing with thousands of people throughout the country. His direct approach, passion, and enthusiasm make him both a compelling speaker and a fierce proponent of free markets.

Mark has authored several books on the topic of investing and economics for both investors and financial professionals; he also hosts *Matson Money Live!,* a weekly live web show about investing, economics, and current events.

TELEVISION: CNBC "Kudlow Report," CNBC "Power Lunch," Fox Business News "Opening Bell," Fox Business News "Power and Money," Fox Business News "Closing Bell," and CNBC Reports.

ARTICLES: The *Wall Street Journal, Investment News,* SmartMoney.com, Forbes.com, *The Business Courier, USA Today, Financial Services Advisor, Advisor Today,* P*ersonal Financial Planning Monthly* and many more.

BOOKS: "Main Street Money: How to Outwit, Outsmart, & Out Invest the Wall Street Bullies," "The Dirty Filthy Lies My Broker Taught Me, 101 Truths About Money & Investing," "Confessions of a Commission Junkie," and "FlashPoint: Mastering the Art of Economic Abundance"

VIDEO: "How the Really Smart Money Invests" and "Navigating the Fog of Investing."

AUDIO: *The Seven Deadly Investor Traps that Destroy Your Wealth & Three Power Strategies to Fix your Portfolio, The Curriculum for Conscious Investing, The Investor Coaching Series,* and *Breakthrough to Abundance.*

ONLINE: *Matson Money Live!* and Mark Matson TV.

Mark is the proud husband of Melissa and father of seven children. He is an avid cyclist and trains constantly for challenging races.

Connect with Mark Matson at:

www.markmatson.tv

www.matsonmoney.com

www.twitter.com/markmatson

www.facebook.com/markmatson

www.facebook.com/matsonmoney   *As of 1/22/2013*